Write Down Deep

• an Alchemy of the Writing Life •

By Jan Fortune

Down Deep Books

Published by Down Deep Books, an imprint of Cinnamon Press, Meirion House, Tanygrisiau, Blaenau Ffestiniog, Gwynedd, LL41 3SU

www.cinnamonpress.com

The right of Jan Fortune to be identified as author of this work has been asserted by her in accordance with the Copyright, Designs and Patent Act, 1988. © 2020 Jan Fortune.

ISBN 978-1-78864-801-1

British Library Cataloguing in Publication Data. A CIP record for this book can be obtained from the British Library. All rights reserved. No part of this publication may be reproduced, stored in a retrieval system, or transmitted in any form or by any means, electronic, mechanical, photocopying, recording or otherwise without the prior written permission of the publishers. This book may not be lent, hired out, resold or otherwise disposed of by way of trade in any form of binding or cover other than that in which it is published, without the prior consent of the publishers.

Designed and typeset in Garamond by Cinnamon Press. Cover and interior design by Adam Craig.

Printed in the United Kingdom.

Cinnamon Press is represented by Inpress and by the Books Council of Wales.

Acknowledgements

Much of this book began as blogs written over a sixteen month period and published on my website 'Becoming a different story' and on Medium. Some of these blogs found their way into material for online courses in creative journalling or writing through the seasons and I am grateful to the amazing community of writers who follow the blogs, have taken part in courses and offered support and feedback.

I'm also grateful to the writers who have attended or helped to lead or organise courses I've co-tutored at Ty'n y coed, in the Peak District, and in my home in Tanygrisiau, helping me to try out and refine material. Thanks to Tricia Durdey, Pete Marshall and Aidan Shingler. A special thanks to the amazing writers who attended and/or led the first Tanygrisiau masterclass: Adam Craig, Mick Evans, Lizzie Fincham, Seth Fortune, David Gilbert, Isabelle Llasera, Michelle Pashley, Heather Prendergast and Diane Woodrow but particularly to Lizzie, Seth and David for contributing material for the writing exercises in Sections 4 and 5.

Enormous thanks to Anne Clarke and Adam Craig who have proofed and copy edited this book with skill and attention.

And huge thanks to Irena Hill who makes amazing launches possible with such grace and hospitality.

Many of my readers made this book possible by pre-ordering and pledging funds to ensure its publication. It's both inspiring and humbling to receive such generous support. Deep and heartfelt thanks to Annie & Bella, Andy Allan, Maria Americo, Francesca Aniballi, Gail Ashton, Valerie Bean, Valerie Bence, Lisa Bray, Sandra Bunting, Hanne Busck-Nielsen, Christine Buxton, Mark Charlton, Anne Clarke, Susanna Clayson, Beverley Coles, David Cundall, Anne Doherty, Anne Dunford, Liz England, Mick & Sian Evans, Katrin Fiedler, Judith Field, Mark Fitzgerald, Yvonne Foreshaw, Rowan Fortune, Mary Beth Frezon, Stan Galloway, David Gilbert, Yvonne Govan, Angharad Griffiths, Jane Harrigan, Jean Harrison, Sandra Hogarth-Scott, Tamsin Hopkins, Gill Horitz, Sue Howes, Edna Hutchings, Nigel Hutchinson, Tracey Iceton, Nick Jones, Sue Lewis, Isabelle Llasera, Amanda Leahy, Hazel Manuel, Pat Metcalfe, Anne McClean, Fokkina E McDonnell, Jane McKie, Terri Mullholland, Shirley Nichols, Aryanne Oade, Fiona Owen, Sarah Passingham, Lesley Preece, Heather Prendergast, Helen Pizzey, Diana Powell, Jonathan Richards, Susan Richardson, Sheila Roe, Denise Sparrowhawk, Clare Stevenson, Kay Syrad, Bonnie Thurston, Julia Wallis, Nicola Warwick, Sarah Watkinson, Clare Whittaker, Rachel Wilson, Diane Woodrow, Patricia Helen Wooldridge, Lynn Woollacott, Mary Wright, Teffy Wrightson, Lee Wyles, Jennifer Young.

· Dedication ·

A few amazing people went more than the extra mile to support this book. The book is dedicated to them with gratitude and in admiration for fellow-alchemists of the imagination:

For Mark Charlton and Anne Clarke

&

For Michelle, a writer of courage and grace who knows the depths of story,

&

for Adam, always

WRITING DOWN DEEP

• an Alchemy of the Writing Life •

• Contents •

Prelude — 13

Section 1: Craving the Writing Life

Chapter 1: Nurturing the Writing Life — 19
Seven Exercises for a Writing Life — 28
100 Writing Prompts for Those Days — 35

Section 2: The Mindset of the Writer

Chapter 2: Diving into the Mindset of a Writer — 43
Chapter 3: The Audacious Magic of a Single Word — 48
Chapter 4: Imperfect is Good — 58
Interlude 1: Writing the Green Blade — 65
Chapter 5: Your Time is Now — 77
Chapter 6: Small Steps and Big Promises — 86
Interlude 2: Writing the Wild Flowering — 89
Chapter 7: It's All in the Words — 102
Chapter 8: A Mind for Play, Love, Imagination and Ritual — 105
Eight Exercises for a Writer's Mind — 110

Section 3: The Evolution of the Writing Process

Chapter 9: Please Read	115
Chapter 10: The Power of Journalling	120
Interlude 3: Writing the Bright Fire	125
Chapter 11: Working at Depth	135
Chapter 12: It's in the Journey	138
Interlude 4: Writing the Soaring Sun	147
Chapter 13: Where Shall We Go?	160
Chapter 14: Making It Up	169
Four Exercises of Chance and Place	176

Section 4: Embodying the Writing Life

Chapter 15: From Dreams to Body	183
Chapter 16: Exchanging Balance for Rhythm	186
Interlude 5: Writing the Sun to Earth	195
Chapter 17: The Habits that Nurture	210
Chapter 18: Is This the Place?	214
Interlude 6: Writing the Light's Balance	219
Chapter 19: Tending the Creature	234
Nine Exercises in Coming Home	238

Section 5: Writing the Soul

Chapter 20: Of Purpose, Quest and Craf	247
Chapter 21: Who Will Make the Quest?	255
Interlude 7: Writing the Darkness	267
Chapter 22: Beyond Ego to Connection	279
Chapter 23: The Alchemy of Your Writing Life	282
Six Exercises in Soul-writing	290

Conclusion: Writing Your Story

Interlude 8: Finding the Still Point of Your Story	301
Chapter 24: Who Are You Becoming?	352
One Final Exercise: a Mandala for Your Story	355
Afterword	365
References and Further Reading	367
About the Author	375

Prelude

Writing Down Deep — the Alchemy of the Writing Life, is a book for writers who want to dive deeply into their creative flow and into the extraordinary power of writing to affect individuals and the world. Whether you are a blogger writing articles, a memoirist, poet or novelist, writing is magical, it offers perspective shifts, leaps of imagination and connections that are vital to how we live at every level. The world is storied and those who tell stories of every kind, from the first shamans and bards to marketers who understand that we crave story, not sales pitches, have a unique role and responsibility.

My premise is that story (including poetry, fiction and nonfiction) is vital to human survival. It is so important that storytellers do well to become congruent with their tales. This certainly isn't the only way for writers to operate. There are countless examples of writers leading dissolute and broken lives yet producing extraordinary works. But whilst this book is not a call for writers to be 'perfect' or to have all the answers, it is a beacon on the path of constantly questing to become a different story as we write. It is a rebellion against the legions of advertisers, politicians and spin-doctors selling stories that are false, misleading or intended to warp the truth.

No one has to aspire to become a different story. It's a conscious decision and many writers never take it and still have 'success' as writers. But you can aspire to become a different story if you so chose. This book is for the wild idealists and alchemists of the imagination who believe that writing is so powerful that it should change us as we push the boundaries of our craft. This book is for those who see writing as an act of radical spirituality, in the broadest sense of 'spiritual' as the antonym of egotistical hubris, rather than as the opposite of 'material'.

The book is a companion on the quest and, as such, you can read it straight through or slowly; make the rhythm suit you. It has five main sections that are interspersed around shorter, seasonal sections. This gives an overall structure of a year of journalling and thinking to accompany your writing life.

Section 1, 'Craving the Writing Life', is an introduction to our motivation as writers and the power of story. Section 2, 'The Mind-set of the Writer', explores how we build on this to establish an evolving practice of writing, from how we keep in touch with the subconscious writer to how we keep on writing and improving. This leads into Section 3, 'The Evolution of Your Writing Process', in which we'll examine more of the mechanics of writing and deepening our writing lives. Section 4, 'Embodying the Writing Life', takes all of this and anchors it in the physical world and in your own embodiment of your writing. Too often writing is cerebral and disconnected, but the state of our planet is too urgent for narrative alchemists to forget about their bodies and the environments they inhabit. Section 5, 'Writing the Soul', takes this depth to a profound level, looking at how creativity, imagination, wonder and personal mythology transform both the work we do and the people we become as writers, body and soul. Section 6, 'Writing Your Story', brings the themes of the book together: what story do you want to write? What story do you want to become?

At the end of each section there are writing exercises. These are not mechanical or 'how to' exercises but instead are aimed at challenging us to dig deeply into our writing processes and writing lives. There are always new boundaries to push, new skills and new ways to embody our writing lives so it can be instructive to return to these from time to time and see how your answers and writing have moved on. At the end of the first section there is also a list of 100 writing prompts for those days when you want something to give you a push and no inspiration seems to be coming.

Woven into Sections 2 to 6 are seasonal pauses. These follow the quarter days and cross-quarter days of the year, seasonal reflections on diving deeply into our writing with thought, prompts, journalling questions and 'rituals', writing exercises or activities to anchor our writing. The first seven of these are 'interludes' of three to four days of concentrated journalling, tracking the cycle of the year. The eighth, 'Finding the Still Point of Your Story', is a longer 'interlude' of five weeks that runs from the beginning of December to early January with daily readings, journalling prompts and rituals.

As writers, we witness to the world and weave stories that make sense of what it means to be human. This takes a great deal of energy, often on top of other work and family commitments, and we will only find this energy for writing if we are nourished. The interludes are part of that nourishment. As they fit into particular seasons of the year, feel free to move around the book and access the interlude that matches the time of year you are reading, or you might want to read right through the book and then come back to it as a workbook, using the writing exercises and interludes through the seasons.

I'm a fan of slowing down in order to give ourselves the time and space to dive deeply, so in the online course that accompanies this book, in the first year we work through each section missing out the interludes and then return to these in the second year while completing an individual writing project, whether it's a novel, a collection of stories or poetry, or a nonfiction project…

Finally, there are Endnotes for those who'd like to follow up references and further reading and an Afterword with some information about courses and the Becoming a Different Story online community.

SECTION 1

CRAVING THE WRITING LIFE

Chapter 1
Nurturing a Writing Life

Why we write

Whatever our reasons for writing and whoever we are now, the craft can improve, our identities can grow and we can deepen the power of story for the world as we both hone our skills and develop our lives. This is always about process, not product. The moment we feel our writing is the best thing or that our lives are as good as they get, we ossify.

So the message of this book is that we should always be in the process of becoming different in order to have a writing life that constantly challenges and moves us, and those whose lives we touch, another step along in the journey.

Writing goes to the core of human identity and as such it can be a strange and demanding compulsion, but at some point, most of us do it (among so many other reasons) for the way in which it transports us to another space.

When we write, we're opening ourselves up. Writing takes us into another space. As Virginia Woolf described it:

> I walk making up phrases; sit, contriving scenes; am in short in the thick of the greatest rapture known to me.

Writing is a journey within ourselves as well as a means to bear witness. In the meeting of the interior world and in writing embodied pieces that encounter the world with all the senses, we expand the understanding of what it is to be human. Writers constantly grapple with the human condition. T S Eliot talks about this desire to make meaning in his poem 'The Dry Salvages' and perhaps the search for meaning is even more important than the search for happiness.

Narrativising gives life shape, connects us to others and to the world we inhabit, to what has gone before and what will come after. Writing allows us to imagine alternatives. Writing can be a lonely activity, but sending our writing

Chapter 1: Nurturing a Writing Life

into the world can be both a public act of hope and a private ritual of remembrance as we make art out of everyday, ordinary moments. So much gets lost. There are too many moments to capture them, to always find the meaning, but some of them make it.

Even if your reasons for writing are as simple as Octavia Butler's love of stories that have to be told, the fact remains that when we love stories so much that narrativising becomes who we are and it is simply unthinkable not to write, it is still the case that those stories will grow a thousand fold if we also pay attention to the stories we are as creators.

Take yourself seriously

Writers hold out a vision for transformation, for reality, for themselves. This demands a high degree of reflection. It requires that you walk around with your senses open, determined to stay awake in a world where so many people seem to be at least half asleep.

Writing demands that you deploy imagination and insight, that you live with an extraordinary internal world that has the potential to transform the outer world. Each time we read there is the possibility of a new perspective and growth. And if the written word is so transformative then the chances are that writers have power and responsibility. It behoves you then not to denigrate yourself or what you do (whilst holding this in tension with not becoming an egotistical, arrogant bore, of course.)

In *The Artist's Way* Julia Cameron challenges writers to become witnesses. This is a lot to live up to, yet it is compelling. There are countless novels that are a testimony not only to inward states, human emotion and condition, but also to events. Books like Primo Levi's *If This Is A Man*, dealing with the legacy of the Holocaust, so that it becomes part of common consciousness. The film *Hiroshima Mon Amour*, from the book by Marguerite Dumas, reflects on the existential crisis of lovers who need to cling to one another after horror. And the list could go on.

In addition to testifying to the human condition, to stories that would otherwise go unheard and to the possibilities that lie ahead, writers deal with how much we can achieve. The poet Adrienne Rich talks about throwing in her lot with those who renew the world. This not only speaks of an extraordinary hope and belief in freedom in the face of suffering, but also gives writers an enormous responsibility for opening up new horizons. Our writing has the opportunity to shift the perspective of readers and widen their choices as a result. Words are powerful things.

Language shapes reality. What do we believe about reality? How do we conceive the nature of our existence and freedom? None of us can transcend the facts of existence: we exist in a universe of physical laws and principles. Environment, language and culture shape us in complex ways. And we never become aware of all these influences or shake free of them.

But we are not reducible to those influences. Neither are we simply the roles we adopt; none of us is only a writer, a mother, a daughter, a musician. Only objects or deities (if they figure in your world view) are wholly one thing. God is God. A table is a table. But human beings are complex and changeable. We are conscious, or should be if we are brave enough to stay awake in the world.

Humans can transcend certain 'givens' —

- the class we're born into
- the racial stereotypes projected onto us
- the social expectations around

These do not have to define who we are. As Sartre claims, we have the ability to negate these expectations and to become anything.

And it's not only philosophers who think like this. Increasingly, research suggests not only that we have plastic brains that can adapt and change, but also that our biology is more fluid than we conceived previously. (Studies in epigenetics are rapidly expanding our understanding of this, for example Nessa Carey's *The Epigenetics Revolutions*.)

This amount of freedom is terrifying and wonderful. It suggests that authentic living requires that we take our autonomy seriously. It implies that I am never identical with my current 'self', yet am always responsible for sustaining, challenging and growing it. It means I can't hide behind phrases like 'this is the way I am' or 'it's in my genes/my past experiences…' If I choose to remain a certain way, it is a choice, and there is no lying to myself about that. To paraphrase Sartre: Whatever life has made you into you still have the choice to make yourself into something else.

The inner world is a powerful place that changes how we experience the outer world. Stories, poems and articles make their way into our subconscious and transform how we interact with the world and impact on it. By being writers who take this seriously we open up a world of new thinking and new ways of being, for ourselves and for those who engage with our writing. Writing is an awesome thing to do and we do it best when we become people who take our freedom and imaginations seriously.

When we write for the trance and take ourselves seriously, we are forces to be reckoned with. In what follows, I'll break down this perspective on the writing life into particular areas: the mindset of the writer; embodying the writing life; writing the soul and observations on the writing process. I don't mean to suggest by this schema that soul, mind, body and process are separate or competing 'parts' of the writer; these are simply ways to approach the subject, taking into account the complexity of the subject and of writers themselves.

Switching Off Distractions to Switch On Creativity

Creativity is deep, attentive work. Whether you are solving a maths problem or painting a picture, writing elegant code or a novel, you have to be attentive, focused and in flow. You need to be in an optimal peak state to create and that means setting aside distractions for key periods. This isn't easy. There are so many things clamouring for our attention, but if we don't find a way to step back, creativity will be one of the many casualties.

Switching Off

1. Technology

Long bouts of social media or aimless Internet surfing can leave us feeling ragged. We end up with our thoughts fractured and innovative thinking out of reach. There's no doubt that technology has changed our lives and, in many ways, for the better. The access to like minds across the planet, the ability to communicate across distances, the tools for writing, research and so much more, can be mind-expanding. But there is also the anxiety that the smarter our phones get, the dumber we become. So many people check their phones over and over that it's a wonder they get anything done.

Why this knee-jerk checking? It might signal a population unable to cope with 'doing nothing' for short (or longer periods) or uneasy being alone with their own thoughts. It might also be that sometimes our devices deliver a reward. We discover an illuminating article, get news of a book we've been waiting to read or hear from a close friend. So we check in case we're missing something. But this can come with a cost: compulsive phone checking makes us feel mentally fragmented but not checking leaves us uneasy. Devices can become security blankets and we check in for fear of missing out, becoming anxious, antsy, miserable and jittery if we are forced to be apart from phones and computers. For some this can almost feel like not existing. Existential rage against obliteration is a strong human compulsion so it's perhaps not surprising that people can feel distraught at the thought of being 'cut off'. The online life taps into the human psyche.

Sadly, whilst anxiously checking social media in case we miss something, we instead miss out on the ability to be alone with our thoughts or being able focus on someone who is with us in person or on building up a deliberate practice that improves our skills and adds depth to life.

The practice of always checking messages or social media, together with the myth of multitasking, robs us of focus. Our brains receive thousands of stimuli and the ability to sift for what's important and ignore the distractions is vital. When we try to attend to a stimulus the brain has to move that piece of information to the frontal cortex. If we are doing three things at once, the constant switching (it isn't multitasking) takes time and leaves us feeling fragmented and fuzzy-minded.

It doesn't have to be like this. Our attention spans are quite capable of being sustained. Think of losing yourself in a great novel or film. Think of the total absorption of a parent in a new baby. What we can't do it sustain focus in the face of a thousand distractions or when our attention is being divided. This means that sometimes we have to switch off (particularly social media, messages, calls, and apps) to switch on our creative flow.

2. Productivity

If your work and your art are of a piece then there's less conflict about how you use your time. However, many of us do one thing to hold body and soul together and pursue our art in addition. You might love your non-writing work, but that doesn't mean you want to be available to it at all hours, seven days a week.

Yet so many of us remain available to work email wherever we are or bring work home with us and it becomes all too easy never to fully switch out of work mode. Working from home, I know the temptation is to answer emails all through the day, to do a last check late at night before sleep. I used to feel obliged to be available all the time. It's only in the last few months that I had the epiphany that it is possible to take weekends off and answer emails only once each workday.

No matter how much you love your work, there will be elements of it that you can delegate or eliminate. So much busyness isn't productive in the first place. The rest you can limit:

- Time-batch essential but mundane administrative tasks.
- Set a time to finish each evening and disengage.
- Promise yourself weekends or blocks of time with no work.

Above all prioritise developing skills over productivity. Getting better and more skilful at what we do takes huge reserves of creative energy. It requires deliberate practice and takes energy that has to come from somewhere, so switch off from work regularly.

3. Daily life

We all need habits that sustain us. It's important to be well-nourished and to get exercise. It's important to have a morning routine that sets up the day and an evening routine that promotes quality sleep. But sometimes we push ourselves too hard and need to take a step back. Exhausted people find it hard to maintain creativity. We need to sleep. It's a wonderful restorative and we suffer when our sleep is out of balance or deprived.

Similarly, switching off constant consumption is healthy, whether it's overeating, constant reliance on technology, pushing our bodies long and hard, staying up far too long or overworking. Switching off can help creativity.

4. Sociability

We need other people. Having family or friends who help and support us and who we are there for in return, is essential, but sometimes we need solitude. Some of us like more solitude than others. Personally, I love the buzz of family gatherings or of a great book launch or leading a writing course that is full on for five days. But I refuel alone and in quiet. I love periods of solitude. Other people find the opposite, but however you work best you need some time with your own thoughts.

Some creativity requires teams — making a film, some forms of music or scientific research. Other creative endeavours, like landscape painting or writing a novel, are more solitary so as a writer you will need time alone for your craft but you will also need some time alone for respite. Even if you prefer to be in a group, bouncing ideas off other people to nurture your own development take some time for solitude. Why?

- You will be more focused.
- You will think more deeply.

- You will be less distracted.
- You will learn more about yourself.
- You will take all this back into your relationships: refreshed you can be more giving.

Switching On

Switching off is essential to creativity but it's not the end of the story. Creativity is intense, attentive work. It requires you to set aside distractions and limit work time. It means knowing how far to push yourself and when to rest and take some time alone. But as well as switching off, there are also positive things you can do to prime creativity.

Some of these will be individual, but these are my creativity primers, which I share with you as examples:

Spend time with family

> I have a big noisy family that is often swelled by friends so close they have become 'family'. Sometimes solitude nourishes, but at other times it's about nurturing these vital connections.

Read

> I read everything from philosophy to how-to books, from feminist theory to poetry, fiction to food writing. But the books that nurture me most are poetry and fiction. To lose myself in language or in a story is bliss. And it elevates my thinking and how I write.

See art

> When I travel, the local art and photography galleries are always high on the list of things to see. Whenever I'm in London I try to visit Tate Modern. I can barely draw stick figures and have a lot to learn about art, but visual image feeds me; try it.

Watch films

> Not anything will do. Some switched-off time demands comfort viewing (but not too much). More often I go for films that deepen my insight in some way. Art films. Foreign films. They may seem demanding but you're not trying to switch off your brain, just the distractions.

Listen to music

I'm on a learning curve with this one. I don't create to music, but it can certainly prime creativity and many people love to write or paint to it.

Move your body

When I'm at my best I have a daily yoga practice. My heart rate drops. I'm more focused as well as more flexible (physically and mentally). I'm more able to get into the trance state of writing.

Walk

An extension of movement. I'm with Nietzsche on how walking and rumination go together. Thoreau, Hemingway and many other writers agree.

Dance

I don't do enough of this, but I love it when I do and it often accompanies my cooking.

Cook and eat

Constant consumption can make us sluggish, but nutritious food cooked with love and a bit of flair is great fuel. For me, the practise of cooking is not only a delight in itself but a kind of meditation and I often have surprising thoughts while doing it.

Bathe

This is my daily luxury. Hot water soothes and rejuvenates and a bath is a great place to simply think.

Meditate

There are lots of meditation techniques and increasing evidence that our brains cycle at slower speeds during meditation. Slow theta waves in the frontal lobe and creative alpha waves in the posterior part of the brain minimise stress and take the focus off tasks, to increase deep relaxation.

Chapter 1: Nurturing a Writing Life

Let the silence in

There are times for music and film, for dancing and positive activity, and times for quiet. I love to create in silence. Take some time that is not filled, which leads me to:

Do nothing

I can't claim to be good at this one, but sometimes the positive thing to do is nothing. Even if it's only for a few minutes. Completely unwind. Let go.

Whatever your creativity primers, take some time for at least one of them today and whatever stage of your writing life you've reached, nurture your art by switching off from distractions to switch on creativity.

Seven Exercises for a Writing Life

Writing is a life's journey, but the creative life doesn't have to be one of continual striving and endless to-do lists. Travelling in Spain a while ago, I had time to think about the ways in which life can be both creative and positive. This is not, by any means, the last word on the creative life, but some of the elements that seem vital when we crave and begin to sculpt a creative life.

- Look for signs of abundance.
- Value growth and move on.
- Take time to gather yourself.
- Face (and quiet) your fears.
- Use discernment.
- Don't move with the herd.
- Be the person you want to become.

1. Look for the signs of abundance

Creative people are often 'itchy'. By that I mean we are always looking for the new project, the new experience… This openness is great for creativity, as is the sense that there is always more to learn and to become. However, it shouldn't prevent us from stopping to realise how far we've come and how much we already have in our lives.

Journal exercises

How far have you come in your life and creative endeavours in the last five years?

What do you already have in your life that makes it abundant?

Progress might be in relationships, in creative projects (those that worked and those that didn't), in health or work… Epicurus tells us that abundance is not about having things, but enjoying life. If we begin by thinking of life as pinched and mean then we are more likely to live in fear than in thanks, with the result that we experience blocks in our energy and perpetuate a downward spiral. Instead, Marcus Aurelius advises that the first thing we think about each day is what a privilege it is to live. Abundance is a way of being. It should be on all our to-be lists.

2. Value growth and move on

If we don't encourage ourselves by thinking about how far we have come, we're likely to feel demotivated. But, equally, we also need to move forward. Lao Tzu talks about letting go of what we presently are in order to become someone new. We are always evolving, which is not to devalue the past. We can be thankful for what has been whilst being forward-looking.

New growth generally requires some pruning of old growth. Making progress, as people, as writers, in whatever passions inspire us, is both exhilarating and uncomfortable. When we grow, take on new creative projects or work on personal development, some parts of the lives we've had will no longer fit with the people we want to become. And sometimes it is not only behaviours and mind-sets, but people that we will feel ourselves moving away from. This shouldn't mean becoming unkind or judgemental, but it may mean wishing some people well while letting go.

Journal exercises

If you have a passion in life or a drive to be the best person you can possibly become, it will inevitably involve decisions.

What has to go to make room?

What are you willing to give up in order to have the time to create?

What do you need to uncommit from to grow and move on?

3. Take time to gather yourself

Working on a big creative project, whether it's yourself or a novel, a poetry collection or a work of art... will require clarity, focus and a great deal of emotional and psychological energy.

Give yourself time to recover and reflect.

Journal exercises

What are your energy drains?

What inessential things are taking your time and distracting you?

In *Letters on Life*, Rainer Maria Rilke remarks on how are lives re impoverished by being in a constant state of distraction so that we are never ready for the moment, for the present. We need to give ourselves time. After all, in the words attributed to George Eliot:

It's never too late to be who you might have been.

4. Face (and quiet) your fears

Creativity takes courage. It's easy to stay in our comfort zones and not change. It's easy to make a million excuses as to why we never started that book, painted that picture, or launched that new project...

Feeling afraid is human. And if we step out of the comfort zone we face the real possibility of failure. But staying stuck is a much worse form of failure, one that will increasingly fill us with regrets.

Journal exercise

What do you fear?

It might be:

- Failure.
- Not being in control.
- Being judged.
- Not being loved.
- Losing money or status.

It might be all or none of the above… But we all have fears.

Learning what our fears are is the first step to being kind to ourselves. And a major step to becoming less reactive and less likely to take on others' negative projections.

Courage is not the absence of fear, but simply moving on with dignity despite that fear.

5. Use discernment

It isn't only all those inessential distractions that can overwhelm your ability to create art, literature and the life you want. You can't make huge progress on 20 fronts at one time. If you are anything like me, you may find yourself not so much distracted as simply overwhelmed by taking on too much.

Some activities go hand in hand. I try to prioritise writing and travel together. Spending time in unfamiliar places has enabled me not only to research real locations and layer authentic details into the novels I've been working on, but also to shift my perspective. This has been a huge creative bonus.

However, if I decided to do all this AND learn to play an instrument AND study Hungarian this year AND keep my business going, something would have unravelled. Perhaps it would all have unravelled.

In terms of big quests in life, aspiring to two or three major goals, supported by good habits of time use and nutrition and healthy living, are likely to be more manageable than seven major goals + family + work + nutrition + exercise + daily routines + journalling + saving the world by last Tuesday. (Though, as a caveat, that's not to say we can't take an interest and delight in many fields of human enquiry.)

Journal exercise

When do you begin to feel burnout and what step can you take to prevent it?

6. Don't move with the herd

A creative life is unlikely to be a conventional one. There are conventions that hold societies together. There are norms about morality that we do well to follow. But so much of what we do is not about large moral agreements, it's about going along with the herd, staying half-asleep so that we don't rock the boat or ask uncomfortable questions.

A creative life, a life in which you continually develop the story of who you want to become, is likely to not only demand that you are wide awake for much more of the time, but also that you take risks with how you live and who you are. Mark Twain puts it something like this (though the popular quote has been a little mangled):

> Whenever you find yourself on the side of the majority, it is time to pause and reflect.

I haven't had a TV for well over a decade. A couple of times when I've told people this, usually because they've asked if I've been watching some particular programme, the other person hasn't only shown surprise, but said something like, 'I don't understand. What do you mean by you don't have a TV?' Not having a TV does not compute, even though it's not really a very radical life choice. The details of what it means to you to not move with the herd will vary. We are unique, creative people, authoring hand-written lives. Some of the things it means or has meant for me include:

- No TV.
- Home educating my (now adult) children.
- Moving away from institutional affiliations, whether of religion, politics or anything else.
- Living rurally in a house that will always be a project, but it is nonetheless roomy and homey.
- Running an independent press on a shoestring, supporting fantastic literature that mainstream publishing won't touch.
- Prioritising writing, travel and family over 'things'.
- Being an optimist who doesn't believe the dogma 'There Is No Alternative'.
- Spending many years as a vegetarian and currently eating a 'Blue Zones' style diet. (It involves a lot of beans!)

We are herded through life in so many ways. None of us escapes from this entirely but we can become increasingly conscious of our decisions. A quote attributed to Gandhi sums it up:

> It's better to walk alone than with a crowd going in the wrong direction.

Journal exercise

In what ways is your life distinctive?

How could it be more so (by your own lights and values)?

7. Be the person you want to become

A creative life requires commitment. It's vital not to let anyone else dictate who you are or who you want to become, and that includes silencing those inner voices that we learnt in childhood or education and that need shutting down before they derail you.

For the last five years I've been working on a trilogy of novels. The protagonist in the first book, *This is the End of the Story*, begins from a position in which she is uncertain of her own identity. Belief is Cassie's gift, so much so that she believes herself to be whoever those in her life tell her she is — Cassie, Kat, Kitty, even Casilda, as Miriam insists, an eleventh century Muslim princess from Toledo who later became a Catholic saint.

In the second novel, *A Remedy for All Things*, Catherine (formerly Cassie) is beginning to have a better sense of herself, but a series of extraordinary dreams shakes her identity again.

It's not until the final novel, *For Hope is Always Born*, that these questions of identity might resolve. But what is crucial throughout the narrative arc is that the emerging identity must be one that comes from within, that is intrinsically motivated.

We can't create if we see ourselves as marionettes pulled around by circumstance. Instead of giving control of our lives to petty distractions, unreasonable demands, fear, conventional notions of the 'average' life or excuses we've got used to living with, we need to follow this paraphrase of Rumi's advice:

> Let yourself be drawn by the stronger pull of that which you
> truly love.

Change relies on congruence. Your desires, your beliefs and your self-confidence have to be of a piece. Your values and your behaviour have to reflect one another. Of course there will be days when it all falls apart. We're all fallible and human, but the direction is always towards matching our inner and outer life. In the words attributed to Mahatma Ghandi:

> Be congruent, be authentic, be true to yourself.

Journal exercise

Take out a set of coloured pens or pencils, and draw, map and write the answer in many colours:

Who are you becoming?

100 Writing Prompts for Those Days

Writing is a muscle. The more we use it, the more flexible and strong it becomes. Whether you are writing morning pages in which you do two or three pages of thinking on paper or work from a writing prompt, whether you are outlining ideas or setting down emotions, the more you write, the more confident your writing voice will become. And so will your self-confidence. Writing needs space and priority but some days, despite having an environment that supports us and putting aside distractions and despite making the time to write, nothing comes. At such times, writing prompts can be great ways to clear the blockage — or simply use these as starter exercises as you get into flow.

10 for Time

- Every second felt like…
- These are the rituals of my morning…
- We played 'What time is it, Mr Wolf?' and…
- It's always at twilight that…
- 'Time flies over us, but leaves its shadow behind.' (Nathaniel Hawthorne)
- Teatime was once…
- It was a time of…
- If time has wings then…
- What was most disconcerting was that it always occurred at the same time, down to the second, and each time…
- 'The two most powerful warriors are patience and time.' (Leo Tolstoy)

10 for place

- This was a place where the stream ran with tears, the grass…
- She was in that liminal space, neither…
- The road ahead…
- 'The streets of London have their map, but our passions are uncharted. What are you going to meet if you turn this corner?' (Virginia Woolf)
- Outside the tent something rustled…
- The river snaked beside them as…
- The whole town seemed empty…
- Love changes your view of a place…
- The most beautiful place I've ever seen was…
- How to describe this city? I can only say…

10 for Character

- Staring at the screen, she knew that what she had refused to acknowledge these past months was now irrefutable…
- 'There is, I believe, in every disposition a tendency to some particular evil, a natural defect, which not even the best education can overcome.' (Jane Austen)
- He had thick dark hair and…
- Although she'd left, the room told me everything I needed to know about her…
- 'I am no bird; and no net ensnares me: I am a free human being with an independent will.' (Charlotte Brontë)
- These are the ways I thought I knew him…
- The person in the mirror is…
- 'It is curious that physical courage should be so common in the world and moral courage so rare.' (Mark Twain)
- …but despite the threadbare clothes he wore the most immaculate shoes I'd ever seen…
- She would change character, she decided, that was all…

10 for Senses

- The light was strange, a glow that…
- Peering through the half-open door, he could see…
- The scent of…

- She reached out and touched…
- Cold gnawed and the air…
- Every muscle ached…
- The shrill cry was…
- The taste filled me with…
- So quiet that…
- I could smell the electricity in the air, taste it on the molecules that entered…

10 for Weather

- The sky was ashes and…
- 'A change in the weather is sufficient to recreate the world and ourselves.' (Marcel Proust)
- It seemed the spring would never come that year…
- After the storm…
- 'Is not this a true autumn day? Just the still melancholy that I love —' (George Eliot)
- It had rained for weeks and now…
- There are five magical winds that blow through…
- A thick fog clung to the earth, shrouding…
- In the distant the lightning shimmered as though from…
- It was the hottest summer afternoon….

10 for Movement

- One step, then the next, that was…
- As the dancers whirled in…
- To move is to be…
- The wings rose first, then…
- It seemed as though the bus would never reach…
- 'I am losing precious days. I am degenerating into a machine for making money. I am learning nothing in this trivial world of men. I must break away and get out into the mountains to learn the news.' (John Muir)
- The only time I took a sleeper train…
- Something moved on the horizon…
- 'All truly great thoughts are conceived while walking.' (Friedrich Nietzsche)
- The movement was unlike any other…

10 for Memory

- 'I can only note that the past is beautiful because one never realises an emotion at the time. It expands later, and thus we don't have complete emotions about the present, only about the past.' (Virginia Woolf)
- It's so long ago now...
- When he left...
- 'Touch has a memory' (John Keats)
- It was the winter when...
- I don't remember this myself, but my grandmother told me...
- He no longer remembers...
- Someone was telling a story and...
- Nostalgia is...
- These are the things I've forgotten...

10 for Emotion

- Hubris, he thought, surveying...
- The tears didn't come until...
- The questions come at night and then I feel...
- She was sitting on a train at the end of an ordinary day when bliss seized her...
- Sadness is what makes me...
- Rain pounded the earth. Head down, she walked, feeling...
- '"Goodbye," said the fox. "And now here is my secret, a very simple secret: It is only with the heart that one can see rightly; what is essential is invisible to the eye."' (Antoine de Saint-Exupéry)
- This was the most frightening moment of his life...
- He knew he had to say no, but the thought of doing so filled him with...
- When I think about my family, I feel...

10 for Story

- What was lost was...
- Whispers, it was only whispers and shadows, and yet...
- It was a Saturday, or maybe a Friday, early evening and...
- I knew it was a lie from the beginning, but...
- 'If you do not tell the truth about yourself you cannot tell it about

other people.' (Virginia Woolf)
- The day after the funeral…
- My parents' bedroom was…
- There seemed to be no way out…
- It started like any other day…
- It was the story he never told that…

10 for Imagination

- It was when the silence fell that…
- He could make out only shapes…
- 'Vision is the art of seeing things invisible.' (Jonathan Swift)
- It was the things that went unsaid that…
- The cat dreams of…
- If you can imagine it then…
- Deep in reverie, I…
- Tomorrow will be…
- It was no ordinary mirror…
- What are you doing here?

Here's to your writing flow and your extraordinary creativity.

SECTION 2

THE MINDSET OF THE WRITER

Chapter 2: Diving into the Mindset of a Writer

The mindset of a writer is a powerful matrix of attitudes that can assist you in staying focussed and finding your flow. It requires the passion to keep the promises you make to yourself, the courage to fail and to value your development more than the outcome, frequent use of the word 'no' and systems that will help you to replace overwhelm with steady steps and positive, cumulative growth.

In this section we're going to dive into that mindset and also take two seasonal interludes. As I mentioned in the foreword, these interludes will appear in each of the remaining sections of the book and are nourishment for your writing. As they fit into particular seasons of the year, feel free to move around the book and access the interludes that match the time of year you are reading, or you might want to read right through the book and then come back to it as a workbook later.

Beyond imagination, my most basic tool as a writer is my journal. I journal as soon as I wake up because this is the time I'm in that liminal space between waking and sleeping. Sometimes I can capture snatches of dreams and tease them into the daylight. My mind is at its most open and creative at the extremities of the day so starting the day with journalling is a way to begin the day well.

It's also the way I end each day. My journal is a framing ritual that allows me to imagine and to reflect. And I come to my journal in an attitude of hope and expectation. Often, I think I will write a certain thing, then find I'm writing something completely different. The journal is a space where I take myself by surprise. And that can lead in all kinds of creative directions. Journalling boosts my:

- creativity
- clarity
- equanimity
- gratitude
- acuity
- passion
- purpose

And these are qualities that build into the writing mindset. So often we have a million things we want to achieve and a million demands calling for our time. Too many people lead stressful, busy lives and find themselves overwhelmed. In this state, dreams and quests are constantly shelved because we don't know where to start.

Creativity

Big changes rarely, if ever, originate from trying to do everything all at once. We need new habits and systems that facilitate shifts, that build into something powerful, almost taking us unawares. Journalling is a fundamental habit.

What is the first thing you reach for each morning? Coffee? Your phone? Your laptop to check emails and/or social media? Don't! These things can wait. Some of them might never need your attention at all. But none of them deserve that wonderful creative burst on first waking. It's precious. All night your subconscious has been churning away and if you went to sleep thinking of a problem or how to write your next chapter or what the precise word in the third line of that poem should be, now is the time to get into the flow.

If nothing comes, use one of the writing prompts from the end of Section 1.

Clarity

At the beginning of every day I think about my quests. The day will be busy and there will be many calls on my time, but by reminding myself of my direction, I'm more likely to take small steps towards it that day. I might:

- Clear a two hour space for writing in the evening.
- Make a concrete plan to visit somewhere that will help with my writing research as well as my passion for travel (perhaps buying a train ticket or booking a place to stay).

- Move from journalling to yoga to keep myself fit enough to write and travel.
- Think about a way to be generous or take a risk that day.

Journalling enhances your ability not only to make decisions, but to live them. There's something about writing visions down that makes you more engaged with them, a first way of embodying them. And you begin to shift your self-image when you journal in this way, which is always a powerful motivator of change.

Equanimity

Journalling is also a wonderful way to absorb emotions. In this sense we write a lot of 'rubbish' in our journals. That's fine. It's better there than eating away at you or spilling out onto others. If I'm journalling every day, morning and evening, even for a few minutes each time, I'm calmer, more focussed and more optimistic. As Kafka recognised:

> In the diary you find proof that in situations which today would seem unbearable, you lived, looked around and wrote down observations, that this right hand moved then as it does today.

This is not only clarity, but depth. I begin to see patterns in my behaviour, to let go of negative feelings. Journalling is empowering because it enables me to see how I can make my inner and outer life more congruent. As the saying attributed to Gandhi goes:

> Happiness is when what you think, what you say, and what you do are in harmony.

Gratitude

I don't often list all the things I'm grateful for in my life but keeping a journal nonetheless makes me much more aware of how much there is to be grateful for, sometimes overwhelmingly so. Managing emotions in a journal often shifts my mood and outlook, makes me aware of how easy it is to follow the ego and helps me to get over myself. And being aware of the blessings of our lives helps us not only to look inwards, but to connect our internal life to those we love

Acuity

My journals are currently colour coded. I keep personal reflections and to-be lists in purple, task lists in black, book notes or notes for articles in green and quotes in red. I use blue for dream journalling and am beginning to need more colours.

Journals are a great way to store and work on ideas as well as emotions. If I'm reading nonfiction books I find writing key ideas down is an excellent way to enhance the learning. And whatever I'm reading: philosophy, books on writing, fiction, poetry — there are always quotes I want to hold onto: to savour. It sharpens my mind to do this and I find myself making connections between ideas from books from different perspectives and across genres.

Passion

The place where creativity and clarity meet is passion. What is it that excites you? What is that makes your life meaningful? Your journal is the place to begin writing the story you want to live. It's a safe space in which to fly. It's a private space where passions can surface and you work things out with yourself.

Purpose

I would recommend journalling to everyone, but for writers there is a particular alignment between journalling and sense of purpose. After all, writers write and journalling is a great training ground where:

- You flex your writing muscle.
- Hone your voice and try it out.
- Play with ideas.
- Produce occasional nuggets of gold.
- Find out who you are.

The writer who flew with imagination, J.M Barrie, sums it up like this:

Chapter 2: Diving into the Mindset of a Writer

> The life of every [wo]man is a diary in which [s]he means to write one story, and writes another; and [her/]his humblest hour is when [s]he compares the volume as it is with what [s]he vowed to make it.

In short, journalling is a powerful way to cultivate the mindset of a writer. It will:

- Prime your creativity.
- Make your thinking and living not only clearer but more congruent.
- Increase your equanimity and appreciation.
- Sharpen your mind.
- Fuel your passion and purpose.

With this in mind, in the six short chapters in Section 2, we'll consider interlocking systems to build and constantly develop this mindset, taking a couple of interludes along the way.

Chapter 3
The Audacious Magic of a Single Word

For some of us, saying no is hard, even anathema. I've been a people-pleaser for over five decades, but the seeds of saying no were sown when I left a vocation. Not only was I assaulted three times at work, but those I worked for were anything but sympathetic and it was time to say 'no more'. But as a publisher and editor I soon slid back into my old people-pleasing ways. This may not sound like much of a problem, but it is. Saying yes every time isn't healthy.

If you always say yes, what's it worth?

When we agree to give time or skills or resources to something it should be of some import. If you say yes to everything then nothing is more important or valuable in your life than anything else. The creative project that is your dream and passion, quality time with your family and friends — are these of no more weight than random requests or unreasonable calls to work more hours than a week contains?

If you always say yes you'll end up in difficult situations

What might seem like making life easy life for the short-term is likely to become the albatross around your neck. It's so much more difficult to extricate yourself from a situation that doesn't fit your values or that fills you with dread than it is to say no at the outset.

If you always say yes, what are you avoiding?

People who say yes a great deal tend to have problems with conflict. Not only with actual conflict but even with imagining that someone might get upset or angry with them. This can be so debilitating that they'll say yes rather than risk not seeming pleasant and appeasing. If the imagined outcome of saying no to someone frightens you, it's time to take stock and learn that the world won't end if someone doesn't like your 'no'. It might be uncomfortable, but you are not responsible for someone else's response and you are not there to walk on.

Saying no gives you space to focus on what matters

If you want to feel time-rich, don't be busy with things that don't matter. Instead focus and pay attention to the things that matter. Be present. The 'more' that matters is not quantity, but depth. Saying yes to things that leave you lukewarm or because you want to appease others is a recipe for self-negation.

Saying no signals choices

If you don't make choices, sometimes difficult ones, then you are not giving anything priority. Whatever comes along, whether it's a pay increase or a distraction, you need to ask whether it is in accord with your vision. If the answer is no, don't say yes for the sake of short-term gain. Don't say yes to appease someone. Don't say yes to something that will take you in the direction you don't want to travel.

Of course there are times when we say yes to something we're unsure of because we want to try something new or test an idea. But when your heart is sinking at the same time as you are saying 'yes' then you know it's the wrong way to go. (A sinking heart isn't the same, however, as fear of the new.)

Saying no prevents burnout

In George Orwell's *Animal Farm* Boxer is the most loyal and hardworking of animals. He's not very bright but he never stops labouring — he constantly tells himself he must work harder and when he collapses from exhaustion the pigs report they've sent him to a vet. But in fact they send him for slaughter at the knacker's yard in return for a case of whiskey.

I'm not advocating becoming closed or ungiving but we do have to make choices if we want to be free of the downward cycle of overwhelm. Saying yes to things that aren't essential or that are more than you can manage will drain your energy.

A few years ago after a difficult financial period for Cinnamon Press I took on more and more work. The trend escalated and we woke up one morning to find our forward list of publications topping 30 a year with only two staff. We also had a poetry journal, several poetry pamphlets, four literary competitions, and three writing courses to manage. When I got an Arts Council grant that enabled me to take time off to research and write in Budapest we confronted how out of control the work was becoming. I came back determined to reclaim the original vision for the press, which meant making hard but vital decisions about what we publish and how we use time.

If you want to avoid overwhelm, you have to learn to say no sometimes. But even if we can see that always saying yes isn't healthy and appreciate the benefits that come from saying no, we don't always have the courage or the skills to do it. It takes practise to learn to say no graciously. Before we get to the stage of saying no, we sometimes need time to think. There are people who are adept at getting a yes out of others because they're good at putting the other person on the spot. Don't be strong-armed. If you feel pressured, ask for time, say you have to check with others, that you need to follow up other commitments first. You can get back in a timely manner, but you don't have to always decide on the spot.

You can also make counter-offers rather than either a yes or no —

- I can't do that for you, but I could…
- I can't make it then, but this would be possible…
- I could do this for you, but it would mean I'd have to drop the other favour you asked to make space…
- I can't help with that, but have you thought of asking…

If it's a definite no, though, you need to communicate that.

Be clear

If we are not clear about our vision and priorities it's hard to say no. But if we have a good sense of our values and quest then it's easier to sense when something isn't for us. When I was taking on more and more work it was because I'd slipped into a survival mode and had lost the distinctive vision I'd begun the press with. Taking time to refocus changed that. It's easier now to say no because I have, once more, a strong sense of what fits. There's a story that Norah Ephron was once asked why she repeatedly worked with the same actors, people such as Meg Ryan and Tom Hanks. Her answer, apparently, was 'because they're the same food group'. With a bit of clarity, we know when a person or a project is the right fit for us. When we have that clarity, we should pass it on. Keeping others dangling with non-committal maybes is much more annoying than a gracious, honest 'no'.

Be firm

A firm no doesn't have to be blunt. We can thank the person for thinking of us. We can listen and empathise without taking on a problem as our own. We can suggest other solutions. We can even avoid using the word 'no':

- I'd love to but I'm completely at capacity for the next…
- It's lovely of you to ask, but it's not something that appeals to me…

Be focussed

You know the value of your time and you know what your priorities are. Every yes is a commitment, big or small, to give emotional energy or time or resources. I'm a fan of giving. I think generosity is fundamental to being human and engaged. But that doesn't mean we should pour ourselves out on a random-scatter principle. This only dilutes your giving and makes it meaningless and reactive to every demand and whim.

You can't do everything. Choices have to be made. When you say yes, mean it.

Be brave

Saying no can make some of us so anxious that there are physical symptoms. The only way through is to do it. There are people who will push us to change the answer. There are people who will show disappointment or even anger. There will be some people who like you less. But what we will discover more often is that our imaginations exaggerated. And it might be that many people have more respect for us when we show we value our time and make thoughtful decisions.

Chapter 3: The Audacious Magic of a Single Word

What about compromise?

Reaching agreements with other people is a valuable skill. To be able to negotiate and find common ground is demanding and rewarding. To reach solutions in which all parties feel satisfied, listened to and taken seriously is a major achievement.

But that's not what compromise is. Compromise is about reaching a settlement, whether or not it feels authentic. Compromise is all too often about accepting an outcome that has lower standards than we want to countenance. Compromise is another word for mediocrity. I'm done with that. Compromise is a way of staying in the shallows when you should be heading for the depths.

Compromise isn't about listening and learning from others, it's about giving in. This is not to say that we should become intransigent. Other people may have visions and perspectives we haven't considered. Learning from others is vital. Those with super-inflated egos or closed minds might claim they don't compromise. But what they are actually doing is refusing to learn and grow.

That isn't what I'm advocating. Being open to new ideas and being able to take advice is a mark of humility and flexibility. But doing whatever anyone else wants of you, or saying yes to everything that comes along, is soul-destroying. By all means, listen and weigh the options, but know why you say yes and no and how each decision reflects your ideals, goals and values. Don't agree to take on work or go down a route someone else suggests because it seems like the easiest thing to do at that time. That way resentment lies. Moreover, what might seem like an easy life for the short term is likely to become the albatross around your neck. And it's much harder to extricate yourself from a situation that doesn't fit your values than it is to refuse it in the first place.

When you make compromises, or say yes to projects against your better judgement, your values suffer. Imagining you are doing it to please someone or out of kindness or for a quieter life doesn't change this. We are what we do. As Gandhi apparently notes:

> Your beliefs become your thoughts, your thoughts become your words, your words become your actions, your actions become your habits, your habits become your values, your values become your destiny.

We will often say yes to things we know are not in our value-set rather than offend or disappoint someone. The regret and resentment that follows is often much more difficult than the initial difficult conversation. And telling someone we can't follow through on a promise is much harder than never making the promise. How much better to know your values and live by them. As Aesop cautions:

> Don't let your special character and values, the secret that you know and no one else does, the truth — don't let that get swallowed up by the great chewing complacency.

Compromises, no matter how small we tell ourselves they are, change our souls. Consistent people with clear values can listen to others and make adjustments as they learn, but they don't 'give in', 'go with the flow', or choose 'anything for an easy life'. If you are passionate about something and give up because it's difficult, you lose something of yourself. If you care for something but walk away when supporting it is demanding, your self-respect is likely to plummet.

Giving up on our dreams and passions is soul-destroying. When we go small on our goals and values, we shrivel inside. When we give away what matters us to most fundamentally, this isn't compromise, but giving in.

When you live by values your integrity shines through and you stand out as someone who is trust-worthy. If we don't live by values; if we compromise to please others, we're likely to be inconsistent. Trying to be people-pleasers is a difficult and circuitous path. It makes us blow with the wind rather than being people of integrity. The knock-on is that not only do we feel smaller and less worthy, but that our motivation, energy and even physical well-being suffer.

So often the reason for compromise is financial. We all have commitments and bills to pay, but when we chase money first we tend to put our big goals on hold. When bills are calling, it's hard to see any income as 'the wrong money', but short-term gain can often add up to long-term drudgery.

A rich life is more than monetary gratification. A rich life can be one that is full of choice, knowledge, relationships, experiences… Money can be a great resource, but it's not an end in itself and living for it will force us into endless compromises.

We each leave a legacy. Even if it's a long way off, there will come a time when it matters who we were and how we acted. Being a people-pleaser can make us feel valued for a short time, but ultimately it's likely to make us the people who are taken for granted and invisible. We don't have to be harsh, intransigent people to avoid being compromisers. In her novel, *The Dispossessed*, Ursula K Le Guin describes a character who is uncompromising precisely because he is neither competitive, nor domineering, but never betrays his gentle values. We want to be remembered for characteristics that are distinctive, generous and note-worthy, not because we always gave way.

None of this means we have to become inflexible people who imagine we have all the answers. Negotiating and learning are good things to do. Listening is a wonderful skill. But giving in on our values and passion, doing things merely to placate others or for a quiet life will lead to a mediocre life lived in the shallows. Life is too precious for that. And if you are a creator of any kind, that way losing your passion lies.

Swapping overwhelm for systems

The best advice we give is usually the advice we most need to listen to ourselves. This is certainly the case for me when it comes to getting overwhelmed. I'm still far too good at saying yes. My to-do list usually contains at least 5 miracles to perform before breakfast. And every time I eliminate a task that isn't important or essential, I have a tendency to think of two things I could do in its place. But I've been making a concerted effort to stop this cycle of wild optimism followed by overwhelm.

It's so easy to overestimate what we can do in a short period, but the converse is also true: we can underestimate the amount of change we can accomplish in a longer time. Getting the flow right is the trick. How? We all needs systems in place that help us work within the laws of physics and our emotional and time limitations.

I recently had a tiny number of publishing slots for a group of talented writers who'd worked hard over a year of intensive mentoring. There were many fewer slots than authors. I've faced this before and in the past I've taken on more work than was sane because saying no was too difficult. Saying yes exempted me from hard decisions. It also insulated me from the possibility of facing others' disappointment or even outright conflict.

This time I came away without increasing the number of books on the forward list. I did this even though I managed to take on the work of three more mentoring students than I'd planned. I achieved this feat by only allowing myself to take on an extra commitment if I could uncommit to something else in the timetable. This still required me to say no, but I gave myself room to choose where was best to say it.

We don't have to become negative and ungiving, but we do have to make choices if we want to be free of the downward cycle of overwhelm. Saying yes to things that aren't essential or that drain you will sap your energy. Saying yes to things that leave you lukewarm or because you want to appease others, is a recipe for self-negation. Having a system in place that lets you know how much you can do, helps to short-circuit that.

Chapter 3: The Audacious Magic of a Single Word

To avoid overwhelm, your system needs to give you time to think. Even if you don't end up saying no to some things, it's good to take time to consider before giving a yes. I've learned to say I'll respond by email rather than agreeing to phone calls. Not everyone who wants to call is trying to manipulate or bully, of course, but email gives me space to think. And it's not only demands on your time that are good to think about. When you are facing a long to-do list or have deadlines competing for your attention, you need time to step back. The reactive thing to do when we are facing five things to be done at once, is to jump in. Sometimes I've found myself going between two or three tasks at the same time, all suffering as a result. Breathe. Think. Prioritise. Do one thing.

In short, forget multi-tasking. It's not a system, it's a cruel myth. There are lots of things we can do at once. We can walk and hold a conversation. We can cook and listen to music. If one of the things we are doing is automatic or simple for us, we can likely combine them together. Daydreaming while washing up or exercising gives the brain a hit of dopamine without getting frazzled. But the idea that we can do two (or more) complex activities at once is a lie.

What happens instead is that the brain switches between the two activities. And the constant switching has consequences. We use up glucose, causing feelings of exhaustion or even disorientation. We store information in the wrong place, making our short-term memory weaker. We produce more stress hormones. Multi-tasking and overwhelm belong together.

A system I find much more humane is to use time blocks. Instead of a simple to-do list, I now load all my tasks for the week into a timetable. They get slots, depending on how essential they are, that are batched with similar tasks. Writing, editing and mentoring get big chunks of time when I'm fresh and awake. Routine admin and maintenance tasks get less time and at less productive times of the day.

If I give myself three hours for email, I'll use it. If I have an hour to update the accounts, answer emails and do five small admin tasks, I'll get it done within the deadline. These kinds of tasks will always expand to fill whole days if we allow them. Batching activities, that are similar, together and giving your most focussed times to the important tasks will go a long way in preventing overwhelm.

I also break tasks down. Having said that you can batch less essential things so they absorb less time and energy, the opposite can be true of bigger tasks. If you have a major quest to achieve, or a project you are passionate about, it's likely to be complex and not something you'll do in one sitting. The novel I want to write this year is getting done in chapters between planning sessions. I'm not going to spill out a whole book in one go. And when it's done there will

Chapter 3: The Audacious Magic of a Single Word

be editing and several other stages. When you break big visions into tiny steps they are much less overwhelming.

It also helps if you have a system for challenging your perspective when overwhelm threatens. None of us have an objective sense of self, but when we get overwhelmed, our perspective is likely to be at its most inaccurate. Feeling overwhelmed often comes with a slew of self-accusations:

- I'm useless.
- I never get anything right.
- I can't manage even…

You know the kind of negative thinking that keeps us wallowing. Whenever you find yourself thinking like this, ask yourself what is inaccurate in your mindset. Make yourself think of five things you've achieved —

- Five big achievements from your whole life.
- Five everyday but essential things you've achieved today (no matter how small they seem).
- Five times you've been generous.
- Five times you've finished something.

Don't let anyone berate you, not even yourself. If something has gone wrong, face it, but don't feel that taking yourself apart will help. Apologise if it's a mess that involves others. Then start again. And start by thinking about what you can do, not what you can't. Show yourself consideration, as you would for others.

There are days when we are so overwhelmed that the energy eludes us. There are days when all we want to do is curl up in bed and pretend the world doesn't exist. On those days time blocks might feel a step too far. Doing anything can feel impossible. On those days it can be useful to do something that has nothing to do with the twenty tasks calling to you, leaving you feeling too dizzy to function. On those days you need a system for recovery. Do something completely different.

- Go for a walk.
- Pour a long bubble bath.
- Read your most 'comfort-book' book.
- Above all, be kind to yourself.

I can hear the argument coming back, *But that won't get anything on my list done.* I'll be even further behind and more overwhelmed. But the truth is often the opposite. By giving yourself this precious pause, you can return with fresh thinking and more energy and positivity. We often solve a problem by not thinking of it for a while. Give yourself a break.

And don't feel it's all up to you. If at all possible, enlist help. People with an 'I'll do it myself' attitude are most prone to getting overwhelmed. A few years ago when I found myself living alone in a tiny rural village with no shops, I had to ask my neighbours for help. The alternative would have been to let my business collapse because I couldn't get to the post office with boxes of books. The responses were unfailingly generous. When you feel overwhelm creeping up, ask for help. Other people can give practical help, offer insights you might not have had, tell you that the thing you are worrying about isn't nearly as important as you imagined or just have a hot drink with you and care. We all suffer from overwhelm from time to time, but you don't have to let it win. You can defend yourself.

- Say no sometimes (and always when it matters).
- Prioritise your dreams and passions over people-pleasing or compromise.
- Take time to think.
- Use time blocks.
- Forget multi-tasking.
- Break tasks down.
- Challenge your perspective.
- Be gentle with yourself.
- Enlist help.

Repeat.

Chapter 4

Imperfect is Good

Success and failure are slippery and complex concepts. Some types of failure, the simple antonym to success, can be devastating. A car fails and people die. A pregnancy fails with the loss of a precious life. Mental health fails leading to breakdown and suffering. No one wants to court this type of failure. There's also failure that arises from negligence. When we fail to live in the moment, when we don't attend to something crucial, terrible things can happen. Anything from an oil spill wiping out ecosystems to emotional damage, to a loved one who knows we're not there for her. However much we manage to learn from it on reflection, it would always have been better to get the learning in another way. Moreover, when we're dealing with the type of failure that comes from our own negligence, it's not appropriate to re-label it as 'success' or 'learning' simply to duck the responsibility. There are times when the things that go wrong are shouting out for us to pay attention and do some deep reflecting.

Yet we also know that the courage to risk failure in creative enterprises is crucial. Even when it leads to repeated failure, such bravery teaches us more than we'd ever guess was possible. This leads me to think that what we mean by 'failure' isn't a monolithic thing. And it's this other sort of failure, the type that involves taking risks, that we can redefine as success. In this sense, you don't need to succeed. That is you don't need to realise every goal in exactly the way you'd envisaged it, to be a success. Why? Because:

Inversion isn't always failure

The common question, *What's the worst thing that could happen?* is a useful shorthand for the Stoic notion of inversion. Stoics, like Marcus Aurelius and Epictetus, practised *premeditatio malorum*, or 'premeditation of evils'. The idea was to consider the worst outcomes of an action. What if this results in bankruptcy or losing my home? What if this leads to everyone disliking me?

The point of the exercise was to anticipate possibilities in order to plan better and think about how to manage worst-case scenarios. And it was also a way to overcome fears. So often it's fear of failure that keeps us thinking and acting small. But inversion isn't always about failing. Not only does this exercise help us to think about what might happen and prepare as far as possible, but it also provides an alternative way of thinking in general.

When we begin to think like this, to have the courage to face our fears and act, then we put ourselves into that group of artists and innovators prepared to challenge the status quo. Inventive art is often an inversion of conventional thinking. Too often the definition of 'success' is being popular, getting the greatest number of 'likes', pursuing the same safe goals as everyone else. Inversion challenges this. What you end up with might not be 'success' in the eyes of the crowd, but it might very well be innovative, ground-breaking and exactly where you want to be.

Courage is better than fear

Courage is not the opposite of fear. Courageous people feel fear, but act in spite of it. This isn't easy. We have a long history of useful fear, but this usefulness has often passed its use-by date. Most of us in the western world are no longer prey to an animal stalking our cave at night. Swathes of us in the western world (though not all and not enough of us, in the west or globally) are not in fear of starvation or lacking the basic requisites of survival.

When we get the concept for a new project or have an exciting idea for the next book we want to write, the lizard brain (perhaps with help from internal voices of discouragement that we've carried with us for years) will kick in. It will start whispering that you don't stand a chance, that you are bound to fail and then what will you look like? And very quickly the idea is dead. Fear, like perfectionism, is paralysing. But your creativity and courage are all about possibility, growth and saying yes to life.

Taking a risk on your ideas doesn't only cultivate courage. It also makes you more persistent and more able to learn. A kindness we can do for ourselves and others is to encourage risks, persistence and learning, to rejoice in the things that didn't work along the way but which taught us so much.

Moreover, being wrong is good for you. The majority of scientists are wrong most of the time. Some of the 'wrong' outcomes lead to intriguing and worthwhile spin-offs. Some lead to persistence and learning. We discover the limitations of certain decisions, rethink or re-evaluate how to proceed, challenge our brains, find ways to cooperate with the world. Humans are good at this. This type of failure is not a flaw, or a failure of character, and this is a problem. Getting something wrong does not make you 'wrong' as a person.

'Failure' shows you where you shouldn't be...

Sometimes we try things that are not a good fit. We try something and it doesn't work. But there's no need to see this as failure. 'Failure' can open new doors. If you never take chances you are much less likely to bump into the unexpected. Once you begin to take risks, whether with your quests in life or with your writing, you will find that even if the outcome isn't what you expected, it is likely to be interesting.

Growth is vital to life and while success is comforting, we can also stagnate in it. Not getting easy success, on the other hand, makes you stretch and move outside this comfort zone. Failure in this sense helps us to change perspective and gives a renewed appreciation of how far we will push our boundaries.

Ultimately, how we work is more important than outcomes. Very little of what we do turns out exactly as we have planned, but the outcomes are less important than the preparation and the attempt. Once we have a quest, the creativity is all in how we approach it. And this changes us, which is why it is so much more valuable than outcomes. In the end, our deepest and most vital achievements will be what we learnt along the way and the quality of person we strive to be.

Success is a perspective and, within the definitions of success and failure that we're playing with, we can view many 'failures' as successes. This isn't mere semantics. Language is powerful and when we view attitudes — like not giving in to fear, having the courage to try new ideas, and valuing each step along the path — then we make a huge internal shift. We have so much more success in life than we often give credit for. We breathe, we love, we practise kindness, we deal with other human beings. We improve. We have experiences. This is magnificent. Just even being able to try new things is something to celebrate every day.

Taking a chance is an antidote to perfectionism

Perfectionism is a kind of paralysis. On the one hand perfectionism demands of you that you can do everything: achieve ten goals before breakfast, produce a manuscript with not one comma out of place... On the other hand, its demands are so preposterous that you will stop in your tracks and procrastinate rather than risk failure. Of course aiming high is good. Of course you should improve your craft. As an editor, I'm a fan of putting in the work, making things excellent, stretching our boundaries as writers. But there is also a time to let go. And there are times when you need to take a chance.

In writing, as in any area of life, perfectionism is a killer. Writing is a wonderful metaphor for life. Writing matters. It illuminates, takes us deeper into the experience of others, connects us with nature, humanity, ourselves. As in writing, so in life. Writing is powerful and we want it to be brilliant. No writer should be content with dull prose clogged with adjectives and exposition. No writer should be happy with didactic, sentimental poetry. No blogger should want to bore people. But it doesn't have to be perfect. In fact, it can't be perfect. Perfectionism relies on a plethora of false premises:

Failure is not an option

Of course it is, especially if it's the type of failure which we've just been examining, the type that is a great teacher. As we've already established, if we fear failure we will never take the risks that lead to real progress. But sadly, perfectionism can dig deep into our sense of self. It whispers malign things that we need to resist, things like:

You are not worthy

Feeling inherently not 'good enough' can lead people to making supreme efforts to fit in, find acceptance and love. The underlying thinking is 'If I'm perfect I won't experience rejection', but it's false thinking. We're all flawed and the writing we do will have flaws. It doesn't make you an unworthy person. In fact, if you have the humility to hold your flaws in tension with always improving without ever feeling you're the finished product, you are likely to be a very worthy person indeed.

You can never rest

On the one hand perfectionism leads to procrastination. We can't fail at what we never begin. On the other hand it leads to a permanent state of anxiety in which we drive ourselves on, never able to rest. Creativity, writing, any activity in life is unsustainable without periods of rejuvenation. You can and must rest. Life is not a puzzle with a fixed solution and writing is not a horse race to be won so we can afford to step down from the continual treadmill and stop chasing the elusive state of having everything in our lives 'just right'.

You can do it all

You can't and you don't have to. This myth seems to spin out of late capitalism run riot: you can have everything, be everything, do everything and if you don't achieve this there's something wrong with you. That's rubbish. And it's also inhumane. You absolutely should believe big, have quests you are passionate about and hold to your vision, as long as it's not a vision of having and doing everything. We all have to make choices. If writing is essential to you then prioritise it, but that might mean you have to lower your standards in other areas. It might be anything from making a bit less money to not having time to dust (big sacrifice!).

Instead of being taken in by the false whisperings of perfectionism, we need another voice in our head that sings that writing and life need joy and kindness instead of self-doubt. Striving is excellent. When we've finished a piece of writing, we should let it settle. Later, revisit it with fresher vision, edit it, then repeat. I'm a strong advocate of edit, edit, edit, wait. Followed by edit, edit, edit...

In the book *So good they can't ignore you*, Cal Newport advises that we adopt a craftsman mentality. We ask what we are good at and how we can get better. We stretch our abilities through deliberate practice, developing skills that bring creativity, impact and control. In this way we give back to the world whilst also developing a higher level of consistency and clarity that will stretch, challenge and delight us.

But there is a world of difference between the passion to improve our craft and perfectionism. Why?

Because it's about joy not fear

Perfectionism presents itself as a kind of rampant egoism: not letting go of any work until it's perfect; not taking joy in achievements, but driving yourself further. Perfectionism is an ego screaming that it must be extraordinary, that it must be better than anyone else, and not just better in what it creates, but in *who* it is. The myth of the superhero is everywhere, a myth bolstered by social media platforms that provide cocooned feelings of celebrity and quizzes to enable you to discover your superpower. But the truth is we're all only human and yet equally extraordinary. The truth is that the world will survive the loss of any of us, even the greatest artist or writer.

The truth is that such egoism is a symptom of the underlying disease, which is fear. Perfectionism brings us full circle back to the courage to find meaning in simply trying. Perfectionism is not your friend. Ironically, it can stop us doing our greatest work. It will keep you small-minded and spiritually crushed. You have this one amazing life and none of us wants to look back with regret on all the chances we didn't take because we were too afraid.

You don't have to be complacent or hubristic to believe that you too can create something. And whatever you create, it doesn't have to be perfect, it has to be the best you could do at that time during a life that is constantly changing.

Perfectionism is a way of sucking all the joy out of writing or out of life at large. It encourages us to look at others and think they have it all worked out. It's easy to see what's on the surface of someone else's life. But everyone, no matter how 'successful', has struggles. What's often amazing is how so many of us get through our days given how much is going on at any one time. Don't imagine the person with the gorgeous house decorated with antique furniture has no self-doubt or suffering. Don't imagine the writer with three award-winning novels doesn't labour to start writing every time she sits down. Instead of comparing yourself to others, take a deep breath and write. In the words of Epictetus:

> We don't abandon our pursuits because we despair of ever perfecting them.

By all means be ambitious. By all means have huge dreams and do what is needful to bring them to fruition. But don't let perfectionism petrify you. Remember:

- It's better to try and fail, learn and move on.
- All humanity is flawed, but you are still worthy.
- Rest and rejuvenation are essential.
- You don't have to do it all: lower your standards in the non-essential areas.
- Striving, honing your craft and making progress trumps perfection.
- You will have a lot more joy in life without perfectionism.
- Don't compare yourself to others who may seem to be doing better. You never really know and, in any case, comparison is odious and demotivating.

Interlude 1

Writing the Green Blade

This interlude is a chance to dive deeply into your writing and your own story. It's planned to be used around the first cross-quarter day of the year, January 31–February 3, though if you are in the southern hemisphere this would fall in early August and your interlude in late January to early February would be 'Writing the sun to earth', found in Section 4.

January 31

All winter things have been growing, quietly and hidden from view; small things — delicate yet strong, and intensely beautiful. It's the long cold season after Christmas, light trickling back into the days little by little, skies grey, frost in the mornings, yet once again snowdrops and crocuses appear before any other sign of Spring is underway.

Life is precious and fragile. When we meet a new-born baby the response can be overwhelming — the absolute vulnerability and dependence is matched only by the fierce power of new life. When I see the first snowdrops each year there is a similar awe that such apparently flimsy plants with their bowed bell-heads and javelin-leaves have managed to spear the hard, cold earth with the force of unstoppable life.

There's a hymn that is often sung at Easter, by John Macleod Campbell Crum, but which always springs to mind for me when I see snowdrops (even though the song refers to wheat):

> Now the green blade riseth, from the buried grain,
> Wheat that in dark earth many days has lain;
> Love lives again, that with the dead has been:
> Love is come again like wheat that springeth green.

Interlude 1: Writing the Green Blade

And the last two lines:

> Fields of our hearts that dead and bare have been:
> Love is come again like wheat that springeth green.

The impulse of life is irresistibly urgent, but it can take a long time to germinate. A baby is in the womb for nine months, a bulb grows beneath the earth through the winter. The growth is off-stage and deep. The bursting forth comes only after a secret life of change and growth and struggle. And the moment of birth is, of course, one where pain and joy collide. The result is something radically tender and sweet, yet with the steely purpose of survival, whether we're looking at an infant only a few hours in the world or an exquisite clump of snowdrops.

This is also how writing happens. There are times when we think nothing is happening, when the germination is slow and hidden. And this secret life can be full of turmoil and doubt and change and then we are in flow again and the prose is supple and the poetry dances and life floods every word.

In the Christian liturgical calendar, this time commemorates the presentation of the baby Jesus in the Temple, a thanksgiving for birth, also known as Candlemas, as traditionally candles are blessed to bring light through the rest of the year. In the Celtic calendar, this time is a new beginning, a liminal time between winter and spring, known as Imbolc (or as *Gwyl Fair y Canhwyllau* in Wales). It is a time of new shoots, protection and fertility, of blessing objects and wells and of feasting. Imbolc was originally associated with Brigid (later Christianised as St Brigid), goddess of fertility, who visited homes, where beds were made for her and food and drink left out.

It's a slow turning back to longer, lighter days and sometimes our writing creeps just as slowly from pen or fingers, inching towards fertility and the blessing of a rich flow of words and images. If you have anything like my lack of patience, you may find yourself wanting to (figuratively) pull up the bulbs to see how the growth is coming along before the shoots begin to show through: of course, that only stunts the growth or kills it entirely.

It's so easy to subvert the creative flow with impatience and internal doubts, or by overwhelming ourselves with unrealistic expectations so that whatever we create never feels 'enough'. When we get to feeling like this we often need to look in another direction, let the subconscious mull over the words while we go for a walk or cook a meal or scrub a bathroom. It

Interlude 1: Writing the Green Blade

can be difficult to trust that the mind is working away beneath the surface, but it is and, if we are to have any hope of diving deep into our creative cores and coming up with the green shoots, then, to paraphrase Mary Oliver in her wonderful essay, 'Of Power and Time', in Upstream, when we feel our creativity returning, 'restive and uprising', we have to give it power and time.

There is no other way work of artistic worth can be done. And the occasional success, to the striver, is worth everything. The most regretful people on earth are those who felt the call to creative work, who felt their own creative power restive and uprising, and gave to it neither power nor time.

How do we give our creativity power? Power is a strange word. Most often it's associated with force, with manipulation, perhaps with money and influence. But the power of a baby or of a crocus is of another kind. Writing about different types of knowledge in The Scientific Outlook, Bertrand Russell noted that knowledge can come from an impulse to control or from love and fascination. Power too can be of different sorts.

The mysteries and wonder of a starry night, a baby, an elegant metaphor, a moving story, a glorious sunset, can all be described as 'powerful' without any of them being thought of as bombastic, manipulative or politically cunning. Wherever there is awe, love or beauty, we are in the presence of power; power of a kind that is not inimical to vulnerability.

We'll consider giving our creativity time tomorrow, but for today, contemplate its power.

Journal exercise

When and where do you feel your creativity is not enough?

When and where do you feel your creativity restive and uprising?

Where in your writing and your life do you experience struggle and awe?

How do you understand 'power' and in what ways do you give your writing power?

What new shoots are there in your writing and in your life and how will you protect and nurture them?

Ritual

Take a double page in your journal or a big sheet of paper you can pin up somewhere and draw an earth line across it about half way up. Now fill the portion below the line with writing that you want to do or may do, with things you may be struggling with that haven't yet emerged or plans for this year that are still only part-formed and gestating. Give them permission to stay in the good earth for as long as they need. Above the line mark the tips of leaves and shoots rising and inside each leaf note whatever is emerging in your life and your writing; your current passions and projects, from political activism to family commitments to writing…

Now commit to nurturing those tender shoots.

February 1

Mary Oliver talks about how not following our creativity on its quests can only lead to regret. Yesterday we thought about giving our writing power. But of course to have power, it also needs time. Time is such a slippery and strange resource. The prevailing story is that time is in terribly short supply. Another contemporary story about time is that we should admire those who are endlessly busy to the point of overwhelm. We can question these stories. How?

- Shift the balance of what you give your time to.
- Batch and limit tasks that have to be done but aren't what you are passionate about.
- Take one step at a time, breaking down big tasks into smaller parts.
- Ask for help.
- Eliminate the inessentials and learn to say no.

Time is as much a quality as a quantity and it's a theme we will return to in the next chapter. Thinking about germination, whether of snowdrops or books, the theological notion of time as kairos, seems more appropriate than chronos, chronological seconds ticking by. Kairos speaks to us of those often unlooked for moments when things simply come together, when the timing is 'right'. Kairos feels different from ordinary chronological time, often it is part of those experiences that feel almost 'out of time'.

• Interlude 1: Writing the Green Blade •

Time is much more than chronos. It is the quality and depth of each fully lived, truly awake and connected moment. We may not be able to add a single hour to life by worrying, to paraphrase Matthew's gospel, but the depth of our experiences is in our gift. Creative people, in this sense, have much more time. When we both curate our time differently and give it intentionally, things change. To give time to what you really care about, you need to shift your perspective and:

- Live by kairos, not chronos.
- Live life not lifestyle.
- Live by less.
- Live to a kinder rhythm.
- Live new.
- Live now.

One of the things I'm most passionate about implementing in my life this year is a gentler pace that pays attention to life's rhythms. Being present, focussed and attentive in a world of distractions is one of the hardest and most rewarding things we can achieve. In the words of David Henry Thoreau:

> The meeting of two eternities, the past and the future… is precisely the present moment…

The present moment, the ability to be attentive and present NOW is both a quality that we cultivate, in the sense of a skill that we hone and practise, and a gift that we give. I am least attentive to those I love, to my writing and passions, to my environment, when I'm stressed, overwhelmed with non-creative work (those emails that make demands but are not real conversations, or the distractions of a too-fast world), preoccupied with small things or have not given time to journalling and the occasional period of silence and solitude. My thoughts get ragged and my behaviour gets cranky.

On the other hand, when I'm doing yoga daily, journalling, taking walks, making time for leisurely meals, then I listen. I listen not just to the surface words but to the emotions of others. I listen to the wind and rain. I notice objects that are small and beautiful, or take delight in making a pot of coffee or stirring berries into porridge.

When I'm attentive, I unbend. I don't carry myself so stiffly. And the physical relaxation shows in my actions. I start to embody the creativity and generosity I want to live when I take the right time needed for any given activity and become more present rather than being elsewhere in my head, full of distractions or anxieties about things that aren't important or that I can have no effect on.

What is true in life is true in writing. We have to pay attention to the rhythm, not force any particular pace, which sometimes needs to be slow and at other times will fly. We have to have extraordinary patience and be prepared to show up and do the work, knowing that at times very little will happen or we'll finish with a meagre page of lumpen prose or a few lines of poetry that have neither song nor soul. And then we have to show up again and again until that deep creative part of us loosens and breathes and trusts. And when we do, the prose becomes elegant and the poetry lithe.

Creative flow is a creature as shy and wild as Antoine de Saint-Exupéry's fox in *The Little Prince*. It requires taming, not by subjugation, but by being impressed that you will wait on it patiently, that you show due ceremony, that you are as serious and reliable as you are playful and imaginative.

Giving our writing time demands a whole new way of seeing time, a new mindset for being in time and a wholehearted embodying of attentiveness.

Journal exercise

What are the ways you scare away the shy creature of creativity?

How do you need to re-envision time, find rhythms that are kinder, that flow with the pauses and the slow periods as well as the flying like the wind times, in order to encourage creativity to work with you and to nurture the new shoots and leaves of your writing that you identified yesterday?

What important parts of your life are you not giving attention to? Why?

What will you do today to show attention, the purest form of generosity, in your life and in your writing?

Ritual

Get out of doors with a notebook and find a place where you can pay attention, where you can see through the exteriors to something deeper. Write notes or (if you don't live in Wales, where it is likely to be raining heavily) a whole piece in progress.

Interlude 1: Writing the Green Blade

February 2

All winter things have been growing, shoots and leaves, green blades rising through cold, hard earth; babies in wombs; ideas for stories, phrases of poems tucked away deep but slowly rising to the surface. The Celtic festival of Imbolc is a festival of hope. The light is returning, the first signs of spring are emerging. We simply have to attend; look and listen, breathe.

Plants grow more easily when there is depth. Souls are similar. Depth is not fashionable in a world where we skim surfaces with increasing rapidity. Deep is the arena of the spirit.

For the green blades to make it through the winter and emerge in the spring, there has to be depth — room for roots to take hold, nourishing soil to grow in, light and water to emerge into.

Change and growth are strange, sometimes mysterious processes, rarely simple and often so incremental that no one sees them coming. Events can seem to happen suddenly, whether they are changes in culture, huge paradigm shifts, or a snowdrop suddenly blossoming in apparently empty soil. But the truth is that there have been deep roots for a long, long time, before anything was visible above the surface.

Big historical changes are often incremental, even when they erupt in revolutions that seem sudden. Birth comes only after long gestation. Plants flourish after germination. The light returns in its season and will not be hurried.

Yet we live in a world where being busy is lauded, where patience is seen as weakness, and where the instant and immediate are the drugs of choice, constant little dopamine hits as we check our phones for the 10th time this minute or our emails or social media in case we've missed something. There's no doubt that technology has changed our lives and, in many ways, for the better. The access to like minds across the planet, the ability to communicate across distances, the tools for writing, research and so much more, can be mind-expanding. But there is also the anxiety that the smarter our phones get, the dumber we become.

Waiting with patience is not a highly valued contemporary quality. We want everything and we want it now. We are increasingly uneasy with 'doing nothing' for short (or longer periods) or with being alone with our own thoughts.

Life encourages a fear of missing out (FOMO) that can keep us plugged in, always busy, always anxious but the ironic cost is that we still miss out — on the ability to contemplate, or on the ability to focus on someone who is with us in person. And we can miss out developing a deliberate practice that builds our skills with deep work.

The natural world offers a different model — life has seasons, the light will return, the shoots will break through, but in their own sweet, unhurried time.

Kafka apparently had a one-word dictum in large letters hung over his desk: WAIT. In the brilliant book, *Delayed Response*, Jason Farman completely re-imagines time and waiting, examining how power structures can use enforced waiting to control populations, but also how we can see our time as intertwined with others' time so that we invest our time and attention in one another in positive ways of waiting that increase empathy. And he rehabilitates waiting not only in terms of what we hope for in outcome but also as a state in which we learn more about who we are.

The Celtic festival of Imbolc is a festival of hope. The light is returning, the first signs of spring are emerging. We simply have to attend; look, listen, breathe and wait.

Journal exercise

How do you understand 'patience' and what part does it play in your life and your writing, whether as themes or in how you work?

In what ways can you value being less busy in your life?

When do you feel most overwhelmed? Why?

What do you feel uneasy about waiting for?

What do you feel comfortable about waiting for? Why?

Ritual

Try to have some unbusy, unhurried time today to do very little at all, not even writing. And preferably take this idle, unbusy time well away from any device or screen.

February 3

Giving our creativity power and time is a radical act in a world that values the 'shallow' and the 'fast'. Look at any click-bait-style blog and you will see how they play on our fears of missing out, of not being rich enough, attractive enough or productive enough. But becoming the writer we want to be and the person we want to be in order to be that writer, isn't an instant makeover scheme. It is a life's work, always in progress. Like the natural world, it has seasons and it takes the time it takes.

As we emerge from winter and as the daylight lengthens, it's a good time to be hopeful and creative, to give our writing time and power, but there's no rush. The shoots emerge incrementally. Each moment is precious and to be savoured. Each moment contains an eternity, as William Blake expressed in 'Auguries of Innocence':

> To see a World in a Grain of Sand
> And a Heaven in a Wild Flower
> Hold Infinity in the palm of your hand
> And Eternity in an hour

When we dive deep and look below the surface of things we begin to see the profound connections between transitory, ordinary life and the enormity of the cosmos and all eternity. We are, Søren Kierkegaard tells us,

> a synthesis of psyche and body, but… also a synthesis of the temporal and the eternal.

Long before Einstein, he points out that:

> precisely because every moment, as well as the sum of the moments, is a process (a passing by), no moment is a present, and accordingly there is in time neither present, nor past, nor future.

He goes on to argue that the 'eternal… is the present… and the present is full'. Giving our writing power and time is not simply about carving out the odd hour to actually sit down and write, but is a way of touching eternity, connecting with all of life. Yet even as we touch eternity we know that no matter how persistent and indomitable life itself might be, each of us is transitory. We have a short time to wrestle soul-powerful, immortal meaning from the impermanent and ephemeral.

Snowdrops and the crocuses do this simply by appearing, green blade followed by delicate flowers. Stars do it by blazing their light long after they have vanished. Too often we humans do it by leaving footprints of destruction, but it does not have to be so. A legacy of story, myths that next generations can find sustenance in, poetry that persists, an extraordinary line in a journal that brings illumination to one other person, are all possible. None of it will last forever, but even the briefest touch of eternity is glorious.

The light is returning. We live and write in hope. Can the light win?

We all know that the world is a mess. We look at politicians and can only wish that the asylum was being run by lunatics — surely that would be so much better? Apparently by 2050 there will be more plastic in the sea than fish. We are living in the midst of the Holocene (or sixth) mass extinction, this one largely caused by human activity.

War continues in Afghanistan, Syria and the Yemen, with more than 10,000 deaths from armed violence in each of these places in the past year. Whilst conflicts in Somalia, Nigeria and Iraq, drug wars in Mexico, insurgency by Boko Haram, ethnic violence in Southern Sudan and Northern Mali claim thousands of lives each year.

While consumerism is a frenzy for some, global poverty persists. Over 3 million children die each year from causes related to malnutrition and more than 10% of the world's population live in extreme poverty (as defined by the World Bank), including 13 million people in North America.

And it's not just statistics. How many of us know someone, perhaps someone very close, who is dangerously ill? How many of us have lost someone close in the last year, five years? The light is returning and yet we are as fragile as the green blades that last a week, a couple of weeks and then they wilt and are gone.

And yet, we make our marks, with words, with love. This is hope. This is why we write. And so we return full circle. The only way to write is to take the power and time now. Give your writing power of love, light and hope. The spring is coming.

Journal exercise

How does your writing connect you to the past, the future and to eternity?

How do you understand 'hope' and what part does it play in your life and your writing, whether as themes or in how you work?

Where is the spring in your writing?

Where is the line between hope and naiveté in your writing and how do you hold that line?

Ritual

Listen to CD Wright reading her poem 'More Blues and the Abstract Truth' (From *Steal Away*) at PennSound's CD Wright page:

https://media.sas.upenn.edu/pennsound/authors/Wright-CD/Port-Townsend_1999/Wright-CD_15_More-Blues-Abstract-Truth_Copper-Canyon-Session_Port-Townsend-WA_7-16-99.mp3

Write a piece of prose, a story or a poem that embodies hope, despite the word breaking over and over again.

Chapter 5:
Your Time is Now

Thinking about the mindset of a writer, becoming people who are able to say no to certain things so that we have the time to write, determining to follow our passions and diving deeply into our writing, constantly brings us back to the theme of time. Giving yourself time is essential. Now is the only moment any of us has and as soon as we try to grasp it, it's gone. Time, Einstein tells us, is not linear. And physicist, Julian Barbour, adds that it is change that gives us the illusion we call time, when all that exists is a succession of 'nows'. Time, or the illusion of it, is mind-bending, but the notion that it is more qualitative than quantitative isn't so hard to grasp when we think about how some people seem to be able to squeeze a lifetime into a month while others feel that time slips away with frustrating rapidity; that some days seem to last forever, while a year can flash by in an apparent blink.

So how do writers and other creative people find ways to give time to their most passionate quests?

There are two ways forward. The first is to take some practical steps. These steps are concerned with how we guard or curate time, the twenty-four hours in each day, even if to conceive of time like this is an illusion. The second is to think, and so to live, from a different perspective. In this perspective, we don't snatch time or take or make it, we give it — to ourselves, to those we love, to the life that delights us and through which we create.

Systems of time

The practical way is to curate our time carefully, with systems in place to shift the balance towards having time to write or create. Curating time is not about packing more in. It's not about being super-beings who run all the time. You cannot be always rushing and regularly achieve the flow state needed to write. So how do you stop running?

Chapter 5: Your Time is Now

A technique I've used several times is to spend a week or two documenting all the ways I give my time to various activities and people. Keep three lists:

A. All the ways you give time to tasks that distract you, annoy you, or that make you wonder, 'If I didn't do this would it make the slightest difference?' (Checking phones and apps compulsively, or cleaning your kitchen for the third time today, might be good examples.)
B. All the ways you give time to tasks that make life keep working, things you see as essential but which might not fill you with delight. (The weekly laundry or grocery shopping, or emails, or work tasks that are not your favourite things but are tolerable within limits, for example.)
C. All the ways you give time to things you love. (This should include your creative work, time with loved ones, favourite ways to relax and recuperate, the parts of your work that you enjoy and find fulfilment in.)

What's the balance?

Putting it into a pie chart or block graph to get a visual idea can help. Now ask yourself some searching questions:

How are you going to reduce group A to an insignificant amount of time?

How many things in group B are essential and how many could you let go of, or at least reduce, with very little impact?

If things are essential (you might sometimes have to reply to an email or do laundry), how can you batch them together so that you're not wasting time on switching back and forth between activities?

I talked previously about using time blocks for email and admin tasks, rather than being reactive and doing them as they come in. This has freed up huge amounts of time for me this year. The first time I did this exercise, I disliked the look of the pie chart. I was giving less than 30% of my time to passion projects, people and activities I love, work I find most rewarding or ways to relax and refuel. Over the course of this year, I've shifted that to nearer 80%.

Ask yourself: What has to go? What can I do in differently?

In both chapters 1 and 3 we've considered systems for using time well. This is not about wringing every last drop of productivity out of yourself. It is not about going faster or boosting your work rate. If anything, using time well should slow you down, but not in a way that will frazzle your brain with anxiety about all the things that 'need' doing. Simple things like:

- Saying no.
- Batching routine tasks together and limiting how long we spend on them.
- Using your most awake times for the activities and people you care most about.
- Refusing to be reactive in the face of competing 'demands'.
- Forgetting that you ever heard the word 'multi-tasking'.
- Breaking our big quests into tiny, manageable steps.

Asking for help is also something we touched on earlier. Likewise, knowing when we need to work collaboratively can release enormous amounts of time and energy. A great deal of what writers do is intrinsically singular work, but the discernment to realise when some parts of our life, even our writing life, require others is vital. When we work together on the right projects, we all have more time.

Other people can give practical help, offer insights you might not have had, or tell you that the thing you are worrying about isn't nearly as important as you imagined. Sometimes people you'd never initially have thought of asking for help can be the most supportive or wise, and this includes children as long as the help is invited and accepted on its own terms, rather than forced. Sometimes you need to pay to get help. The right course or mentor or retreat at just the right moment can be the lifeline your writing was looking for.

Perspectives on time

There are practical things we can do to curate time differently. And there are deep shifts in perspective that we can make that will, slowly and by increments, change our paradigm dramatically. This is Jean Jacques Rousseau:

> The (wo)man who has lived the most is not (s)he who has counted the most years but (s)he who has felt the most life.

We've already discussed how important it is to be gentle with yourself in order not to get constantly overwhelmed. But we can also go even deeper in our quest to give our writing and inner life more of our time. The short version is to live by *kairos*, not *chronos*.

Chapter 5: Your Time is Now

The most important perspective shifts we can make for everyday life is to realise that time, like so many things, is not an absolute. Time, like any other experience, is as qualitative as it is quantitative, if not more so.

In a former incarnation as a theologian, I'd have explained this by using the Greek concepts of *kairos* and *chronos*. *Chronos* is the ticking of seconds on a clock, chronological. But *kairos* is 'the right time'; it is ripeness, the moment of truth. *Kairos* FEELS different — it is related to those experiences when time seems to slow down or stop. Having a perfect life is unrealistic and perfectionism, as we've seen, can be a toxic myth. But having perfect moments is possible and time-expanding.

It's not something you can fake or force but the more you take moments to slow down, breathe deeply, notice the small pleasures of a day, simply inhabit your day more fully and with more attention, then the more you'll find yourself living by *kairos*. Some *kairos* moments will be the extraordinary times of life. The seconds after each of my children were born or meeting my grandson for the first time are *kairos* memories. These were huge life events and not something I can repeat or call up to order. We can't always construct such moments, but we can at least put ourselves in the path of them.

When I spend lots of time with family members in an attentive way, when I take the time in a morning to set up a slow breakfast with beautiful plates and a pot of drip coffee doing ever so slowly, then *kairos* moments come about unlooked for. You can live more life in one excellent day than some people experience in a lifetime and when you we spend one day and then the next and then the next putting yourself in the way of living by *kairos*, then it will become how you spend your life.

Not only is this an enriching way to live, but it is also a perspective that is about getting a life, not a lifestyle. We're sold things all the time. If your inbox is anything like mine, it will be full of spam — a million offers of products and services nobody needs. Investing in ourselves, whether through courses and books or through experiences of music, adventure, travel… can be deeply fulfilling and mind-expanding, but too often all we are being sold is a lifestyle that costs our lives.

Do faster cars or bigger mortgages make anyone more fulfilled? Far too much of life is infected by fear: fear of missing out is everywhere. There are adverts constantly warning you that you need these 3, 5, 15, 100 products just to make it through the next month. Don't give them credence.

If you find yourself working to maintain a lifestyle that you don't need or want, it might be time to reappraise. Similarly, given that work takes up a huge slice of life, if you spend most of your life on work you hate, then time will hang heavy but disappear fast. Sometimes we have responsibilities that demand we take work we don't welcome. But this shouldn't be the norm. Work should be integral to who we want to be, not something that consumes us to no good end.

What can you unsubscribe from? What is trying to sell you a lifestyle rather than a deeper life? In what ways do you want to invest in yourself and what has to change to allow this?

We live in a world that urges us to have more, do more, be more, it can seem counterintuitive to enrich our lives by having and doing less, yet making fewer and better choices does just this. If you want to feel time-rich, don't be busy with things that don't matter. Instead, focus and pay attention to the things that matter. Be present. The thing we often genuinely need more of is depth, not quantity. In the words of David Henry Thoreau:

> A (wo)man is rich in proportion to the things (s)he can afford to let alone.

When we are not distracted by what doesn't matter and not seduced by all that glitters, we are rich in other ways. We begin to focus: on loved ones, on deep life quests. We understand what we want and live less fragmented lives. Less distraction gives us more and deeper time and we find ourselves living more slowly. I'm not suggesting we can abandon work and responsibility, but there are always ways to slow life down and often it begins with shifting perspective to look at what we most cherish.

At other times a *kairos* perspective can be found by deliberately seeking out new experiences. We often notice how, when we're on holiday, a week can seem to last forever whereas at home days blur into one another, time moves on at a sprint. Being in new places, exposing ourselves to new experiences, helps us to perceive time more slowly Of course, taking one holiday after another is likely to be impractical, but we can all expose ourselves to new ideas. Challenging books, a foreign language film or a long walk can all contribute to changing our experience of time. And if you have the opportunity to travel, grab it. The challenge of unfamiliar places, the space to devote time to walking and soaking up other cultures, is perspective altering.

But most of all, the shift to a *kairos* perspective is about living now. Being present, focussed and attentive in a world of distractions is one of the hardest and most rewarding things we can achieve. To quote David Henry Thoreau again:

> You must live in the present, launch yourself on every wave, find your eternity in each moment.

Chapter 5: Your Time is Now

Now is the only time any of us has and as Rumi puts it:

> Happiness is now.

Time, as we noted in Interlude 1, is much more than *chronos*. It is the quality and depth of each fully lived, truly awake and connected moment. We may not be able to add a single hour to life by worrying, to paraphrase Matthew's gospel, but the depth is in our gift. Creative people, in this sense, have much more time. When we both curate our time differently and give it intentionally, things change. To give time to what you really care about, you need to shift your perspective:

- Live by *kairos*, not *chronos*.
- Live life not lifestyle.
- Live by less.
- Live to a kinder rhythm.
- Live new.
- Live now.

As with eschewing perfectionism in order to free your writing and creativity, a great deal of living with a sense of no time is about fear. There are people in your life who will tell you that you have to do X, Y and Z, or else. There are people who will try to make you feel guilty or manipulate you into using your time in ways that drain your energy to no good end. You need to stop listening to such people.

Of course, it's not always other people who undermine you. There will be voices inside that whisper that you cannot create your own life, that biology predetermines your life, that the creativity you long to nurture is an empty dream. There will be inner voices that tell you that you can't do the depth of work it takes to write a book or have a fulfilling relationship. These people, demands and inner voices will consume your time at extraordinary speed. But you're not going to allow that to happen. Don't speed up. Don't jump at every call to fear. Excise these voices from your life by every means possible. Determine to live a life that aligns with your quest, let go of the rest and you will find that you do have the time to give to your creativity.

A non-linear view of time, mind turning as it is, implies that you can change yourself at any moment. We each create who we want to be. This view of time frees us to live more wide-awake, more consciously. It frees us to spend more of our precious time in deep flow on the projects we love. When we spend more of our time on intrinsically motivated activities, time feels as though it slows down. We can see this in toddlers. A young child will take an hour to examine one pebble, or a tiny stretch of beach. Why? Because it absorbs her attention and she is following her own motivation to learn.

When we are doing something we are passionate about, time takes on a different quality. Life, David Henry Thoreau tells us, is precious. We do not want to find ourselves at the end of it having not lived. So how do we know that we are living, that we are sucking out the marrow of life? This question has made me think hard about my art and my work and about what I need to let go of in order to write.

Shifting to a *kairos* perspective can be done both by what we let go and by what we embrace. In theology, the *via negativa* (negative way) describes divinity by what it is not (for example, to be 'God' is not to be evil or capricious...). This is also known as the apophatic way. When so much of what consumes our lives and our time is inessential, we can consider what we need to let go of in our lives in order to pursue great things. For me, some of those things are qualities or mindsets that limit me. Things like:

- Making excuses for not keeping promises to myself.
- Small thinking.
- Fear.
- Attaching to outcomes rather than to process.
- Complaining instead of problem-solving.
- Self-sabotage.

Other things that I'm acutely aware of needing to let go are those things that so many of us tolerate in life and that, once tolerated, set the tone of our days, weeks, months and more... Life is too short and too precious to tolerate:

Wasted time:

I don't mean day-dreaming or rest or play or creative mooching. What wastes time (and our lives) is more often those small inessentials that pile up — hours on Facebook, demanding emails, inessential nonsense...

Bullying and harassment:

Sometimes aggressive and difficult people can teach us a great deal about ourselves by how we react. It can also make us much more clear about setting boundaries and what we should not tolerate.

Bad literature:

Story is my way of making sense of the world. I have no time for stories that lie. I don't mean stories that are imaginary or fantastical. I mean those that deliberately mislead, that sell hatred and division or promote the myths of fascism or greed. Story is too urgent for that.

What do you need to let go of in your life?

The tradition of katophatic theology deals in what we can positively say. We need to know what and who we don't want to be; we need to be aware of what to let go of, but we also need to know what we want to embrace. We will each have different answers to this, depending on our passions and our values, but there are constants that we can all benefit from:

Commitment to our intrinsic motivation

That is, the courage to follow our passion and our quest.

Gratitude

Those of us living in rich countries or those of us not handling current tragedies, often have a lot to learn about valuing the small, vital graces and connections of each day.

Expectation

We need to live in hope, not to allow cynicism to take over.

Keeping promises

To ourselves and those who are most important and transformational in our lives.

Courage

None of us have charmed lives. We all know illness, loss, grief… Yet some navigate this with a grace and dignity that is awe-inspiring. To have the courage to face whatever a day brings, and to take risks for what is right, is powerful. In short, we have to live as if we are the person we want to become. And in addition to the big values, we have to remember to show ourselves some compassion and give the things that matter to us the bigger portion of our time. For me, this includes:

- A daily morning and evening routine of journalling and yoga.
- Cooking and eating whole foods.
- Writing.
- Travel.
- Time with family and friends.
- Work I love.
- Reading.
- Bathing.

What about you?

Each of us is a work in progress. Each of us has twenty-four hours in a day and a chance to see time differently, but only if we're willing to make vital decisions about our precious lives.

Chapter 6
Small Steps and Big Promises

Change is essential to life. We're always changing. But sometimes we get carried away. We sit down to think about how we want to move forward in life and find ourselves listing twenty areas of life where we can make strides. Pretty soon, we've got tens of major goals all calling to us at once. And not long after, we get overwhelmed and end up doing none of them.

Not only is it all too easy to burn out before we begin by setting too many goals, but we often we set goals for life as though we are corporate entities rather than human beings. Goals that are all about figures, like achieving a turnover £2 million by 2022, are not motivating. Such goals are abstract and contain no meaningful milestones that people can relate to. Despite this, we often adopt these kinds of goals in our personal lives. Goals like: I will lose 30lbs by the end of the year.

Instead, choose goals that have intrinsic motivation. Not: I will lose 10lbs in the next six weeks. But: I will fit back into my black jeans for Kit's birthday party. This is something concrete, life-related and something you actually want. It's so much more likely to be achievable than an indeterminate 'ought' hanging over you.

Even more powerfully, break goals down into incremental stages. No matter how enormous the quest you are on, it will have ways to break it down into steps that don't overwhelm you. Last year I injured a hip. Nothing serious, but painful and it brought a halt to exercise. As it was healing I set a target to get back to doing yoga morning and evening plus stationary cycling at least 3 times each week. There was no possibility of doing it all at once. So I broke the goal into increments:

- Do the gentlest 20-minute yoga routine every morning for at least a week.
- Go for daily walks, adding to the steps each day.
- Add another two yoga sequences, continuing with mornings only.
- Do all but the most demanding yoga routines, staying with mornings.
- Begin to regain confidence with the harder balance poses and press-up style poses.
- Add a gentle evening yoga practice.
- Finally add the cycling 3 times a week.

I didn't put an overall time line next to the increments because I wanted to work at the pace the injury would allow and not make it flare up again. At the end I bought a new pair of yoga trousers to celebrate. If I'd attempted too much too soon, I would have hurt the hip. I might even have jeopardised being able to travel around Spain to research the novel I was working on.

It doesn't matter how small the steps are as long as there is movement. In fact advocates of *kaizen* (Japanese for 'continuous improvement') will say that the smaller the better. We often have inbuilt resistance to change, but if the steps are tiny we can short-circuit that resistance. Kaizen proponents will advise starting with two minutes exercise a day for someone who has always been sedentary. It's so small it's hard to fail, but gradually it builds.

Once we have a system of small steps, we can begin to mark the milestones. By breaking down the quest, we allow ourselves to experience moments of pride and achievement along the way whilst the ultimate aim becomes feasible. I've been working on this book for more than two years. I began with individual blog posts on the theme of writing and the writing life. I knew that not every post I wrote would be a fit and that there would be a great deal of editing to transform the elements into a cohesive book, but starting with blogs allowed me to test ideas and get feedback through the responses of readers.

The first milestone was to produce a 9-chapter PDF book to give away to people who followed my blog and then to develop an associated course for it. The blogs later cohered into a much bigger course on journaling, complete with over sixty audio units, and others have become a series of seasonal online mini-retreats. The next milestone was to sketch out how all the elements fit together using a huge sheet of paper and coloured pens. When I began thinking about the project it seemed too huge and nebulous. I couldn't initially envisage the structure of the book but many blogs, spider diagrams and maps later, the increments have built into something I'm excited by.

You can also strengthen the steps of your quest with implementation

Chapter 6: Small Steps and Big Promises

intentions. These are simply routines that we develop for situations that might otherwise derail us, or ways of thinking ahead — if X, then Y. They set up not only the target, but the how, when and where. They become automatic so that we're not constantly depending on gritting our teeth and relying on willpower and they can cover a multitude of situations:

- If I crave chocolate, I'll open a jar of olives.
- If it's the last day of the month, I will do a breast exam.

They are also useful for thinking about tricky situations. If you've ever found yourself too shocked to know what to say when someone makes a sexist/racist remark, for example, you could have a small stock of things to say in the moment rather than freezing and kicking ourselves for the silence later:

If I hear X, I'll respond with Y.

Even when we are taking small, feasible steps. life can get in the way. The quest might be to develop a morning routine of early waking, journalling and exercise. It's all going well and then we get a head cold. A couple of days can unravel weeks of habit building. Or we just have one bad day and feel like we've lost the thread.

The principle of kaizen not only relies on continual small steps, but also on making corrections as soon as possible. That way, going off course doesn't build into total disaster. When an airplane is in flight, it is often off course and the pilot makes constant adjustments so that it reaches the correct destination. We are the same, more so. We're human and fallible. But it's easier to lose 5lbs in weight after a holiday than to let the weight-gain build up over the next holiday and the next until we're faced with 30lbs to lose.

In short, change is essential to growth and development, but it doesn't have to be enormous and overwhelming. A quest taken in small steps is still a quest.

Interlude 2

Writing the Wild Flowering

This interlude is a chance to step back and nourish your writing flow. It's planned to be used around the first quarter day of the year with days either side, March 20–22, though if you are in the southern hemisphere this would fall in September and your interlude during March would correspond to 'Writing the light's balance', found in Section 4.

March 20

All winter things have been growing, quietly and hidden from view; small things — delicate yet strong, and intensely beautiful. If we live anywhere with marked seasons, the transitions become meaningful. Our environments change, the light changes. Spring sees a warming of the earth and a lightening of the skies and with it comes growth, bringing associations of growth and hope.

The Venerable Bede (673-735), mentions that Eostre was previously worshipped in April, in *Temporum Ratione* or *The Reckoning of Time*. We know little else, although Ostara or Eostre has become associated with a goddess of dawn and light, and later traditions have associated her and the Easter season with hares and fertility.

Easter varies in time from March through to late April in step with the Jewish celebration of Passover, but the Spring or Vernal Equinox, which falls around March 21, is also associated with Ostara and with traditions of new birth and new light. Themes of death and rebirth occur across many belief systems (think of the gods Attis, Adonis, Osiris and Dionysus, as well as the Christ-figure). Similarly, spring equinox festivals stretch from ancient Persia to Mexico.

The season is also linked with notions of eternity, which takes on different resonances depending on our beliefs. For myself, I have no belief in a personal deity, though, on the principle that we can't know what we can't know, I'd describe myself as a spiritual agnostic rather than an atheist. What I do believe is that the stream of consciousness within this body, with its memories, will not survive this life. But this doesn't make me less in awe of the splendour of the universe, the raw beauty of the mountains outside my window, the fierce moments of joy that can come at the most unexpected times. It doesn't prevent me from having moments of epiphany when I feel the connection of all life and its extraordinary preciousness.

In theological parlance, this is a kind of 'realised eschatology'. The theory, spearheaded by theologians like Joachim Jeremias and my former New Testament tutor (who famously spoke at the court case against the censorship of *Lady Chatterley's Lover*), John Robinson, is that even those with Christian faith don't need to wait for a second coming of Christ or far off end-times for the Kingdom of Heaven because it is already here on Earth, right now.

It's a view that privileges life and becoming, over destruction and an afterlife. And, whatever our faith position, all writers can contribute to this sense of eternity and infinity, not as future paradise but as the ability to be in the moment where past, present and future coalesce. All writers can attest to eternity and infinity breaking into the now. And anyone alive can appreciate that moments of enlightenment and epiphany are to be found in diverse places. From acts of generosity to standing in a shaft of light in a forest; from the small daily rituals that dignify and simplify our lives to a sunset over the ocean.

Watching the world wake up in spring, we feel an upsurge of hope. The world that seemed dead is alive again and our sense of finitude shifts. The longing for certainty, for eternity, for survival beyond this life, is as old as humanity. There is evidence of burial and caring for the dead as far back as 50,000 years ago. And this hope is not in vain, whatever our religious stance or lack of it: our finitude does not diminish the grandeur of life.

Concepts like constancy, endurance, connectedness and soul, for me, need no external referent beyond the mysteries of life itself in order to be of value and truth.

This chapter was first written for a series of online courses to provide mini retreats at home for writers. One of the participants wrote to me about an extraordinary experience of transcendence:

> Very late on Saturday night I stood in my garden, wrapped up warm and made notes. My imagination caught fire and I

was amazed. The cat tootled about checking now and again whether I was about to go inside. I felt a quiet, unrolling kind of epiphany as ordinary objects seemed to show me their own 'personalities' and testimonies. It's hard to explain but I felt a connection and it was just wonderful.

Such profound experiences of being at one with the universe need no proofs. Their power resides in the experience. Nature, the soul, and love are things 'one recognises through the heart', to quote Dostoevsky. There is no tension here between a scientific and a spiritual discourse. Instead we are saying that reality and experience are not either/or but both/and. There are certainties and categorically unequivocal 'facts' that we might never know or that might be unknowable, despite our yearning for answers, but the human condition is one of ambivalence. We relate to the world as rationalists and as visionaries within a breath.

For some of us the assurances extend to another life. For others, like me, they reside in the here and now, in the stories we are becoming, in love, generosity, humility, vulnerability and courage. They reside in transcendent moments that dwell in the experience of our connectedness to all life, all matter. Yet, wherever we locate ourselves in this tension between transcendence and imminence, as writers we need to write of resurrection. Resurrection is the narrative of:

- finding a way to reclaim our injured and sick planet from the maw of destruction;
- love re-found, grief lived through and transmuted into memory;
- political struggle, movements for justice and peace, whether in poetry, fiction or nonfiction;
- largeness and persistence in the face of whatever the universe throws at us and those we love and the world we inhabit.

Resurrection is the immortal words of Maya Angelou, in her poem 'Still I Rise', which speaks not of afterlife but of the indomitable spirit. And for many, resurrection is the consideration of how we live now, as I wrote in 'How to rise again', first published in *Particles of Life*:

Find dandelion clocks,
and count to twelve,
tie talismans
of fresh sweet lavender
beside your gate
and by south facing doors.
Grow tulip bulbs
on every window sill
and walk a moonlit beach
at equinox.
At Easter, bury chocolate;
foil-wrapped eggs
like secret seeds
in every scented room,
and cook a feast and laugh
with those you love
and open windows,
even in the rain.
You will not live forever,
but for now;
not wasting life
on how to rise again.

Journal exercise

For you, when and where does the world seem to be 'heaven now'?

How is this reflected in your writing and your life?

Have you ever felt connected to all of nature… a grand and eternal unity? Write about a moment of transcendence, from memory or from imagination.

How do you understand 'transcendence' and in what ways does this affect your writing?

What notes of 'resurrection' are there in your writing and in your life (whether you see this as personal, spiritual, ecological, political…) and how can you give them more expression?

• Interlude 2: Writing the Wild Flowering •

Ritual

The images of spring and rebirth are not merely picturesque, simplistic and sentimental. Birth comes after struggle and labour. Rebirth assumes death, loss and grief. In the natural world, new growth often comes after harsh pruning, long winters, scourging fires. In the political realm, change is sometimes violent or takes huge courage and resistance. In our personal and writing lives, any huge leap of life takes enormous passion and energy and may come only after loss or deep inner work.

Take a double page in your journal or a big sheet of paper you can pin up somewhere and draw two overlapping circles (like a Venn diagram).

In the left hand circle list those things that are current causes for grief or that are presently losses in your life, your world, your writing, but where any of these are ambivalent, show even the slightest sign of hope, let them overlap into the area where the circles intersect.

In the right hand circle list those things that are current causes for joy or hope, that are presently signs of connection, transcendence or resurrection in your life, your world, your writing. Again, some of these might be slightly ambivalent, so let these overlap into the area where the circles intersect.

Now commit to honouring the losses and celebrating the new life.

March 21

Writers are often cerebral and sedentary, but when writing loses touch with the body and the natural world, it loses impact. As the world comes to life and Spring flourishes, this is good time to reflect on embodied writing. Despite being someone who can get lost in my own head, forgetting to move, eat or drink, I'm also know that this undermines my writing and that writers need to adopt more holistic outlooks.

There's a long history of dualistic thinking in writing, as in many other areas. In seeking to find metaphors for aspects of our experience or in seeking to find ways of talking about something particular, we often slide into language that sets body against mind or sets one subject against the other as object. And yet these distinctions, between body and world, even between one mind and another, are increasingly hard to defend, either from a scientific or philosophical perspective. It is no longer only Buddhists who posit that none of us is discrete and separate. The idea that millions of individual minds can be tucked away safely in the cupboards of millions of brains finds little support in any realm of enquiry.

Whatever model of consciousness we adopt, it is hard if not impossible to argue that I am two separate and opposite 'things', flesh and disembodied mind. That's not to say that we can't have meaningful conversations about 'soul' and 'spirituality' (whether as metaphors or as part of belief systems), but it is to assert that we are physical systems with emergent properties of thinking, values, consciousness. It is to assert that there is no 'ghost' in the machine, but rather one integrated and exquisite animal with language and thought.

If we stop thinking of ourselves as compartmentalised pieces, some of which we can neglect, then holism is inevitable. So too is writing that is more embodied and a writing life that integrates the whole person. In order to be writers who —

- witness to the human condition,
- make the connections,
- detect the patterns of events and name them,
- bring to light things that might otherwise remain hidden

— we need to join to the body.

We need to get outside, breathe deeply, focus on what our senses are telling us and interact with the natural world. By fully inhabiting a place with an awareness of your body and senses you not only appreciate on a deep level that you are skin, bone, muscle, sensations, but also tap into information from the world travelling through you. The effect is to evoke emotion and memory, to bring into consciousness what you hadn't been aware of a few minutes before.

I'd never been a fan of nostalgia until I was reminded that its etymology is from two Greek words — 'to return home' and 'pain'. The body is our first and abiding home and some of us are so out of step with our physicality that we forget this and need to return. All the grief and pain we experience doesn't simply get buried in the unconscious. We have to open this up. As writers, we need to take notice of Walt Whitman, who says:

Interlude 2: Writing the Wild Flowering

> Understand that you can have in your writing no qualities which you do not honestly entertain in yourself.

This isn't a simplistic 'write what you know' dictum. It's a call to inhabit ourselves and write from the senses, from authentic, embodied human experience. It's a call to dig deep in ourselves in order to connect with others. When we write from sensations, listen to the emotions and consider what interests, intrigues and fascinates us, then the writing becomes whole and more lucid.

Writing takes a great deal of energy. If we're to direct it attentively to the body and outwardly to the world, then we need to guard that energy fiercely. This is why we are in the midst of thinking about the mindset of the writer before we move on to writing process in Section 2. We need values, habits and systems that enable us to creatively nurture our time and energy if we are not to be derailed by all that life will throw at us. Too often, writers have a poor record when it comes to self-care. We have to redress the balance.

Journal exercise

Do you ask what your body wants or do you ignore and repress signs of discomfort, pain and illness?

How will the mind and spirit continue to soar if the home is tumbling down?

Do you fail to eat or even not go to the bathroom because you're 'too busy'?

Only when you see yourself as body, do you begin to inhabit the present moment.

In what ways do you hear and trust your body?

What is your body telling you it needs? For me, it is sometimes comfort, sometimes challenge. My list would include:

- To feel the sweat of work and the cleansing of hot water.
- To feel nourished, but not bloated.
- To savour wholesome food.
- To be supple and flexible.

- To relax with a massage.
- To feel sunlight and rain and wind…
- To be hydrated.
- To wander in beautiful places, from Toledo to a forest.
- To taste the tang of sea air.

What is your list?

How will you integrate it into your life?

How do you embody this in your writing?

Find and read the poem by Mary Oliver, 'Wild Geese'. (You can hear Mary Oliver reading the poem on YouTube. It's in her collection, *Dream Work*, and also in the Bloodaxe anthology, *Staying Alive*.)

In what ways is the world offering itself to your imagination?

How are you honouring this in your life and in your writing?

Ritual

(This is similar to a ritual from the Writing the Green Blade interlude, but bears repeating with a variation.)

Get out of doors with a notebook and find a place where you can pay attention. Be aware of all your senses, of your emotions and your body as you walk and name what your senses bring you. It can be a quick list, taking the pulse of each sense. Then go into detail. Focus on one sense at a time or interact with an object. What stories begin to emerge? What symbols or images come to mind?

March 22

All winter things have been growing, shoots and leaves, green blades rising through cold, hard earth; babies in wombs; ideas for stories, phrases of poems tucked away deep but slowly rising to the surface. Now the world is bursting into life and if we are to flow with the seasons and honour ourselves as bodies and creatures, connected to all life, then it behoves us

Interlude 2: Writing the Wild Flowering

to be writers of resurrection.

It's spring, but spring isn't an end point. Any art undertaken with commitment and seriousness becomes a metaphor for the artistic life and, I suspect, for life in general. Our quests as writers call us to be people writing resurrection, which in turn requires that we remain hopeful. Hope isn't blind optimism or glibness, but the courage not to become cynical and jaded.

Hope is fundamental to becoming a different story. And the world needs different stories; those that are radical, transformative, challenging and nurturing. To evolve the stories, we have to foster hope and expect great things. But we should also be open to outcomes we didn't expect or may not have desired. We have to be willing to learn, regroup and hope again.

Journal exercise

a. Imagine the quest: What is it that you want to happen?
b. Break the quest down into steps: How will you make it happen?
c. Align your passion and your motivation: How committed are you?

Now journal on those questions (you might want to include a drawing of a path, mark out the steps and put clouds of passion and motivation in the sky)

What is it that you want to happen?

How will you make it happen?

How committed are you?

Hope and intrinsic motivation go hand in hand. We only expect transformation and change (words of resurrection) when:

- We value the quest for itself.
- Believe that the quest is possible.
- Believe that we are effective in the world and can make things happen.

And we will only value and believe in a quest and in ourselves to pursue it

Interlude 2: Writing the Wild Flowering

if the aims are:

- clear
- desired
- believed
- expected
- invested in something

But investing in something is not synonymous with attaching to outcomes. If we fixate on the end we lose the ability to respond with flexibility to whatever happens along the way. If we make the quest all about one specific outcome, then we will become cynical and disillusioned when other things happen along the way. Instead, expect everything, attach to nothing.

The quest is the decision you have made. It might be to complete a novel or sequence of poems. It might be about personal transformation or a decision to prioritise transformative relationships over transactional ones. It might be about changing your work or lifestyle. It might be to prioritise political activism. Whatever happens, you have changed the story of yourself. When you have shifted perspective and whatever the specific outcome then:

- You remain hopeful and expect good things whatever happens.
- You won't abandon the quest or allow defeat or success to sidetrack you.
- You will keep moving and changing.
- Your values are not shaken by circumstances.

We should set quests and pursue enormous visions with indefatigable persistence, recognising that it is the learning that matters. When we do this we live in congruence with our values, always:

- growing
- dignified
- clear
- free

It's certain that life will give us plenty to practise with. When I experienced a series of workplace assaults years ago and my health and vocation unravelled, it wasn't the outcome I was aiming for, but it forced me to rethink my life. A huge boulder on the path eventually made me take

Interlude 2: Writing the Wild Flowering

another path that turned out to be a gift. Attachment is to people. Attach to those you love and commit to, not to things and outcomes. When we internalise this, then, win or lose, we stay with the quest.

A life of wonder, that welcomes even the unexpected, makes us more grounded and gives us equanimity. Abraham Maslow saw wonder as a key feature of peak experiences and a sense of wonder makes us know that more is possible than we might have imagined. Wonder, like hope and expectation, prevents us from becoming jaded in our thinking. As Kierkegaard put it,

> Life is a mystery to be lived, not a problem to be solved.

Cultivating wonder requires:

- A willingness to explore, play and create.
- A narrative sensibility to weave stories as we grow.
- Always identifying as a learner.
- The openness to observe, listen and move about the world with all our senses open.
- Receptivity to new experiences, to unfamiliar places and situations that stimulate creativity, thought and deep work.
- Trust in your own intuition.

How do you maintain a sense of wonder in your life and in your writing?

How do you practise gratitude in the face of the unexpected?

We hear a great deal about mindfulness, but I think that living in hope, expectation and wonder requires something more radical and holistic. We need not to be mindful, but 'bodiful'. We'll return to this in detail in Section 4 but, as previously noted, it's so easy for those of us involved in creative tasks, especially writing, to become cerebral and sedentary. Yet great art and great writing demand connections to the body and to the world. Travelling to places we write about is not always possible, particularly if we are writing about other time periods or imagined worlds. But writers need to find ways to connect; not to cut ourselves off, not to imagine ourselves as disembodied minds. The urgency of the times we live in, both politically and ecologically, scream against this.

- Breathe in.
- Feel your breath reaching every part of your writing body.

· Interlude 2: Writing the Wild Flowering ·

- Become tuned to its blockages, discomforts, tensions.
- Walk in the world that feeds your senses that nurture your imagination.

You are not a mind (subject) looking at body (object) but a whole creature tapping into the awareness that you — an intelligent body — have. You may not be as separate from the world as contemporary individualism has suggested.

The question of where the individual mind-body complex ends and the rest of the world begins is one that has exercised philosophers for generations. Husserl asserted that the lived body is the centre of experience, whilst Merleau Ponty talked about the world as the realm of experience, not thought, in which everything we touch in turn touches us. We don't understand the world from the perspective of disembodied mind. The body is the primary vehicle of knowing. Mind is rooted not only in body but in the body's interaction with the world. Ultimately, distinctions between mind, body and world are arbitrary.

Writers, creators, all of us, are 'enworlded bodies' imagining quests, breaking down the steps, making commitments as we write resurrections and become the people we want to be, as we become different stories.

Journal exercise

What is your quest?

When does the fabric of your life feel woven from wonder and hope?

When does this desert you?

How can you protect and nurture yourself, soul and body and oneness, to stay with your quests in wonder and hope, even when the outcomes are unexpected?

Ritual

Spring is a time of wild flowering. It is a time of life bursting through the surface and into the warming light and air. What one thing can you do today to assist your own wild flowering? Give this some time and attention.

Chapter 7
It's All in the Words

In this section we are thinking about the mindset we need as writers in order to be able to write and embody the writing life. In the last interlude we considered our deep connections to all of life, to the universe. When we express this, when we write stories and poems, articles and memoirs, geographies and histories… we do so in words and the words we choose matter; they sculpt how we and our readers see reality and act. Writing gives people ways to express experience… The stories we tell let others know who we are and what we hold dear. Narrative and meaning go hand in hand. We all need stories that make sense of experience, particular and universal. But if the language functions to exclude our experience then how do we find this meaning?

Almost three decades ago I completed a PhD in feminist theology. One of my main concerns was the lack of inclusive language in organised religious structures and in liturgy. I was particularly impressed by research done by Dale Spender into how language functions. In her book, *Man Made Language*, Spender argued that since language is crucial to how we form identity, patriarchal language has a detrimental effect on women.

Her studies of mixed sex gatherings demonstrated how men maintain dominant positions. She found endless examples of how men exercise linguistic control by diminishing female talk on the grounds of its style rather than content. For example there was a consensus that women's language is more irrational, emotional or aggressive. Spender also found that women are more often interrupted, their opinions more often discounted and that men will hold private conversations while a woman is talking.

Spender went on to describe how, in 1746, the male grammarian John Kirby made it a grammatical rule that the male gender is 'more comprehensive' than the female gender. He encoded this personal opinion, with the support of other male grammarians, into the language structure. By 1850 the rule had become an Act of Parliament. In the '90s, when I was doing my PhD, women stood accused of 'tampering with the language' when they challenged this rule.

This was particularly the case with liturgical language. Such an accusation assumed that language was the property of males. In fact, women were doing what men have always done: producing linguistic forms that did not diminish them.

Research shows that people think 'male' when they hear the word 'man'. Aileen Pace Nilsen showed this with young children, using the sentence, 'man needs food'. In the same year Schneider and Hacker came up with the same conclusion about college students. They used such phrases as 'Political Man', 'Urban Man' etc. Linda Harrison showed that science students think male when presented with the phrase 'the evolution of man'. We are thus led to project male images onto the world and become blinkered about perceiving female images.

For males, identity is constant. But females must then look for clues about whether a reference includes them. Moreover, we often regard males as the whole species. Eric Fromm's assertion that, 'man's vital interests are life, food, access to females etc' is an apt example. On the other hand, females are never the whole species. We never talk about man having a hard time with pregnancy.

Kirby's grammatical 'he/man' rule makes women the outsiders. A woman achieves humanity by labelling herself a man and this means losing her identity as a woman. Religious communities can exacerbate this by addressing women as brothers, sons etc, or in hymnody and liturgy that excludes female pronouns. With such language the image of woman as an equal part of the species soon disappears.

Things have moved on since I did that PhD, but has language moved with it? There is some progress, but reading *Man Made Language* now, it's depressing how fresh it feels.

And there are other voices raised in concern. In an entertaining but pointed performance piece in *The Wave in the Mind*, Ursula Le Guin parodied herself as 'man'. The piece is wry and witty, but it becomes more poignant as she talks of herself as a 'second rate' or 'imitation' man. And it's not only that language fails women by defining them as 'men'. The he/man rule is only one aspect of exclusion.

So many of our metaphors, for example, are drawn from war or conflict. Yet if we shift the language — talk about resistance, learning, out-thinking, changing, unsettling... then it is not only words that change but our consciousness and behaviours. Language either diminishes or enlarges our understanding of our own experience. Many of our ways of imaging experience assume that not only is there a normative gender, but that conflict is the major symbol of experience. If our metaphors don't come from battle, they are likely to come from competitive sport, which has already borrowed a military vocabulary. This is not only the case in politics and business, which use adversarial metaphors all the time, but also in relationships:

- He won her heart.
- She fought for him, but lost to his mistress.
- He had to fend off women.

It's the case in many forms of dialogue:

- I shot down his arguments.
- I left her without a leg to stand on.

It's particularly worrying that it's how we view disease, often to the detriment of those suffering. Conflict metaphors can leave those whose illnesses are incurable feeling that they are guilty of 'losing', as in:

- He lost the fight against cancer.
- The war against obesity.

It's also the case in personal development. Rather than talking about questing and exploring, we are likely to read about:

- How to crush your goals.
- How to dominate your morning routine.

Metaphors shape our thinking and behaviour. Metaphors of excelling, flying, being alight, realising a vision, are all available, as are many more that do not rely on internal conflict. If our language only represents men, or largely uses metaphors of conflict, then we are leaving vast swathes of experience unspoken and silenced. Surely the task of the writer is to enlarge experience, not collude with its diminishment?

Language is rich and nuanced. As writers it's our most basic tool. It behoves us to use it to include and to make experience meaningful. When language is a battlefield or a no-go area for a particular group, whether this is women, children, the sick, the elderly, the full panoply of racial identities… it's not working. As writers, we can do better than that.

- We can make language fresh and inventive.
- We can narrativise in ways that enhance meaning, even in dark times.
- We can refuse to use language that excludes or to use metaphors that set us in opposition.

Chapter 8
A Mind for Play, Love, Imagination and Ritual

We are beings capable of change. So often we feel stuck and yet it is possible to effect profound changes in ourselves. But how? Day to day it's so easy to slide into negative thinking or to become so busy that our environment overwhelms us. But there are ways to take control. We need to cultivate a daily practice that elevates each day and gives us a sense of the extraordinary.

To do this requires a holistic sense of the self. We need to have habits and systems in place to support deep thinking and living. And, of course, we need these habits and systems to be sufficiently simple that we can find them a help rather than just more things to do that will exhaust us. The aim is to energises and nurture, not burden. An holistic practice also needs to take account of all the elements of human life:

- physical
- emotional
- intellectual
- spiritual

A tall order? There are certainly lots of voices telling us what to do to live well. Much of it may be great advice, but being on the receiving end of 'preaching' isn't motivating. If we see ourselves facing uphill struggles that demand gargantuan willpower, sooner or later, we give up. For example, eating well won't last

- if you are not intrinsically motivated to eat well,
- if your environment is full of sugar and white carbs.

Chapter 8: A Mind for Play, Love, Imagination and Ritual

Similarly exercising will grind to a halt if

- you don't love your body,
- you don't want to move your body and keep it in great condition.

Play

Instead of exhausting ourselves with willpower and effort through gritted teeth, we need to reclaim a sense of pleasure and play. No one needs to tell a toddler to do 10,000 steps a day. Play in children is joyful, creative, problem-solving. It's never about productivity. Instead of making healthy eating and exercise serious burdens on a never-ending to-do list, get playful. Experiment to find the way of moving that energises you, something you *want* to do instead of forcing yourself to do. Find a recipe book full of healthy food that makes you want to cook.

Love

This is advice from St Augustine:

> Once and for all, I give you this one short command: love, and do what you will. If you hold your peace, hold your peace out of love. If you cry out, cry out in love. If you correct someone, correct them out of love. If you spare them, spare them out of love. Let the root of love be in you: nothing can spring from it but good.

This is a dictum taken up by Joseph Fletcher in his development of Situation Ethics: the idea that we make decisions according to circumstances rather than according to rigid and fixed principles. The only absolute is Love and this motivates each decision. As a complete ethical system it's far from flawless, but it does point to the need to pay attention to our environments and to emotional life every day. It's vital that you have the support of those you love and who love you. Mutual support is life-giving.

On the other hand, those who poison every encounter, who are always negative or who drain your energy, are entirely another matter. We can't always avoid these people completely, but whenever we have the choice, it's better to not spend time with them. Relationships without mutual regard and respect can be damaging and the more we can limit and avoid them the better. Conversely, the more time we can spend with those we care about and who care about us,

Chapter 8: A Mind for Play, Love, Imagination and Ritual

the better.

There are different kinds of relationship in life. Some are transactional — they revolve around what people can get. Others are transformational — they revolve around giving and the relationship develops so that the whole is more than the sum of the parts. You need to make the most space for transformational relationships, for being with those with whom you share mutual love and support. You need to be happy. Easier said than done? This is what Robert Louis Stephenson says:

> The habit of being happy enables one to be largely freed from the domination of outward conditions.

We can cultivate more contentment with simple steps like not taking every remark we hear personally or reminding ourselves to live in the moment. Simple relaxation techniques can be a boost, as can challenging our own negative thinking about ourselves. Too often we are harsh about ourselves in ways we would never be towards someone else in a similar situation. Of course we want to improve as people, but we won't grow by being unkind and unforgiving to ourselves. Of course we don't want to become delusional egotists, but that doesn't mean we can't have a healthy dose of love of self as well as of others.

Imagination

And, just as importantly, if our minds are not engaged and learning we ossify. To thrive and change, to become a different story, new ideas are essential. Where do we find them?

- books
- stories
- groups of people who talk ideas (not gossip)
- solitude

Deep thinking and elevated living happen when you are intellectually stimulated, when you engage and stretch your mental faculties. We need intellectual stimulation from a variety of sources and the imagination to see ourselves as the people we intend to become. Of course, change doesn't end with imagination. We have to act on it, but imagination is where we start the transformations we desire.

Ritual

People of all faiths and none need myth. Myth is the story we live in. And the language of ritual, borrowed from religious language, indicates a basic attitude to life. It's one in which life has dignity and meaning. D Stephenson Bond talks about the need to foster a religious outlook that has nothing to do with following a particular creed or belonging to a religious movement. Such an outlook includes the notion of reverence. When we revere life, we treat the self and others with imagination and empathy.

When we have reverence for human life and the earth we live on, life not only becomes more imaginative, but we live more intentionally and with thoughtfulness. Instead of seeing life as endless goals to tick off, we see how our participation in life makes a difference. This is analogous to the language of devotion, which is so much richer than the functional, pragmatic language of goals because it is essentially about passion and caring.

Our daily rituals don't have to be complex. Living well can be a simple thing. As simple as the pleasure of

- a regular walk,
- at least one meal a day eaten with appreciation and/or with conversation and sharing,
- quiet time in which to think...

In short, your environment and habits should support you. Instead of berating yourself to be a better person, choosing play, love, imagination and ritual allows you to develop habits that nurture you. Habits are like the clothes we put on each day. We choose them and we can change them. To support a life that takes account of your physical, emotional, mental and spiritual needs, these habits need to be simple and powerful. And this is often set in motion by starting your day with them. In this way, the tone is set for everything that comes after.

You don't need a prescription for a morning routine or to be told what time is best for you to wake up. Love your body and listen to it. For most of us, our mornings are determined by two things: the night before and the demands of the day, including where you work and when you start.

For me, the previous evening tends to be a mix of writing, reading, journalling, a hot bath, then sleep. Ideally it also includes yoga and not being on a screen for at least the last hour before sleep. Sleeping isn't my problem. I love it. I'm not an early waker, I fill up with energy in the evenings, but I work from home so I'm able to meditate, journal and exercise before the rush of the day begins. My journal contains everything but in the mornings I try to include a

Chapter 8: A Mind for Play, Love, Imagination and Ritual

commitment to doing at least one thing that will move me forward with a passion project that day. Small steps lead to tangible progress.

You know what works for you. And you know if your current practice isn't serving you well. Whatever elements you need to include, give them some time and do something that reminds you that you are your body — move and eat. Days of play, love, imagination and ritual need a strong foundation. Set that up every day and, at the end of the day, reflect on it. What have you done today to support your whole self on its quest? How have you nourished yourself:

- physically
- emotionally
- intellectually
- spiritually

And if you didn't do this today? Start again tomorrow. Don't worry about what's past. The time to start is now.

Eight Exercises for a Writer's Mind

1. Just write

Look at a tarot card or postcard and write about the image. (I'm not talking divination, but inspiration and we can find it everywhere). Alternatively:

- Pick a card from Brian Eno's *Oblique Strategies* deck and keep writing from it.
- Listen to the world outside your window and see where the sounds take you.
- Write a list of ideas for your next creative project.

2. Playing with words

Take a bunch of coloured pens and, constantly switching between them, write at least 50 words — try not to associate as you go, make them as random as possible and choose words you like the sound of. Use lots of different colours as you go along (constantly changing pen will help to break the association chain that your logical mind wants to impose).

Now take the words and make them into a poem in exactly the order they occurred to you. You can add a minimum of joining words or the odd extra words to keep a modicum of sense going, but don't overthink it. (Yes, it will probably be an awful poem, but you are playing with words not writing for publication).

Now write a descriptive scene or short prose incident using all 50 of the words.

3. Congruence

When our inner life and actions work together, we feel more congruence and our confidence as writers rises.

> How congruent do you feel your life is?
>
> Are your thoughts, speech and actions in alignment?
>
> What values or qualities do you want to live more fully?
>
> How will you do this?
>
> How do you appear in your writing?

4. Gratitude

List at least 20 (and possibly 50) things you are thankful for in your life and why you value them.

Try telling someone how grateful you are for them, today.

5. Focus

What two things have you learnt or been struck by in your reading in the last week?

A sharp mind is a great boost to a writer. The more imaginative you are, the more connections you can make, the richer and more nuanced your writing will become. Do something new today — a different route to work; shopping at a farmers' market instead of a shop with plastic-wrapped veg; cooking from a cuisine you're not familiar with… Then journal about the experience.

6. Imagine

Where do you find new ideas? (Make it as long a list as possible and perhaps colour-code your favourites.)

What are you reading currently? How is it inspiring you? Do you keep quotes from your reading in your journal? If not, try this today and over the next few days.

Spend 30 minutes imagining and writing about who you want to be. (Be bold and ambitious — this is imagination.)

7. Rituals

What are the rituals and habits in your life that either derail or support your writing?

How can you shift the pattern to be more supportive?

Write about at least one thing you can do today to move you toward your vision of the writing life you desire.

In the evening, check back with your journal — did you do it? If you didn't do this today, start again tomorrow. Don't worry about what's past. The time to start is now. How will you do this tomorrow?

8. Pen-picture of writer

What is it that excites you? What is that makes your life meaningful?

Write a description of the 'alternative' you. Write it in the first person present tense.

Now think about the areas where you feel least congruent with that 'alternative'.

What is the one thing you can do today to shift the congruence a little closer?

(It's worth revisiting this exercise from time to time and looking at how far you've come and what the next small step and the next might be).

The Evolution of the Writing Process

Chapter 9: Please Read

Section 3 is about the writing. We'll explore journalling as a support system for your writing; ways of keeping going; working at depth and valuing the journey, and we'll look at some issues in fiction writing and the intersection of writing and travel. But we're going to start with the most fundamental requirement for any writer: reading.

It's depressing as both an editor and a writer when I hear writers (or more usually aspiring writers) saying they don't read. Getting books out into the world is difficult. It's a huge amount of work for publishers, booksellers and writers and the only way it's possible is if there are people out there who read. If you are a writer who doesn't read the work of others, what would make you imagine that others would want to read your book?

Writers have to read:

Because reading is your world

Imagine a chef who hates to eat, an artist who's never been to a gallery. It's not credible — neither is a writer who doesn't read.

Influence is good

Sometimes writers tell me they don't read because they don't want to influence their work. This is the height of arrogance and flawed thinking. No one creates *ex nihilo*. No one is that original. Of course you shouldn't be copying others or never finding your own voice, but what has gone before you is a treasure trove. Tradition and inspiration are all around you in books. You can learn structure, technique and so much more by reading. We become innovative by building on the past, not by writing it off.

For the love of language

Great writers are those who have found wonderful ways to use language. Their language might be supple or taut and honed. It might be rich or lyrical. It might be rhythmic or urgent. You will discover an infinite kaleidoscope of vocabulary and style in the pages of books written by others.

To encourage imagination

If you don't let your imagination run free as a reader, you will impoverish it. We need imagination to solve problems, to comprehend ourselves and the world we live in. Reading fires the imagination.

To see what works

We can learn the theory of grammar or read 'how to' books on how to make decisions about plot or pacing. We can find cheat-sheets on building character and endless texts on point of view. But we learn a great deal of this not as a cerebral activity but in our bones, simply by reading. Writers should read deeply and widely. When we read books that have stand-out characters or tight pacing something in our gut 'gets it'. We learn what works.

To see what doesn't work

Not all books will thrill you as a reader. There are varieties of taste, but some books don't work. Others may have one flaw that nags at you. I used to force myself to finish every book I started. I've decided life is too short for that, but I do give every book a good try, at least the first fifty to a hundred pages, and if it isn't working for me, I ask why. Someone else might love the book, but ask yourself what it is that doesn't resonate. It will help with the decisions you make about your own writing.

Because the more you read, the more you understand the human condition

Understanding the mental states of others is vital not only to everyday relationships but also to writing. The area known as 'Theory of Mind', how we develop this skill, is vast and complex. But research suggests that reading literary fiction enhances our understanding of others. Engaging with works of art gives us deeper thinking and empathy. Is that such a surprise? If you want to write about the human condition, it behoves you to have some understanding of it.

Because the diversity of history, culture and thought is all contained in writing

Ray Bradbury pointed out that burning books isn't needed for cultural destruction, it happens all by itself when people stop reading. Conversely, reading gives us insight into people and places we might never otherwise access, it lets us into the mind of others, which is extraordinary and powerful.

I love to travel. My idea of heaven is to be able to stay for weeks in a place I'm writing about. If I can eat the food, smell the streets, see the art, hear the language first hand, I know it will enhance what I write. But there are practical and logistical constraints on this kind of research. Even a wonderful Arts Council grant can't pay for me to go back to 1950s Budapest or eleventh century Moorish Spain. Reading can take me into the past or into realities that might not even be possible. The diversity is endless and available: cheap and easy to find.

Because it will encourage you to take more risks with your writing

When I was writing the book that became *Stale Bread & Miracles*, I got stuck. I had a long novel on a subject that was important to me. But it was miserable. There were good reasons for that. Nonetheless, I couldn't imagine why anyone would want to read it. While I was pondering how to move the book forward I was editing a book of prose poetry. It occurred to me that I could take each long, self-pitying chapter and crush it into a prose poem. Each piece would be pithy, allude to the darkness, but also let in some light, even humour, to an awful situation. The resulting slim collection has since sold out two print runs and is well into the third. And it's accessible to people who don't generally read poetry.

The more we read, the more we expose ourselves to the range of possibilities for our writing. Reading not only expands your imagination, vocabulary and empathy but also your ability to reshape your writing in unexpected ways.

Because it's good for you

Even if you are not a writer, reading helps to keep our brains active and is an activity that reduces stress. If you *are* a writer, you need those benefits. Reading is a pleasure and if you don't think so, what business have you asking others to do it? As Virginia Woolf says, writers should love books for their own sake:

> When the Day of Judgment dawns and people, great and small, come marching in to receive their heavenly rewards, the Almighty will gaze upon the mere bookworms and say to Peter, 'Look, these need no reward. We have nothing to give them. They have loved reading.'

Because books are the best place to escape

When your own writing hits an obstacle, you can hole up in someone else's world. Get some nourishment before you return to the hard graft. Gustave Flaubert puts it like this:

> The one way of tolerating existence is to lose oneself in literature as in a perpetual orgy.

There are times when this escape is life-saving, as Maya Angelou comments, talking about how reading gave her a sense of herself in a dangerous world.

Because reading increases your ability to be alone with your thoughts

Swathes of humanity appear to be losing the ability to be alone with nothing but their thoughts. Both writing and reading are solitary acts and if you can't be alone with your thoughts as a reader, then forget about being a writer. The more we reduce experience and reflection to status updates on Facebook, the less we allow ourselves to encounter and ponder the distance between the world we live in and our inner world. Why does this matter?

Because immediacy

- makes us write differently.
- encourages us to use metaphor less.

- makes us less likely to craft our writing
- is about numbers — of friends, fans, comments, followers — rather than quality.
- is not about giving our souls time to luxuriate but about ensuring we don't have a moment to let uncomfortable thoughts in.

Because the best writers read.

Reading is part of the total immersion of writing. If you don't love it, do it anyway.

Because you know what it's like to want readers.

When you've written something that's made for the world, it's a terrible feeling to see it overlooked. As writers, we long for others to read our articles, our poems, our books. You owe the return favour to other writers.

Please read.

Chapter 10

The Power of Journalling

Writers need to read. And they need to write. Not all writers keep journals, though most will have notebooks that have story ideas, timelines, scenes, poems… But for me, journalling is the source of my creativity. I'm currently writing in journal number 135 in a 26-year-long run of journalling. There were journals before this 'set', some lost in a house move, others disappeared in my teens. I write everything in these journals:

- random thoughts and observations
- notes on books I'm reading
- goals
- how the day/the week /the month/the year went
- to do lists and to be lists
- deep reflection
- shallow thought-dumping
- writing exercises
- ideas for books, stories, poems, blogs…
- dreams

The journals are beautiful. Many of them were handmade by my daughter or have been gifts. Each one is an artefact. They're also a problem in that they're not written for anyone else to read, so what will become of them? Nonetheless, I persist. I often feel I don't know what I'm thinking until I write it down. It's my act of processing. It's also the fount of my creativity. Why?

To practise

Great musicians practise. They go over scales and arpeggios, études and exercises. When tackling concert pieces, they go over and over particular phrases, gradually building speed and confidence. Writing about the diaries

Virginia Woolf kept over 26 years, she says:

> The habit of writing thus for my own eye only is good practice.
> It loosens the ligaments.

She left twenty-six volumes of these practices. I'm with Woolf. Writing is a muscle. The more we use it, the more flexible and strong it becomes. Whether you are writing morning pages in which you do two or three pages of a writing prompt or outlining ideas or setting down emotions, the more you write, the more confident your writing voice will become. When I teach writing courses and set exercises for the group I'm working with, I do the exercises myself in my journal. It's an interesting way to see how I respond to the same pressure to write in the moment and one I can look back on.

Do you keep morning pages or use a journal for writing exercises?

To record

A journal is a great source book. We can store away quotes. We can jot down overheard conversations that might later become dialogue in a story. We can name the world as we go about it and then go deeper to record the details with precision and note our reactions so that stories begin to emerge. And we can go back to our journals and mine them for inspiration and ideas when they seem scarce.

Some writers have separate books for notes. Often something small and portable works well for capturing a bit of overheard conversation on a train or a description of exactly how light falls on a river at dusk. I carry my journal everywhere and it all goes in amongst all the other sorts of writing.

Where do you keep the notes that become articles, poems or stories?

To keep lists

In her journals, Susan Sontag also moves between various forms of writing. There are episodes of detailed autobiography and passages which are philosophical or academic. But running throughout the journals are lists. She lists movies she's seen, books to read, places to eat and drink. She lists words, not only in English but in French, German, Greek, Italian and Spanish. She lists writers, poets, painters… There's something fascinating about lists, perhaps because we are a pattern making species, perhaps because they can encapsulate everything from sensory details to our hopes for the future.

I have 'to-do' lists in many forms, but will often put my to-do list for the day in my journal the night before. It's a way of prioritising and impressing each item onto my mind. And, like Sontag, I keep lists of books I want to read or make lists of places I want to visit when travelling. More recently I've favoured 'to-be' lists over 'to-do' lists — ways of thinking about the story I want to become.

Where do you keep your lists and what do you list?

To set and reflect on goals

Goals are a subset of lists. At the end of every year I do a huge journalling exercise thinking over the highs and lows of the last year. I look back at the goals I put in my journal the year before and think about what I've achieved. What are the gains and what are the gaps? How have aspirations changed or developed... I often remind myself of my goals in my journal as I go through the year. And I break them down into steps that I can reflect on during a particular week or month. My current quests centre around writing, travel, family and the person I want to be.

I'm conscious from my 26-years of journals that I've sometimes felt completely stuck and incapable of change. I've sometimes felt that I was journalling the same stuff over and over with no movement or momentum. But when I look back over a long period, I can see that huge shifts have occurred. Journalling has been an important part of finding the resolve to make those changes because it's where I do the thinking that begins each project

Where do you write about your hopes and dreams? Where do you envision change?

To celebrate

I often feel there is something artificial about some forms of gratitude journalling. Perhaps this is because it's often advised for people who are going through dark episodes of life. I'm wary of the notion that simply counting our blessings will counteract major problems, like grief or clinical depression, but with this caveat, when there are joys to celebrate, however small or simple, a journal is a great place for it and honest appreciation goes a long way.

Where do you record the best moments of your life?

To rant

The privacy of a journal is a wonderful space in which to dump all manner of emotion. It's a private space for wild ideas, bad moods, and all the things we struggle with and don't want to shout our loud to the world. A lot of what we write in journals is rubbish. It can be self-pitying or harsh or judgmental. If we keep writing and reflecting, journals are places to work through negative emotions and come out the other side. As Eugène Delacroix puts it:

> I am taking up my Journal again after a long break. I think it may be a way of calming this nervous excitement that has been worrying me for so long.

Where and how do you defuse your negative emotions?

To get creative

Journalling is a powerful way to tap into our creativity. This can be particularly the case when you establish a journalling practice of writing last thing before sleep and when you first wake up. The subconscious seems closer to the surface at such times and we are more likely to dive into a deep stream of consciousness. Journals are places where we capture the oddest of moments and, with no thoughts of polishing for an audience, we sometimes hit a rich stream that we can come back to in other writing or find out something about ourselves that is a revelation.

How can you use a journal to tap into your deeply creative self?

To appreciate solitude

Writers are not strangers to solitude, but to write without any trace of an audience in mind not only frees the writing but also enables us to delve deeper into solitude, which is becoming an increasingly lost art. In a journal we don't only write alone. We create something that is internal and reflective. It's a place where we plumb our own human spirit. Going away alone from time to time, without noise or distractions, preferably without devices, and being with ourselves and our journals, is an extraordinary experience. In solitude, we are invariably taken by surprise by what surfaces and by the creativity that begins to flow.

Where do you practise solitude?

To reconcile with ourselves

We can use a journal to pull in the outer world and reflect on it. But we can also use journalling to go within. Journalling is both an act of remembering and a way of making sense of the self. Journals are fascinating accounts of who you were ten-years/a year/a month ago. And by keeping a record of this former self we learn how to change the future, how to become a different story. Virginia Woolf sometimes addressed her diary to her older self and, during periods when she was struggling, noticed the therapeutic value of writing:

> Melancholy diminishes as I write. Why then don't I write it down oftener? Well, one's vanity forbids. I want to appear a success even to myself. Yet I don't get to the bottom of it.

A journal can be a safe space to throw off vanity or the pressure to pretend we are more successful than we feel and simply write.

Where do you find your past self?

To become a different story

Of course, journals also enable us to reflect on the self we want to become in the future, they are space to create ourselves, to try out new stories. We can always change. My journal is a testimony to that. Journalling is a way of creating yourself and then checking back on that. It offers an alternative, a way to become a different story.

What story do you want to be?

In short, journalling is a powerful way for writers to dig deep into:

- their own practice
- observation and note-keeping
- lists and goals
- joys and frustrations
- deep creativity
- past and future selves

How do you use your journal?

Interlude 3

Writing the Bright Fire

This interlude is a chance to celebrate your writing, to examine how far your writing has grown and is flourishing. It's planned to be used around the period from April 29–May 1 when the summer is emerging, though if you are in the southern hemisphere this would fall in late October and your interlude during April/May would correspond to 'Writing the darkness', found in Section 5.

April 29

In a universe of endless motion we yearn for stillness, something that T S Eliot captured in the first poem of Four Quartets, 'Burnt Norton' talking about the still point of the turning world.

The bringing together of movement and stillness, of dance and contemplation and of fire and creativity, is at the heart of the Celtic season of Beltaine, which falls around May Day. Traditionally the beginning of summer, it would once have coincided with driving cattle to the summer pasture. Its rituals were related to protection and to encouraging growth. It was a fire festival (Beltaine means 'bright fire') and a time for weddings and feasts.

So why think about stillness at this celebratory and active time? Because stillness and action are integrally linked if we are ever to do more than skim the surface of our creativity and our lives. Because without the still point, there is no dance. But being still is not what the world encourages. We drown in images, in short bursts of texts, instant messages and immediate 'likes', 'fast', 'more', 'bigger', 'multi-tasking', '10x-ing' your life and 'productivity' are our contemporary watchwords. We hurtle from task to task, juggle commitments and live with increasing levels of speed and stress. To soothe us, we shop, watch vacuous entertainment, surf the

Interlude 3: Writing the Bright Fire

Internet or hang out on social media that is, for the most part, anything but social.

Increasingly, more and more people are afraid to simply stop and be. To do so invites a gap into which all kinds of thought and questions might enter. Better to spend hours browsing in order to buy a cute sweater than to face what is inside. But is it? This is life in the shallows. Not because people are inherently shallow or thoughtless but because in such a breakneck world all of us become dazed, fatigued and more likely to reach for the quick palliative than to dig for hidden water with which to refresh our lives.

If we are going to write and make a difference, even if only to a couple of people, even if only to ourselves, then we have to break this cycle and be still. Ironically, we often tell ourselves there is no time in our lives for being still. We can list all the work we have, the domestic responsibilities, the commitments we've made… Of course, they are true but, despite the modern mantra of productivity, many of us in the western world still have a huge arena of choice in how we spend a good portion of our time. What if we give some of that time to being still?

In *The Art of Stillness*, Pico Iyer talks about interviewing Leonard Cohen during the song-writer's five years of seclusion in the Zen centre at Mount Baldy. Cohen told him that sitting still had become a passion, that stillness was a luxury, a feast. In other words, feasting and the fires of creativity are not about rush and hurry. When we are still, when we stop rushing around and go nowhere, do nothing, when we are simply being, we make space for a different kind of movement, not of busyness but of profound thought. The artist Joan Miró was acutely aware of this in his work, discussing how a motionless object could suggest infinite motion or how we find the hidden sound within silence.

When our minds are full of work, shopping lists, tasks to be done, or when we focus on producing more and faster, our thoughts become clogged and we risk burning ourselves out, often only to start again and repeat the awful cycle. When we de-clutter our thoughts, refuse the distractions and stop for a while, we start to see and hear and attend. We may find that there's a cacophony inside, that we have to practise stillness repeatedly. But when we do, our thoughts change. They become less frenetic and fragmented. They become less ego-centred and switched to survival mode. Gradually our thoughts go deeper and find fresh pools of inspiration and imagination.

Why is this particularly important for writers? Creative people of all kinds need space in their minds. When we overload our lives with frantic

Interlude 3: Writing the Bright Fire

activity we're less likely to live in the moment. We are always concerned, instead, with the next thing on the list and the next and the next... This is inimical to creating anything.

To achieve flow states as artists, creative scientists or writers we need this space. To have a shot at being people who care about the world we live in, we have to be able to see what is happening in the world. We won't do that in a state of high-speed distraction.

Stillness, whether it's five minutes of meditation the instant you wake up; cooking in silence, rhythmically chopping vegetables in the company of your thoughts; or taking ten minutes in the middle of the day to do nothing but sit quietly, is not only good for your sanity and health, but for your creativity.

Of course, as Eliot intimates in his lyrical meditation on time in 'Burnt Norton' stillness is not fixity. The paradox between stillness and movement is at the heart of what Miró was attempting to touch on in his art. And, as Alan Lightman points out in *Searching for Stars on an Island in Maine*, every atom of us is an extraordinary nexus of motion, electrons whizzing around a central nucleus in mostly empty space.

Restlessness is perhaps at the core of the human condition. And as writers we're as restless as everyone else. We're as liable to distraction. And yet, if we are to move the world with our words, we need to rest in the questions and the paradox. We need to make a place not for 'fixity' but of stillness. It's from this stillness that we can move towards the bright fire of our creativity.

Journal exercise

In what ways do you need to change rhythm, say no or do less in order to make room for the bright fire of your creativity?

How do you find your still point and how do you move out from it in your writing and in your life?

What experiences set loose great movements in your mind and how can you have more of such experiences?

When and where do you experience the eruption of the infinite in the finite in your writing and in your life?

Ritual

Take some time to be still today. You might walk and find a beautiful space to sit. You might meditate or take an extra long shower or bath, just drifting... Try to have a period with no electronic devices — an hour, three hours, the whole day? Notice how you feel. Do you feel more centred or more restless? Do you feel anxious or released? What do these reactions tell you about your relationship to yourself and doing deep work on your writing and your life?

Take a double page in your journal or a big sheet of paper you can pin up somewhere and draw three columns.

In the far left column list all the times when you are busy, feel most fragmented or overwhelmed.

In the far right column list all the times you are most still, most composed, most thoughtful and/or contented.

In the middle column list the times you feel most creative. Are there times when the movement/creativity flares up from the stillness? Do you notice any patterns or relationships?

April 30

With our creativity protected and centred, we can begin to let it burn bright. Any gathering around a fire will evoke stories to flow. As writers the hearth or the bonfire is our territory. This is where our ancestors were at their peak, weaving myth and history and meaning. But what sort of storytellers do we want to be?

We don't have to look far to see how many powerful myths of our day are leading people wayward. Myths that control is better than collaboration led the whole of the UK over the Brexit-cliffs. The myth that we can go on consuming more and more and more and somehow it will be alright has led the planet to the brink of disaster. We are all flawed. Faced with this, it's all too easy to resort to complaint, criticism and even cynicism. But tearing things apart doesn't motivate change, it just leaves destruction, hurt and anger in its wake.

In Anne Lamott's most recent book, *Hallelujah Anyway*, she discusses the need for radical kindness to ourselves not as self-indulgence but because we need to feel unthreatened and acceptable if we are to have the capacity to show kindness and empathy towards others. Feeling secure is a step towards having warmth and generosity. And writers need this heart because we are the ones telling the stories. Whether it's the story of how the universe or technology works; a life that illuminates humanity; a science fiction or crime thriller that gives us insight into the human condition and our connectedness; or a poem that reflects on an overwhelming emotion at the heart of everyone, we are the ones shaping the dough of reality and humanity into story-bread. Will our story-bread nourish or poison those who read it?

This is not to say that our stories should all be La-la Land illusions of a world that is sugar and spice and all things nice. Our stories might be of incredible deprivation and cruelty, or tell of tremendous struggles that end in ambiguity. But our stories should come from a heart that cares, that has empathy for even the most flawed characters in our novels, that resonates with even the most difficult emotions in our poetry.

Writers need to cultivate warm and generous hearts but we don't need to be perfect. Being aware of how we need to develop and become a different story should not be an act of self-flagellation, but a joyful project of self-love. Lamott is right to note that not only is kindness crucial, but that it's vital to extend it to ourselves. We don't get warm and generous through engaging in a fight to the death between willpower and self-loathing.

Of course, nor does the pursuit of compassion and generosity entail tolerating abuse or relationships that diminish us. Sometimes, no matter how much mercy we are able to feel, there are relationships in which we realise it's more life-affirming to wish the other person well, but need to move on. Some relationships will always be a losing scenario of pouring our energies into negative cycles of reaction, blaming, and trying to change someone who has no interest in changing.

And of course, having a generous heart does not mean condoning atrocities so unspeakable that we struggle to make sense of them. Some events are so horrific they leave us bewildered as to where the lines of moral responsibility, evil and the unforgivable might be drawn. (It's a topic brilliantly illustrated in the conversation between Mary McCarthy and Hannah Arendt in *Between Friends*, a discussion that came after Arendt published *The Banality of Evil*.)

But notwithstanding that we don't want to self-delude nor stay in relationships that harm us, nor trivialise atrocities, it remains the case that, in an everyday sense, real transformation and progress only happen when we are not on the defensive, when we feel loved, seen, heard and valuable and when we extend the same graciousness to others.

So let's return again to that central question: Why is it particularly essential that writers should cultivate generous spirits? Because we write about the human condition in all its incarnations. We do this not as judges but as observers, and as those who allow understanding to grow and flourish. We write flawed characters, not only because perfect ones are boring but because, by writing of flaws with empathy and kindness, we change human relations.

This is about a quality of living that connects us with the Numinous. When the philosopher, Simone Weil, was dying from tuberculosis she refused to eat more each day than the rations given to her compatriots in Nazi-occupied France. Albert Camus described this as a kind of generosity that is about refusal and resistance; that is radical and future-oriented. It's a generosity that not only brings us full circle back to compassion, but also back to those underlying attitudes of living by more humane rhythms, taking time to be still, and being present.

When we live out generosity it is impossible not to feel compassion, extremely difficult to operate from pride, hubris and fear, and it prevents us from being hard, impervious and invulnerable. We need to be generous, for all that is life-giving's sake and, as writers, for the sake of the story.

Journal exercise

How, in your life and in your writing, do you cultivate a warm and generous heart?

Think about how you carry differing emotions in your body. Weil talks about tightening or setting our jaws. Other emotions may soften and relax us. How can you use your awareness of your body's signals to change the feelings that stiffen and stress you?

Think again about the image of hearths or bonfires is our territory and your connections back to a long line of story-tellers. What sort of person do you want to be as a writer? What story do you want to write? What story do you want to be?

Ritual

What can you do today that would be an act of radical kindness towards yourself? Do it.

• Interlude 3: Writing the Bright Fire •

May 1

We began with stillness in order to have a still point around which to whirl. We drew near to the fire, cultivating a warm and generous heart from which to tell stories. And so we begin to tell a narrative of hope.

I recently completed a third book in a trilogy of novels, the final part, *For Hope is Always Born*. The title, like the other titles in the trilogy, is a quote from Cervantes' *Don Quixote*:

For hope is always born where there is love.

It's a trilogy that charts a great deal of suffering, loss and grief, but despite everything that life throws at the characters, it resists despair. Writers often highlight events and lives that are tragic, but to do so without giving way to cynicism and without losing all hope is a blessing the world greatly needs. Hope is not a glib or simplistic outlook. In *All Said and Done*, Simone de Beauvoir talks about finding the balance between optimism and realism, about how shocking it is to encounter suffering yet feel that it must be written about, even at the risk of being dubbed a pessimist, because in fact to speak the truth is the most hopeful thing we can do.

Starting from the truth in order to go forward in hope is something that would resonate with the ecologist Lauren E Oakes. In her book, *In Search of the Canary Tree*, she recounts her hunt for the yellow-cedar tree. They have survived centuries of change and are traditionally revered by native mystics as well as being commercially valuable for their golden wood. Related to the giant sequoia, they are true cedar.

But in Alaska, Oakes found only a graveyard of trees, corpse after standing corpse. The largest remaining coastal temperate rainforest on Earth hit by a tragedy of epic proportions that mirrored global mass extinctions. We, like those trees, are 'Nature'. We are not separate. Our fate and their fate are intertwined.

Oakes describes her feelings of fragility in the face of ecological crisis, but also a sense of hope because the sight of the trees was so shocking that it changed her, motivating her into a newfound activism and into a search for answers about how we cope with climate change. Like de Beauvoir, Oakes believes that truth is the starting point of any narrative of hope. She recognises that hope in the face of such odds can become facile and ridiculous and yet, it's the only way to live.

We live as if what we do matters until it becomes the truth. This is the essence of becoming another story and it is most powerful when we know ourselves to be intimately connected to the world we inhabit. Separateness is not a defensible position. And the planet we live on is not a commodity.

How do we bring this back to the writing life? We, above all people, are committed to telling the stories. Hope is a vital element of the story of our time. It is neither 'everything will be alright', nor 'we may as well give up now', rather it is that we live in tension.

After WW1, his marriage recently torn apart by his wife's mental illness, Hermann Hesse moved to Switzerland and became a signatory to Romain Rolland's 'Declaration of the Independence of the Mind', a manifesto of pacifism also signed by Albert Einstein, Bertrand Russell, Rabindranath Tagore, Jane Addams, and Upton Sinclair. At the same time he wrote to a young correspondent about how a state of doubt and 'not knowing' is preferable to one of hard certainty.

In *The Gay Science*, Nietzsche offers a similar thought in aphorism 268:

> What makes Heroic? — To face simultaneously one's greatest suffering and one's highest hope.

Hope is not simplistic. It exists in the midst of real sorrow and doubt. It is not a claim to having all the answers but a refusal to become bitterly sceptical or to give in to desperation and utter anguish. In *Hope in the Dark*, Rebecca Solnit frames such tension in a manner that recalls Dickens' opening of *A Tale of Two Cities*: the best of times and the worst of times. Living from hope requires that we acknowledge both.

Hope is not the blasé notion that everything will be fine. Rather it looks the complexities in the face and does what it can anyway. It recognises that we live in uncertain times, but that uncertainty gives us room to manoeuvre. As writers we know that new shoots don't appear from nowhere. Suddenly it is spring and there are flowers blooming wildly and in a blink we are on the verge of summer with the hawthorn blossoming and the air full of green scents and fertility. But the truth is that things have been happening underground or in bud for the previous months to make this so. The same is true with change in the human story. All those writers, artists, activists, essayists living as if what they did mattered suddenly create momentum and there is change.

Beltaine is a time for transformation and change, not easily won or without roots, but grounded in the persistence of life. Change is rarely simple. But as writers, we work for it, knowing that hope is always born where there is connection, where there is love, where there is life.

• INTERLUDE 3: WRITING THE BRIGHT FIRE •

Journal exercise

What causes you to feel despair and how do you deal with this?

What does 'hope' mean to you?

When do you feel most hopeful and how can you nurture this?

In what ways do your stories (including poems) and your life fuel hope and transformation (on any scale that is meaningful to you)?

In what ways does your life and your writing act as if it mattered?

Ritual

Beltaine is a time of protection, celebration and creative fire. It is a time for feeling our writing rooted in our bodies, sensual and connected to all life and not giving up hope. What one thing can you do today to light the fire of your creativity and hope? Light a candle and commit to this.

Chapter 11
Working at Depth

We shape who we are with the choices we make. How we act shapes the story we live out. All too often we know there is a gap between who we want to be and the person we experience in private. And we know that making changes requires deep work; that we need time and focus to take the stories we write to innovative levels. We also know that the more congruent we are as people, the more we close that gap between the person we project and the person we aspire to become, the more our creativity benefits.

We know all of this but we live in a world where shallowness rules. A few months ago I read *Deep Work* by Cal Newport, about how we find more time in our lives to do deep work. This is work that demands increasing levels of craft and knowledge; that requires commitment and concentration. It's the work we are passionate about and want to push boundaries in. But all too often it's also the work that gets pushed aside by a million competing demands on our time, including the demand to be active on social media.

These demands often fracture our attention and divert us from what we love and aspire to. Yet we go along with them not only because they are easy to comply with but also because the prevailing wisdom is that it's unthinkable to be a writer without social media. Fear of missing out (FOMO) is a widespread contemporary anxiety. Moreover these platforms are designed to keep us coming back for more. Retweeting on Twitter or posting on Facebook delivers short-term rewards. We feel like we've taken some time to connect with friends or potential readers or clients. We also tell ourselves that we've achieved something and that we'll read that book on writing techniques another evening. We'll write that article next week. We'll begin the novel after this busy period is over.

But the truth is, the more time we spend in the shallows, the less likely it is that we will engage with the rigours, as well as joys, of deep work. The more we fill life with quick dopamine shots of the kind delivered by social media, the less likely it is that we will value the commitment and flow states needed for

Chapter 11: Working at Depth

extraordinary creativity.

I appreciate that we can't spend all our time in deep work. It's demanding and we need breaks, but social media is the kind of 'break' that, in my experience, doesn't energise, but drains. It doesn't allow the mind or the unconscious to freewheel. In short, it doesn't provide quality relaxation and recovery any more than it inspires creativity.

Of course depth needs to be balanced with routine tasks that maintain the logistics of life but I'm increasingly suspicious of the rhetoric that social media plays an essential part in the logistics of keeping things running well so in 2018 I decided to leave social media platforms, both for myself and for the independent press I co-run.

Innovating is what keeps me loving what I do and I've never fitted well into institutions. I eat differently. I avoid Google and Amazon, going for smaller and indie. I do long distance travel by train and favour slow travel. I home educated my (now adult) children and haven't had a TV in the house for over a decade. I live in a tiny village without a single shop, in a quirky, rambling house that is a constant project. And I run a press that aims to be innovative and non-mainstream. How had I ever got swept along in the tide of posting, pinning, tumbling, linking, tweeting…?

Deciding not only as an individual but also that Cinnamon Press should quit social media raised some questions and consternation. Surely these tools were critical to any business's survival. Without them, how would people know about our books, our launches, or even that we exist? They were good questions, but not good enough to outweigh the conviction that my whole *raison d'être* was incongruent with these platforms.

Not only has the decision been anything but detrimental, it's been a huge boost to my time use, sanity and sense of putting values first. Beyond the pragmatic considerations and the balance of deep work, I couldn't escape the feeling of being in pernicious environments. They are multi-million dollar corporations in which profit trumps every other consideration. Frequently it is us, the users, who are the products and this comes with a staggering lack of privacy and an increasing culture of fake news. Hate-mongers, of course, always find a way to spread their fear and violence. Not having Facebook didn't slow Hitler down and it would be naïve to believe that hate spreading would cease without social media. I'm also aware that there are genuine activists on any platform. My concerns were not a reflection on the people I engaged with but I couldn't escape the conviction that the platforms, with their dubious morality, become integral to whatever message anyone tries to convey.

I lost no friends from leaving social media and am no less in contact. I feel more focussed, less fragmented and more committed to deep work. Conversely,

Chapter 11: Working at Depth

I have more time to devote to people who choose to be in touch. And more time to:

- spend with those I love
- write my next novel
- work on this book
- travel and immerse myself in places that will feed my imagination and inspire new ways of working.
- walk in the Moelwyns (the hills above the village where I live)
- journal, read, cook and do yoga…

Most importantly, not being on social media is more congruent with my story and who I want to become, a writer who values people and deep work.

Chapter 12
It's in the Journey

Doing the deep work isn't easy, it's a skill that requires motivation, the desire to hone our craft and huge reserves of passion. Writing is a long game. You won't sit down and write a book. You'll have ideas, make notes, flesh out parts of it. If you're writing fiction you may have a timeline, character studies, chapter ideas. If your project is nonfiction you might start with articles, heaps of notes… If you are working on a poetry collection you may have fragments, drafts and images. In short, it's small steps that build into something complex and inspiring. It's consistency and dedication.

First you have to start. How obvious is that? Very, but how many people do you know who want to write, but… If you make a start, you're already ahead of a lot of people. Sketch out your ideas — make it concrete. Don't only think about what will be in your book. Commit it to your journal or to a folder in Scrivener or to notes on your phone or laptop or a filing card system.

Then, keep going. There are so many calls on our time, so many distractions. Give yourself a chance. Have regular writing times and deadlines and make them sacrosanct. This is how you get to the end. You might be a slow writer. You might take a year, or two or longer, but don't give up. An unfinished book is just another thing to beat yourself up about. But the way of steady increments is an honourable path; so break down every stage into small steps and persist.

Breaking down the start:

1. What's your subject?

Novels come from a myriad sources. It might be a chance encounter, an image of something you saw on the street or a snippet of overheard conversation on the train. A character might come to you in a dream or a story might spin out of watching a documentary or seeing an art exhibition. This is why you should never move further than the bathroom without a notebook.

Similarly, ideas for nonfiction projects have all kinds of origins. But whatever your genre, people are going to ask, 'So what's your book about?' What will you reply? Write it down now. Make it no more than one or two lines and make sure you have it engraved on your heart. This is mine for *This is the End of the Story* (the first novel of a trilogy):

> Belief is Cassie's gift. So much so that she lets others define and even name her, until an act of betrayal causes her to rethink the stories she tells herself and allows others to tell about her.

2. Have a plan

Where you go next will depend on whether you are writing fiction or nonfiction. It will also depend on the kind of writing patterns you have, but for most of us there will be some kind of organisational document at this point. It might be a contents page with a couple of lines sketched out for each chapter. It might be a timeline for a story or a group of character sketches and main plot points. It doesn't have to be complex or prescriptive, but think of it as a route map, one you might takes divergences from along the way. It's there to give you an idea of main stages to land on along the way and, if it's nonfiction, where you are going to end.

Depending on your subject and genre, you might want to set a rough word count at this stage. For fiction, this could change. Someone I know started a short story a couple of years ago that is now a published novel; it kept growing and found its form. If you are writing a thriller or historical saga you might have a chunky word count in mind. Over 80,000 words is a good-sized novel and over 100,000 words gets into saga and epic territory. In nonfiction having a word count plan can help you map out the chapters and stages of writing.

3. Find your corner

Sometimes we need to write in places that add to the creativity by disrupting the norms. But most of the time, especially when we're not travelling, we need to stake a claim to a writing place. A while ago, I took over a spare bedroom that is now 'the writing room'. It has a selection of my most important books, a desk and a couple of treasured ceramics that make it 'mine'. Your spot can be anywhere. It can be outdoors if you live in a climate that makes this possible. It can be in a library or café or a corner of a room where you can go inside yourself and write. What's important is that the place signals to you that you are writing now. You are not answering the phone, messaging, checking email, cooking, cleaning... You are writing.

4. Give yourself targets

Over time, consistency will trump everything. Having an occasional marathon writing session can feel great, but if you don't keep up the regular writing it will leave you with fragments that you have to continually reconnect with because of the gaps between sessions. Make the goal sustainable. 200–300 words every weekday. Two pages a day. If you write more, it's a bonus and if you often write more you can adjust the goal. Regular and realistic gets the first draft of your book written.

5. Block out a time

People with busy lives will always have something else they could be doing at any time of the day. If it works for you, get up early and give yourself an extra hour. If you work well in the evenings, write rather than watching TV for an hour. If you make a promise to yourself and don't keep it, how will you feel? If writing is vital to you and you don't do it, how will you feel?

Give yourself a regular slot that only urgent emergencies can interrupt and keep to it. This not only protects your writing time but also makes it automatic — it's 7 a.m. I must be writing…

Breaking down the momentum

Making a start is great. Keeping going can be hard. There will be other calls on your time and focus. There will be distractions that tempt you away so that you find yourself making bargains with yourself, knowing you are on the path to breaking the promises you made to yourself.

1. Be a writer

To BE a writer you have to DO what writers do. If you have a day job, think of it as the thing that supports you as a writer. Think of yourself as a writer and behave like a writer. How do writers behave? They write. And they own up to being writers when asked.

2. Protect your environment

Your place to write has to be sacrosanct. And your writing environment has to be this place ++. By that I mean that you need to make as many features of your environment as possible support your writing life. This will sometimes mean clearing your environment of distractions but it also means:

- Letting people in your life know you are taking writing seriously and you need their support.
- Reading constantly. Books should be your natural medium.
- Making connections. Some areas have thriving writing groups and some of these are helpful. If they turn out to be people patting each other's backs, leave. But check them out. You might find writers online or connect through blogs or writers groups on social media. You don't want to spend masses of time on this, but shift some of your social time towards others who share your passion. And go to book launches. It's a great way to support others' writing along the way.

3. Make and keep deadlines

You're already writing every day. You have a daily target. Now add a weekly one. The easiest way is to track a word count: 2000 words a week; 5000 words a week. Whatever it is:

- Write it down.
- Make it public (you don't have to tell the world, but tell someone who will check with you. If you don't tell anyone you'll play mind-games with yourself to let yourself out of promises).
- Review it honestly.
- Celebrate the wins.

4. Give yourself a break

Distractions are tempting because we get a little shot of dopamine and a few moments away from the pressure of writing. Instead of becoming antsy and reactive, plan for breaks. Do some stretches midway through your hour. Have a weekend with no writing. Build in ways to let your subconscious mull on what you're writing. Sometimes breakthroughs come when we're looking the other way.

This isn't a call to procrastination, but to getting your whole self into the work Half an hour of yoga might be more creative than pushing yourself for an extra hour. Going out for a walk (with your notebook) can get a cascade of ideas moving. In other words, make your life support your writing.

5. Get help

There's a balancing act here. If you let others into your work at a too-fragile and early stage, they can derail it. If you show it only to people who would love you for writing a shopping list, you won't be any the wiser about whether your writing communicates. But if you write a 100,000 word masterpiece, then begin editing, spending years on it without any input, you could find you have something even your grandmother doesn't love you enough to read. There are lots of ways to get help:

- A high-functioning writers' group offering intelligent feedback.
- A short residential writing course (get recommendations and read the tutors' work first).
- An author or editor whom you know and trust.
- A mentor who will give you critical and valuable engagement for a set period.
- If your project is nonfiction, trial some of the content and ideas on your blog or a platform like Medium. It's a great way to see how people respond to what you are offering.

Some of these cost money, but you're a writer — if you have any disposable income you should invest some of it in yourself.

Breaking down the end

When you've finished writing the book, you have a first draft. You still have miles to go before you sleep. Let's imagine you've done the editing (over and over) and have put the book away for a while to give yourself some distance. And then you've gone through setting up whatever route it is that will get your book into the world. You might have a publisher, who will have his or her own editing procedures. You might be self-publishing or using the book as a giveaway to promote your writing. Whatever the case, there will be a deadline.

1. Respect the deadline

When that date comes, have a finished book. Then hit Send. I work with authors all the time who feel sick when they let me have their book to edit. It's not a lack of trust, it's that this is their baby going into the world alone. It's terrifying. But you have to do it. Parents have to help their children emerge into the world as autonomous adults. Writers have to do the same for their books. LET GO.

2. Love it

Your first book might be a stunning success. It might meet with total indifference. It's still yours. It's the book you learnt on. It's the first of many. However it fares, have a party. Launch the book into the world. Tell everyone and their cat about it. Be proud.

My first poetry collection is now out of print. The publisher disappeared without trace and that was a tragic story, but I'm grateful that collection is now hard to find. It was awful! Yet it started something. My early novels are 'okay', but…. Yet they did the work of getting me to the next and the next book. Similarly, it took until my fifth nonfiction book (about autonomous parenting and education) before I hit my stride there. But I love them all.

3. Breathe and start again

Take a deep breath and remember:

- Be a writer.
- Writers write.

Some writers have pauses between books. You might need time to focus on promotion or need to refuel your creativity. If you pause, keep the notebooks going. Keep a writing practice whether it's blog articles or your journal. Don't let the writing muscle get stiff and flabby. Then, when the gestation period is right, start the next book.

And never forget — the greatest reward of writing is the journey.

Chapter 12: It's in the Journey

Make the journey the reward

I work with authors who want to be published. I'm a publisher, so I certainly don't want to play down the joy of seeing your work in print, but I'm also aware that publication is often not quite what people imagined and that it still leaves a hunger for something further. It's not that publication is irrelevant, but it's far from the whole story and there are other aspects of writing that are vital and more overlooked.

So what do you want from your writing? Whatever it is, try to have some distance from the outcomes. The creativity is yours, anything else is a bonus. By all means promote your work but don't fixate on it. I recently worked with an author who wanted to know how to streamline her schedule for 'the most effective outcome': publication and sales. But this is the wrong way round; passion has to come first and for its own sake long before we start to wonder where our work will fit in the market.

When you give someone something, you choose a gift you hope they will love, but once it's given, the present has been let go and it's up to the recipient to have her own response to the gift. Writing is similar. We offer it and then it has to make its own way, whatever the responses.

Which brings us back to the question: What do you want from your writing?

Creative people often live in a state of hyper-awareness. At our best, we walk around with all the senses open making connections and bringing into the light things that would otherwise go unseen. Writers function as prophets. Writers provide insight into the human condition. We dig deep into the human psyche. Writers entertain and delight and make us think. Writers don't do all this to stay invisible and silent. As a writer, you spend a lot of time alone, creating. So when you emerge into the world you want your writing to make an impact. You want someone to notice this awesome gift you've crafted.

There's nothing wrong with the fact that you want a response. After the incubation period in which you've dug deep within yourself, followed by putting your soul and guts on the page, it's heartening to have some kind of acknowledgment. Writing is lonely, but at some stage you want it to connect:

- You want other writers to nod and say it means something.
- You want to share ideas with peers.
- You want readers to engage with what you've written.

You want your writing to be visible, responded to and engaged with. If you put it away in a drawer you get none of this. And so writers are keen to find a publisher. I'm not saying don't do this, but I am cautioning you not to make this so important that the journey becomes insignificant. Not all writing is meant to be public, of course. Journalling or many forms of therapeutic writing, for example, are vital to many writers, but not intended for others to read. And even for the writing you intend to make visible, it's worth thinking about what publication means. Publication is a proclamation. It's an act of making something known, something public. And there are many ways to achieve this in addition to or even instead of publication:

- An open-mic reading.
- A local writers' group.
- Attending a residential writing course and sharing work.
- Reading at a conference.
- Blogging.

The point is that when we focus too much on the outcomes of our writing, we can lose the joy of it. First and foremost, you are your own reader. There are hundreds, thousands of serious writers who are never published. They are still writers. They do it for the trance. They do it for the deep connection to an inner life, to nature, to the world. They do it for the sheer joy of it. In W H Auden's poem 'Atlantis', the journey is beset with obstacles, despite which the journey itself becomes the vital event. It's on the journey that learning takes place, that the traveller digs deep within, even if s/he never reaches the shore.

If you write with only the end in mind you will sabotage yourself. Writing is a calling. You honour it in the act of creation that should be its own reward. If it's not, then why write? Too often it is ego that goads us with questions like: shouldn't you have published ten books by now? Shouldn't you be making a living from all this time spent writing? But writing that speaks to the inner self isn't concerned with ego and apparent success. The inner writer feels compelled to write because:

- Writing makes sense of life.
- Writing is play and work rolled into one.
- Writing is a form of breathing.

This kind of writing takes risks and doesn't try to people-please. When we over-focus on the destination, we are more likely to cut off any creative impulse that might seem too strange, too deep, too radical. We are likely to lose the willingness to fail that is vital if we are to go deeper in our writing and learn

Chapter 12: It's in the Journey

important lessons. In Auden's 'Atlantis', it's not about getting to the light at the end of the tunnel, but about the tunnel itself, with the glimmer of light making it worthwhile. Of course, it's good to have goals and great expectations. But true joy is to be found in the work itself. When it's only about a fixed outcome, no matter how hard we try, the lights at the end of the tunnel somehow keep moving further and further away. You don't need to find the light. You're already in it.

What do you want from your writing? If the answer is fame or fortune, writing might not be your passion for long. But if you care about —

- delighting in language
- discovering more about yourself and others
- taking yourself by surprise as images and characters emerge
- the creativity that flows through you
- voyaging on the 'ship of fools' where you can learn as much from failure as you can from success

— then keep writing whatever the outcome. Writing is its own reward.

Interlude 4

Writing the Soaring Sun

This interlude is a chance to celebrate your creativity. It's planned to be used around the Summer Solstice period when the light is at its height as the seasons shift. This is a time of light, fertility and creativity, though if you are in the southern hemisphere this would fall in winter and you may like to use a few days from the longer interlude 'Finding the Still Point of Your Story', found in the Conclusion, but also return to this material during the Christmas/New Year period.

June 20

Creativity is powerful. It's like green sap rising, unstoppable. It is restless and can even feel overwhelming, dizzying. Creativity and imagination are like the summer world, flowering everywhere. And we want this in our writing too; we want the summer solstice to be a time of imaginative and fertile flow. At the height of summer, the light reaches its peak. We have the longest day and the shortest night, but the next day the length of daylight will shorten by a fraction, step by step moving back towards the dark. There is always this to and fro. At winter solstice, in the cold and dark, there is the joy that the shortest day is done, each one now will be a little longer... At summer solstice we are in the fullness of that joy, yet we also know the winter will come again.

Life is rarely, if ever, all one thing. And in the flow of this both/and life that is dark and light, fertile and barren, we need stories, and for those, we need imagination. To keep soaring with the sun, even when the darkness comes, we have to imagine.

In a fantastic essay, 'The Operating Instructions' (in *The Wave in the Mind*), Ursula K Le Guin notes that imagination is humanity's single most important tool. She considers that while the concept of the 'creative' has become watered down, 'imagination' retains its power. It is a fundamental way of thinking, she argues, something that is innate but which we can learn how to use well, in a similar way to training the body.

During a period of travel around Spain, as I took time out of my normal life and immersed in imagining and writing, it was encouraging to consider how vital imagination is. So, how do we train the imagination? Le Guin is adamant that we learn it best from literature, whether oral or written. Through story every culture defines itself and teaches its children how to be people and members of their people.

- This is powerful encouragement to a writer. As I work on a complex story that has at its heart questions of identity and how we transform ourselves, it's timely to remind myself that flying with the imagination promotes:
- a sense of identity and renewed self-image
- autonomy within community
- deeper understanding
- listening
- alternative possibilities
- a sense of purpose and quest

That is a powerful tool with vast potential. Imagination gives a sense of identity and renewed self-image. Imagination is fundamental to how we see ourselves. If you think about how you saw yourself as a child, it's likely that imagination played a huge role in what you decided to do as an adult. We play with dolls to imagine parenting. We have pretend cookers, pretend surgical kits, write plays that we make our families perform… Imagining leads to decisions, to seeing ourselves as a doctor, teacher, priest, writer, mother…

As a writer, I'm fascinated by the intersection of imagination and identity. My protagonists in the Casilda Trilogy have searching questions about where identity begins and ends, about how we make connections across time and culture.

Imagination and identity are both internal states. We have to imagine who we are before there are any external manifestations. Being comes before doing. Spontaneity then becomes a vision that we hand over to the unconscious and let it do its work. Moreover, imagination is a safe place in which to take risks; we can imagine outcomes before trying them out.

The philosopher, Paul Ricoeur, sees imagination as productive and creative. Ricoeur argues that imagination transforms reality through

Interlude 4: Writing the Soaring Sun

creative acts. Moreover he considers that the imagination that helps us form identity is most clearly manifested through fiction, which creates meaning. Similarly, Sartre saw imagination and narrativity as necessary for the formation of a coherent and meaningful sense of self. In short, the story of who we are is an act of imagination.

It takes generations for a community to arrive at an agreement of what life should be. Sadly, these traditions, over time, can ossify into dogma. This is a problem. Yet the converse is also problematic: with no sense of tradition and no social consensus, the proliferating alternatives become disorienting. Rather than finding ourselves shaped by dogmatic traditions, we find lives conforming to a multiplicity of exterior voices, including powerful media. In the face of this, we have to learn how to invent ourselves, but we need trusted guides to help us.

The ideal is to have the freedom to imagine life within a wider stream in which others have imagined a life that makes sense. This balance of listening and freedom is the ideal when the myths of our society are alive and life-giving. You have to think something is possible in order to work toward it. But how do you move from having a dream to seeing it come to fruition? The long answer? Many things need to be set in motion and accomplished. The short answer? It begins with imagination.

Imagination is the only state of mind that allows us to be free from the limiting reality we live in. A few years ago I had not imagined that I could take time out from my work as an editor and director of an independent press to nurture my own writing. I wrote, but it was always squeezed into the margins of a life consumed by working seven days a week. But, despite loving my work, this was unsustainable. I had to re-envision my life not only to stay true to myself as a writer but to maintain the joy and passion for the editing work.

It began with imagination, which fostered the autonomy to reshape how I use time with benefits to both the independent press I run and the writing I'm doing.

How do you need to imagine and invent your life? Imagination and empathy are close cousins. The philosopher, David Hume, believed that the sentiment of empathy is what motivates us to act well towards other people. Whilst we may have no direct access to the minds of others, imagination allows us to empathise. If you scald yourself by dropping a pan of water, I can imagine that pain and consequently care about it.

Conversely, when we don't imagine what something feels like for someone else the consequences can be dire and far reaching. Robert McNamara, who was the US secretary of defence during the war in

Vietnam, has since said that this human catastrophe was due to a failure of imagination. A failure of imagination that is in turn a failure of empathy takes its toll in human life. A failure of imagination about what the earth we are living on is suffering takes its toll in horrendous ecological disasters that will in turn blight the lives of future humans as well as animals. We need to imagine in order to care.

And story is a vital form of imagination for empathy. As I edited the third novel in the Casilda Trilogy, I found that certain scenes still moved me to tears after several reads. This is because I have imagined these characters over the last four years. I've lived with them. They may be fictional, but the act of immersing in the story of other people whom we can imagine as real is a powerful way of honing empathy.

Imagination promotes listening and brings us together. And where do we find such imagination? Within stories, Le Guin notes that reading is a perfect mode of listening, which allows both autonomous thinking and yet joins us to others. Reading has a huge range of benefits to commend it as a way of taking in the stories that feed the imagination and unite us with those who have gone before. Don't be sucked into the trend to listen to audio books at speeds faster than speech — at 1.25x or even 1.5x. Reading should be done at your own pace. It is an activity that is within your control, something that is not selling you anything yet puts you in communion with another mind.

Failure of imagination is everywhere. In politics the doctrine of TINA (There Is No Alternative) has been with us for many years, but it remains a lie. The problem is that envisaging the alternatives is difficult. This is once again an area in which imaginative literature can break the impasse. Imagination is everything. It is the preview for life's coming attractions. We only get that preview if we stop thinking that there are no alternatives and allow our minds to roam more widely. Whatever culture or conditions we have currently created, they are not absolutes but the products of previous imagination. The possibilities are endless if only we will imagine them.

We act in accordance with what we believe to be true about ourselves and our environment. In short, if you imagine that you are a failure or that you live in a context that will not permit you to change, grow or expand, then you will fulfil that belief. On the other hand, if you make a conscious decision to change, imagine what that change would be like to live and embody, and then communicate this to your self-image, it will have enormous impact. In short:

Interlude 4: Writing the Soaring Sun

- You must have a wholesome self-esteem.
- You must have a self that you can trust and believe in.

Once we begin to value ourselves and to imagine other ways of living and recreating our environments, huge shifts occur. Every new development at some stage has to be an act of imagination. Five years ago, I did not believe that I could take two months (or more!) out of a year to travel and write and still sustain a small press. Now I think I need to imagine more deeply, to nurture my creativity and imagination more and trust what follows. As Jung puts it:

> Without this playing with fantasy no creative work has ever yet come to birth. The debt we owe to the play of the imagination is incalculable.

Every quest begins with imagination. Imagination is what makes us fly and as J M Barrie, author of *Peter Pan*, warns:

> The moment you doubt whether you can fly, you cease forever to be able to do it.

The sun is at its height. We are approaching the longest day. There is fertility everywhere, including our imaginations, if only we will celebrate it.

Tolkien insisted that he found his stories. In *The Lord of the Rings*, the symbol is a ring so powerful it has the power of a Sun and the only way to handle it is to return the power to its source. But the journey (made by Frodo) is arduous and the guide is his Shadow (Gollum). In not grasping at the power of the Sun we can journey to its source, but we will return changed, having learnt who we are, both light and shadow.

Journal exercise

List all the places you've found stories in the past.

Where else might future stories come from?

What stories have been most powerful and transformative in your life (whether from books or lived experience or oral telling…)?

• INTERLUDE 4: WRITING THE SOARING SUN •

Ritual

Find a place that is quiet and where you can be comfortable and not disturbed. If music or scented candles or incense help you to focus and get into flow, then use these, but they're not essential.

One style of meditation is Open Monitoring Meditation in which the aim is to simply attend to whatever thought or experience might arise. Sit quietly, breathe deeply and relax. Don't select thoughts or images, just observe your body, the room, the sounds and smells, the images that come and go. Don't judge and don't focus on any particular object. Maintain this for five–ten minutes (longer if the mood takes you).

Now write, beginning with the words: 'I journey(ed) towards the sun…' and keep pen and paper working together for at least five minutes.

June 21

Writers not only need huge imaginative powers, for their material and to sustain the writing life, but also need to embody their work. In the spring equinox course, Writing the Wild Flowering, we thought about embodiment. Now it's summer solstice, the mid-point of the year, a time of fecundity and warmth, and we are going to revisit and deepen this theme.

The state of flow, the optimal state for writing, is a strange experience. We tend to feel weightless, out of time and forget we have bodies that need to eat or drink or go to the toilet. It's such a powerful sense of being other and elsewhere that writers can easily fall into the trap of forgetting to connect. But soon after that the inspiration dries up and flow ceases. In *The Heart of William James*, James says:

> A purely disembodied human emotion is a nonentity.

Long before there was any scientific backing for his ideas, James wrote about how emotions and our corporeal existence intertwine, emotion reverberating through the body as effects such as 'surprise, curiosity, rapture, fear, anger, lust, greed…' James argued that we generally think a mental perception leads to an emotion, which in turn is expressed in the body. X happens, it makes us feel Y and so we do Z. But he argued that we have feelings because of what we physically do. Feeling sorry comes after

Interlude 4: Writing the Soaring Sun

and because of crying. Feeling anger comes after and because we have lashed out at someone physically.

Without the bodily states following on from the perception, the latter would be purely cognitive in form, pale, colourless, destitute of emotional warmth. We might then see the bear, and judge it best to run, or receive the insult and deem it right to strike, but we could not actually feel afraid or angry. We are physical beings and embodiment is fundamental to what we are.

If we fancy some strong emotion, and then try to abstract from our consciousness of it all the feelings of its characteristic bodily symptoms, we find we have nothing left behind, no "mind-stuff" out of which the emotion can be constituted, and that a cold and neutral state of intellectual perception is all that remains.

The notion that cognition and emotion are embodied is much more rooted now in both science and philosophy, following on from such thinkers as Martin Heidegger, Maurice Merleau-Ponty and John Dewey. We see it most simply in our use of metaphors. We talk about being 'up' as a metaphor for happiness or 'down' for sadness for example. The physical, embodied directions become metaphors. Similarly, several metaphors originate in physical interactions from childhood, so that, for example, affection becomes synonymous with warmth.

Thought requires a body, not in the obvious sense, but in the sense that the structure of thought itself arises from the body. Nearly all of our metaphors are based on shared bodily experiences. In short, thinking is embodied. And if metaphor is fundamental to who we are as humans and if this in turn is embodied, it behoves writers to embody their work. Despite the seemingly disembodied state of flow, in fact we always remain bodies in context. We see this when we realise how easy it is to disrupt flow with interruptions or distractions. Rilke understands this perfectly in *Letters of Rainer Maria Rilke*: when he talks about how mind and blood are continuous with each other.

Our writing should take note of embodiment not only because we are bodies but because it is how we connect — to others, to animals, to plants, to the universe, to the seasons, to this mid-point of the year when we feel the sap of creativity everywhere. We are intimately connected to everything and unless we wake up to this, as individual writers and as a species, we will run out of a planet on which to live and think and love and write. The substance of the stars and of our bodies is the same. We are linked to every other atom of the universe and we survive or perish with every other life.

Writers, now more than ever, cannot afford to be creatures of the mind labouring under an illusion of separateness. What we are about is not cerebral, remote, and of no consequence. It is urgent. We stand at a point in history when we either speak up for our embodiment and intimate connection to all that is alive, to all that is material, or we face extinction with it. This is not to decry a state of flow that can be experienced as otherworldly and mystical and touching on the Numinous, but it is a call to bring back what we find there and connect it, to speak it around midsummer fires.

Being connected, being embodied, being in flow; experiencing the Numinous of nature or of the profound transcendence of writing are not dichotomies, but of a piece. Like the naturalist writer, John Muir, when he first encountered Yosemite, if we are to be writers who make a difference to the world's story, we need to feel ourselves part of all nature.

Journal exercise

In what ways do you feel yourself part of and/or apart from 'nature'?

When do you experience the Numinous and transcendent in Nature and how does this affect your writing?

Ritual

Write a story or a poem that uses embodied language related to Summer Solstice — metaphors of 'up', 'soaring', 'warmth', 'bursting'. Make the language as visceral and as concrete as you possibly can.

June 22

Imagination empowers us to soar to the sun, to get into flow and write. Embodying our writing connects us to all that is alive. The solstice is a time of fertility, of blossoming, of the body. It is a time of deep connection and this, in turn, is an act of transcendence, of writing your soul.

Souls aren't very fashionable but the 'self' and all that it implies, including our value as individuals as well as the myriad ways in which we are part of a bigger stream of consciousness or life itself, is a live concept that has perhaps never been more written about. Shifting the ground, however, doesn't get us out of the conundrum of the meaning and boundaries of self and everything else. As Virginia Woolf notes:

> One can't write about the soul directly. Looked at, it vanishes.

We live with a profound sense of subjectivity, such that what we believe affects how we experience and describe reality and yet we feel that we are experiencing the objective truth about the world. Moreover we have a profound sense that being human is linked to temporal flow, with memory intimately linked to identity, creativity and to how we relate to others and to our experiences.

Yet, whilst all of us will recognise the role of memory, relationality between the body and consciousness and the temporal flow that connects us to the language of 'self', there are traditions that question this language and it seems increasingly clear that our sense of 'ongoingness' is very far from any monolithic conception of the self as fixed and discrete. We discover ourselves only to find that the 'self' is a slippery notion. That we are ever self in isolation or self as separate seems illusory. The essayist, Lewis Thomas, has captured this persuasively and beautifully in the eponymous essay of his collection, *The Medusa and the Snail*. He notes that we are more conscious than ever of ourselves. And yet language gives us a different perspective on 'self'. The original root was 'se' or 'seu', simply the pronoun of the third person, and from an extended root, 'swedh', derives the Greek 'ethnos', people of one's own sort, and 'ethos', meaning the customs of such people. 'Ethics' is simply the behaviour of people like oneself, one's own ethnics.

Not only does the etymology point to something altogether more collaborative that hints at the necessity for connection in forming a sense of self, but Thomas also goes on to discuss how the idea of being 'unique' and 'individual' is commonplace. Even individual, free-swimming bacteria are unique. Moreover, it appears that biology did not have segregation in mind when it developed distinct selves. Thomas illustrates this insight through the relationship of a common sea slug and the medusa of a tiny jellyfish. The parasites seem to live not for themselves, yet they still procreate, producing full-grown jellyfish while the snail's offspring become engulfed in medusa's tentacles, but not as prey. The snails gorge on the jellyfish until they become mature sea slugs and all that remains of the jellyfish is the parasite, safely attached, ready to begin the cycle again.

It's an extraordinary and powerful metaphor of the connectedness and interdependence of everything, so compelling that it questions the

Interlude 4: Writing the Soaring Sun

whole notion of a discrete self and echoes the sentiments of the naturalist, John Muir, who notes how impossible it is to pick apart one part of matter from the next.

Our sense of self and the delusions we take on in order to maintain a sense of separateness is something considered by Dag Hammarskjöld in the collection of his diary entries and musing, *Markings*. Like Whitman, Hammarskjöld agrees that the surrender of self to other in relationship is illuminated by the surrender of self to nature. Whitman puts it like this:

> After you have exhausted what there is in business, politics, conviviality, love, and so on, [and] have found that none of these finally satisfy, or permanently wear — what remains? Nature remains; to bring out from their torpid recesses, the affinities of a man or woman with the open air, the trees, fields, the changes of seasons — the sun by day and the stars of heaven by night.

Unless we are at peace with our natural environment, how can we be at peace with one another? And how can we be at peace with either if we are busy defending the boundaries of 'self', shoring up the illusion of a fixed persona that cannot be assailed but instead lives to dominate, conquer and consume? To honour the other and to recognise our connectedness is deeply soulful and demands a largesse that requires humility and flexibility. What does this mean to us as writers and creatives standing at this mid-point of the year, celebrating the light?

It seems to predicate an unselfconsciousness of the type Madeleine L'Engle explored in *Glimpses of Grace*. The self is neither constant nor rigid and to behave as though it is undermines our attempts at creativity. We have to cease from thinking the universe revolves around us. We have to rid ourselves of hubris and instead give ourselves over to play, joy and self-forgetfulness. These are states that the writer knows, loves and seeks:

- play
- love
- flow
- timelessness
- fluidity
- openness

They are states that decry holding ourselves aloof in stiff pride, trying to

• Interlude 4: Writing the Soaring Sun •

be free of risk and in thinking of ourselves as 'apart' or as sovereign individuals. Deep diving into writing and creativity instead requires:

- risk
- vulnerability
- courage
- surrender
- connection
- generosity
- humility

The sense of being beyond 'self' is so vital to the artist's practice that the more tentatively and flexibly we can hold our opinions and their worth, the more likely we are to create. The idea of a fixed self-image that we zealously guard is more prison than liberation. We are who we are becoming, and this is an endless narrative with leaky boundaries.

Of course, we all have interior lives, but the enormity of our subjective experience of consciousness can be held in creative tension with the realisation that the monolithic ego is a prison. It's a tension that Walt Whitman describes lyrically in *Leaves of Grass*:

> Do I contradict myself?
> Very well then I contradict myself,
> I am large, I contain multitudes.

These multitudes become an interior consciousness for Whitman. But there remains the need for transcendence, for not allowing consciousness to solidify into a self-important overarching ego. This transcendence is easier to conceive of when we see ourselves not as discrete lumps, separate, other and (too often) superior, but as narratives in the making. Stories unfold, they curl back on themselves, pick up influences, are symbiotic and complex and fluid. Stories are soulful, brimming with consciousness but always alive to the other. Stories soar to the sun.

Journal exercise

This summer solstice, what story are you becoming?

'There is, in sanest hours, a consciousness, a thought that rises, independent, lifted out from all else, calm, like the stars, shining eternal...' (Whitman) — How, when and where does such a consciousness (whether we call it muse, trance or transcendence) erupt into your life and into your writing.

Ritual

Summer Solstice is a time of soaring to the sun, not as Icarus on wax wings and filled with hubris, but as part of all in nature that is rising up green and fertile and bursting with energy. It is a time to bring stories of connection to the fireside, to tell them, sing them, dance them and embody them.

What story do you want to tell your family/your community/your country/your planet? Write it and, be brave, send it to someone (whether it's your mother or your MP will depend on the story you tell at the moment).

Chapter 13
Where Shall We Go?

Travel is an extraordinary thing, especially in combination with writing. It makes us change gear, it takes us out of our comfort zone and normal routines, it makes us experience life as the outsider in some small sense. In short, it teaches us a great deal that should make the writing stronger and deeper. I got a sense of this when I had the opportunity to research my latest novel, *A Remedy for All Things*, the follow-up to *This is the End of the Story*, in Budapest. But what I learnt subsequently, when researching the third book in the trilogy, *For Hope is Always Born*, massively added this. Being out of my own element pushed my boundaries and led to some interesting insights, including that:

1. Exhilaration changes us

Pivotal experiences are those that excite us. They are profound, invigorating, or even mystical. They interrupt our day-to-day routines and give us an experience of awe so that we see the world differently. When we stay in one environment we can become static in how we see ourselves. Shifting environment doesn't only expose us to the newness of a new place but to ourselves. How do we react when things go wrong? What do we miss? What aspects of life feel most important when you are away from the day-to-day routines? Travel reveals an enormous amount about how we see ourselves, what our passions and values are and who we want to be. I never return home quite the same person. It's not only that I come back shaken out of the humdrum, but that travel makes me question how I spend my time and how I work and live when I return.

What's most profound about travelling while writing is that we discover ourselves as much as the cities we visit. For me, the centrality of writing and how I pass on a passion for the writing life becomes clearer with every trip. In discovering new places I also discover myself.

2. Time is precious, yet it's possible to be time rich

Travelling and taking time out to focus on my own writing and creativity always makes me think deeply about how I want to use my time. I returned from Budapest knowing that I could no longer marginalise my own creativity and expect to be an enthusiastic editor and writing mentor. In the following year, moving from Zaragoza to Burgos and about to head for Toledo, I was keenly aware of how different time was experienced in another culture. The day had a different shape and ended much later, more in tune with my pull to a night owl rhythm, but it was not only about the difference in culture and shape of the day but also the sense that, in taking time to focus on writing in unfamiliar places, time expanded.

In his poem 'To His Coy Mistress', Andrew Marvell writes an extraordinary 'carpe diem' poem:

> Had we but world enough, and time,
> This coyness, Lady, were no crime
> We would sit down and think which way
> To walk and pass our long love's day.
> Thou by the Indian Ganges' side
> Shouldst rubies find: I by the tide
> Of Humber would complain.
> I would Love you ten years before the Flood…
>
> But at my back I always hear
> Time's wingèd chariot hurrying near;
> And yonder all before us lie
> Deserts of vast eternity. …
>
> Now therefore, while the youthful hue
> Sits on thy skin like morning dew, …
>
> Thus, though we cannot make our sun
> Stand still, yet we will make him run.

The more we take control of the short time we have, the more it appears to expand; the more we feel that there is 'world enough and time'.

3. Travel enables us to see life from a different perspective

Day to day, I run an independent publishing house. I'm busy. And every decision is up close and personal. Getting into another environment enables me to see my everyday life from a greater distance. And distance can be a wonderful way to see things more clearly. Reality is, after all, largely what we perceive it to be. So by altering this perception we change our reality. Each time I travel, I know I will return with a different perspective on how I want to live, how I want to work, how I want to use my time.

This can be challenging to those who don't want me to change. I'm extremely blessed to work with a great many authors who are as delighted that I take time for my own writing as that I spend time editing and publishing theirs. But this, of course, isn't universally the case. Whenever I change and grow there will be a few people who find it disquieting and unwelcome. Recognising that what's happening is a perspective shift enables me to stick to my quest without being judgemental of those who find it difficult.

4. More than novelty

There's a cult of novelty in our present culture. From seeking the next dopamine rush of 'likes' on Facebook, to chasing the exotic in the hope of experiencing the chemical high of 'newness'. As the outsider living in a place for only a month, I'm wary of the tendency to romanticise and exoticise a culture I don't live in long-term. But the fact remains that when we travel everything is new and this adds interest to a place and challenges perceptions. New experiences can be as various as:

- negotiating a wide range of public transport including long delays and cancellations (okay, not new to anyone who uses trains in the UK, but different in a foreign language a long way from home)
- launching a book with a Hungarian audience, testing my impressions of a tiny slice of Budapest's history and culture against the reality of those living here
- new foods and shopping at the markets with little or no common language, yet managing fine
- a klezmer concert in Hebrew, Yiddish and Hungarian
- the view at the end of the street — straight across the Danube to fairy tale, floodlit buildings

- living in a city apartment (rather than a rural village) with much closer (and sometimes noisier) neighbours than we have in Wales

Newness is a wonderful thing as long as it's linked with some sense of self-transcendence, a willingness to dig deeper than first appearances and openness to other perspectives. Novelty can be delightful, and we can add depth to it by our local interactions. Moreover, novelty reconnects us with experiencing the wonder we had as children; the joy of not knowing everything.

5. We can maintain our boundaries without losing compassion

Travelling for a long period whilst also running a busy small publishing house demands a lot of preparation. To buy the time away means putting in extra hours before I leave to make it work. The creative people I work with are wonderfully understanding. They have their own sacrosanct creative writing regimes and so empathise with my need to be largely incommunicado (barring real emergencies) for a period.

Yet each time there are one or two people who react strongly against the idea that I might not be 'there for them' for a few weeks. I'm all for win-win solutions, but travel and taking focussed, intense periods for my own writing have taught me that there's a big gap between making sure everything is well set-up for me to take time out and compromising in a way that will eat into that time. Compromise in this sense is always about lowering our standards. I've got four weeks to do a huge amount of writing. If I waste it, the time is gone forever. Of course, some things will demand a modicum of this time away, but I'm always surprised that there will be at least one person who seems affronted that I should be doing my own work. It's this we must resist. We can remain compassionate for those who feel threatened when we announce this time is for our quest and as such is protected. But that compassion shouldn't make us compromise, not unless we are willing to break promises to ourselves to nurture our creativity and our quest. And if we can't keep promises even to ourselves, how will we feel about who we are? In the words attributed to Mahatma Gandhi:

> … there can be no give and take on fundamentals. Any compromise on mere fundamentals is a surrender. For it is all give and no take.

6. Physical movement is a metaphor for how far we've come

I journal a great deal wherever I am, but especially while travelling. Physical movement makes me mindful of other types of movement in my life. Despite elements of continuity of memory and narrative, I'm not the same person as I was five years ago. Physically, many of the body's cells regenerate over periods of a few days to fifteen years, and our consciousness of being 'me' is also ever-changing, yet this hits me most when I'm in an unfamiliar environment. When I'm out of my environment I'm most acutely aware of how much has changed, in the last five years, in the last five months…

7. Openness is a virtue

Zaragoza and Burgos were cities that seemed to have much less English-speaking tourism than many places I've visited. In Toledo, my woeful lack of Spanish was no barrier to shopping, eating out, negotiating transport… Whilst our wonderful host/apartment-owner, Jesus, in Zaragoza, had fantastic English, most people had only a couple of words or less. The result was a marked and rapid improvement in my ability to make myself understood, both non-verbally and in a language that I was sure my accent (or lack of it) was butchering. Nonetheless, the willingness to 'try' to speak the local language elicited a great deal of helpfulness and reciprocal attempts at English.

Travel is a wonderful way to stretch our flexibility. Coming up against new ideas, places, perspectives, shapes to the day and people, demands that we dig deeper for responses. We eat different foods at different times of the day. We acclimatise to the long shut down during the middle of the day and find alternate rhythms to match it. We take a more relaxed view of planning travel and trust it will work (and despite a train strike and different cultural patterns it did all work on the trip through Spain).

Openness reminds us that we are fallible and limited, things we have thought 'set in stone' really aren't. And it also reminds us to be more tolerant and patient. Change and the unexpected don't only happen when we're travelling. All kinds of circumstances arise in life that require the ability to deal with uncertainty and the unforeseen, but travel is a great way to practise our responses to all the inevitable changes that will come our way.

8. Travel deepens curiosity and creativity

Thrown back on my own resources, with time to think and journal, more sense of openness and flexibility, I find that whenever I travel, my thirst to learn and to use that learning grows. Writing needs a lot of focus and a great deal of inspiration, and travel provides both. Away from the distractions of the phone or work email and in a place where we have to make sense of unfamiliar environments, we not only become more adaptive, but also more creative.

9. Creative flexibility

Every time I travel I experience a greater sense of flexibility and openness. I tend to travel for writing and to have a 'plan'. But last year in Budapest, even though I had a lot of writing I wanted to do I ended up writing something completely different. Although I had both nonfiction and fiction projects in mind, the fiction didn't happen. It's not what I'd describe as writers' block. I knew that the material hadn't had long enough to germinate in my unconscious. I had a story arc and a character who'd appeared unbidden at the end of *For Hope is Always Born*, the last in the Casilda Trilogy. But I knew the new novel lacked something crucial and that I couldn't force it. Commenting on one of my blog posts, Nick Jones put it like this:

> For me, some of my best ideas or most inspiring ones come when I don't force them. They seem to come when I've almost turned my back on them and from where I don't know. The best ones aren't produced after a 'sit-in' but from somewhere else.

This is exactly what I needed to be open to. It wasn't what I wanted and at first I resisted. I'd travelled to Budapest to start the novel but the material was telling me, 'not yet'. In the creative hiatus, I wrote a 25,000 word journalling course for Advent and New Year that took me over, body and mind, and left me dizzy and elated by the time I'd finished it (a week later). On the same night that I finished the course, a new character turned up in my dreams and, by the end of the next day, had overturned everything I thought I knew about the next novel. I had no idea where he came from, but he gave the project exactly what was missing, and I was excited to be working with him.

10. Intense time to create

Travel, it seems to me, is valuable to anyone, but my particular interest is in how it affects writing. An important element of my fiction is sense of place and with the trilogy I recently completed I began with masses of reading — place, history, literature from the areas… It made a huge difference to do this research but each time, the visits were crucial. There's a texture to place that is physical. Small nuances of local character and mannerisms. A particular wind or colour or scent. Even though a great deal of my material was historical — from Moorish Spain to 50s Budapest — being in a place gave me so much more sense of place that made its way into the books.

And the intensity also extends to time. When I'm deep in flow, whatever I'm writing, I lose time. I forget to eat or find myself working at 2 a.m.. We give ourselves a different sort of permission to write or create when:

- we shake up our norms
- embrace the new with humility
- allow changes to take place without trying to control everything
- and immerse ourselves in transformative experiences.

11. It's good to be the outsider sometimes

There's a wonderful humility in not knowing how things are done or what the right words are, especially if we are able to let go of ego and ask for help, however haltingly. Travel is a great way to learn more about ourselves. Pitted against the unfamiliar or placed in the position of having a lot to learn quickly, how do you react? There are times when feeling unsettled, slightly ill at ease and unsure, helps our creativity and growth.

12. People are good

Anywhere you go, some people will be difficult. But the more I travel, the more convinced I am of the decency and humaneness of the majority of people.

13. We live more simply

Unlike snails, we don't carry everything we have with us wherever we go. It's always interesting what we choose to take. When we travel, we take essentials — a few clothes, the odd book (and maybe an e-reader as back up), a journal and laptop… It's a good way to realise that 'stuff' is just that. I love the pictures on my walls at home, the book collection, the kitchen full of pans and implements I've gathered over years. But I'm not synonymous with any of those things and I only appreciate that fully when I'm on the move.

14. We are less sedentary

So many of us spend large amounts of time sitting at desks, working sedentary jobs or hooked to electronic devices. When I'm travelling, even if I spend several hours a day journalling or writing on a laptop, I move much more. I walk miles every day, drinking in new sights and sounds and smells.

15. Connections without controlling it all

I'm someone who lives in my head a lot. I dream characters, stories and even non-fiction projects (I dreamt the structure of my PhD many years ago). Travel pulls me into the world and into my body and makes me so much more aware of connections. When you know hardly any of a language, tone, facial expressions and body language go a long way. I begin to use my senses differently in an environment that isn't so easily read. It's another way to push at the boundaries of our thoughts, expectations and assumptions.

In travel, we have to let go of the notion that we can control everything, that life is a cerebral exercise. Journeys go wrong. Trains are cancelled or sit for two hours while animals are cleared from the line. Schedules and reservations are at best sketches of what might happen. When we accept this, we become calmer, the frustrations abate, we are less concerned with the outcome and destination than with the journey.

16. The value of experience over things

There's a gorgeous craft shop in Budapest that hand-designs papers, prints them and then uses them to bind journals. As an avid journaller, I can never resist bringing one home with me. But for the most part, the 'bring-homes' are not objects but memories and often the simplest of those are what last:

- standing by the statue of Attila Jozsef facing the Danube
- drinking coffee in our favourite local cafe
- the fact that two people in two different restaurants remembered us from 18 months ago and picked up conversations

Chapter 13: Where Shall We Go?

- the quirky kitchen knives in the apartment
- buying ground coffee from the wonderful little stall in the Hold Utca market; one word of shared English, one of Hungarian and one of German between us
- the amazing buildings everywhere in Budapest

Placing memory and experience first, makes me live more in my senses, makes me embody days in a different way, and, of course, that impacts on what I write about and how I write. Most of all, it makes me become a different story. We carry all of our experiences in our bodies and travel enriches this.

17. We have more focus and clarity

When I'm at home there are a thousand potential calls on my time. When I set time aside to travel and write, protect my boundaries and open myself to new places, the focus follows. I do the work. At the beginning of the second week of travel in Spain a couple of summers ago, I realised I'd done a second full draft of my novel and written several new scenes incorporating things I'd learnt from the places we'd visited without any stress or thought for word counts. There was nothing extraordinary about this. It was simply that by changing environment I had changed what I was attending to.

18. We make quantum leaps

This brings me full circle. Pivotal experiences don't have to be rare. At home or wandering, we can learn ways to change our environments and ways to rethink how we use time in order to ensure that we have more moments of epiphany and deep joy. Travel is one great way to promote such pivotal experiences. When we become the outsider, risk being in an unfamiliar place with unfamiliar language, food and customs, then we shift perspective and this in turn requires a measure of humility that shakes us up. We disrupt our body clock, our ideas and our certainties. We expand our horizons, thinking and experiences.

When we are in such an expansive, open mindset, not only is our writing likely to be more connected and creative but we become more as people. We are more likely to have deep, meaningful and transformative experiences. Travel is a powerful thing. It's not only that time seems to move differently and normal routines are completely shaken up, but that perception itself changes.

Chapter 14
Making It Up

At any given moment, life is a mess of contradictions. It seems to be true that it's always the best of times and the worst of times. A new baby is born and a good friend is facing appalling illness. A loved one is celebrating, yet the political landscape looks grim. In the midst of joy and loss, writers keep writing. In a world crying out for global solutions, what business have we writing stories and poems? There are so many reasons why writing, or any art, is vital, no matter how uncertain the times. It has many functions, including:

1. Offering different perspectives

Of all the books I've written, the books in my recent trilogy are the ones I'm most passionate about. The novels say that the personal and the political are not disparate, but intertwined. They say that when the world is going to hell, when culture is being harried, when divisiveness is on every corner, then we need other ways of seeing. Sometimes these are perspectives that only story can provide.

It may feel self-indulgent to write while people suffer, but shutting up artists — whether visual or of the word — would assist the tide of insanity. Downing pens, paintbrushes and cameras would let the rise of hatred and suffering overwhelm us and have its way. My novels are not salvation. One exquisite photograph, one exceptional poem, one inspiring sculpture, will not save the world. But each of these acts of art is something — something that has the opportunity to agree with Cervantes that:

> When life seems lunatic, who knows where madness lies?
> Perhaps to be too practical is madness. To surrender dreams —
> this may be madness ... — and maddest of all to see life as it is
> and not as it should be.

Chapter 14: Making it Up

We can resist madness where we see it. We can mourn with those who mourn and rejoice with those who rejoice. We can refuse to dumb down. Above all, we can make art and literature that will not accept the way things are. Stories offer the possibility of an alternative. This, at least, is one good reason to write fiction in an insane world.

2. Questioning the facts

Life and fiction are rarely hard and fast boundaries. In writing *This is the End of the Story*, I wanted to explore how fact and fiction merge. How they blur into one another, are subjective and slippery. It was a line of thinking inspired by *Don Quixote*. In Cervantes' novel, Sancho tries to make fact and story congruent — for him a story has to be 'true'. He has to tell a story in a certain way and it has to be conformist and not invite trouble —

> ... the ancients didn't begin their stories just as they pleased ... your worship must stay quiet and not go anywhere seeking harm, ... turn up some other road, since nobody is making us follow this one, where there are so many terrors to frighten us.

Quixote will have none of this. Seeking truth (rather than facts) and justice, makes him live 'as if' these things were already the way of the world. Quixote has an extreme utopian vision that changes reality through perspective. But this doesn't make for an easy life. The giant windmills (corporations, media, war-machines) want to destroy what is humane, hopeful and visionary. When we write, we have the opportunity to pose important questions. And we can do it with elegance and subtlety.

3. Witnessing to the personal and the political

This is the End of the Story is set in the UK in the 1970s, an era of strikes, the three-day week, and rising unemployment. An era of hot summers, droughts, psychedelic clothes, the Yorkshire Ripper... Life is so often both the best of times and the worst of times and I wanted a fiction that would reflect that. How? I have a lot of sympathy with Keats in hating poetry that has a palpable design on us. In the same way, fiction that is didactic can be tedious. I didn't want rants or great expository lumps intruding in a novel that is character-driven. I opted instead for a device used in the film version of *The Children of Men* (which is even better than the original P D James novel). In the film, the politics is in the background. Dystopian devastation, protests and bombings take place behind the main action and go unmentioned. A C Clarke does a similar thing in her excellent poetry collection, *In the Margin*, using events from the IRA's mainland bombing campaign as asides, barely noticed by the persona and her lover, caught up in an affair.

A Quixote-inspired novel with a major character bent on the pursuit of justice can't ignore political realities. But I used vignettes, interleaved between the non-linear chapters in which the coming of age story plays out. This hints at an ambivalent attitude towards political engagement. In each vignette there is also a report on the current music charts and the weather. This is partly because the weather is a metaphor for the story unfolding in the main chapters. But it's also because we live in a society that undercuts the seriousness of world or domestic crises by placing them alongside the frivolous.

4. Raising questions of tolerance

Cervantes has remarkable sympathy with Spain's Moors. Towards the end of writing *This is the End of the Story*, I went to Toledo to look for traces of Casilda. She was a young Moorish princess who later became a Christian saint buried near Burgos, in Northern Spain. Casilda is fascinating as someone who converted from Islam to become a Christian saint. Her unrequited lover, Ben Haddaj, returned to the religion of his ancestors, Judaism. And Casilda's faithful nurse remained a loyal Muslim, as did her brother and father, though they made alliances with Christian princes. There are times when belief and tolerance lived together, but that didn't last in Spain, as in so many other places.

The stones of the Mosque of Cristo de la Luz, one of the few buildings that would have been there in Casilda's lifetime, record this breakdown of tolerance. There is an apse built onto the beautiful little mosque, painted with Christ triumphant, surveying all. The exquisite synagogues in Toledo were also 'Christianised' when the Jews were later expelled from Spain. The move from cosmopolitan to myopic, from tolerance to hatred was often swift and brutal. A familiar story.

I wanted to reflect that tension in *This is the End of the Story*. Miriam is the only Jewish girl in an otherwise homogeneous school, whilst Cassie is Christian, but stands out for being Catholic. They encounter intolerance from anti-Semitic bullies and a well-meaning, but insensitive, Anglican curate. The nature of belief — not only religious, but in humanity or goodness itself, is a key theme in the book. It's a theme I return to in the second book, *A Remedy for All Things*, when Cassie, now Catherine, dreams the life of a young, Hungarian Jewish woman imprisoned after the 1956 uprising.

5. Exploring the human condition

In the trilogy, I also wanted to explore how fiction gives us a window into the human condition. While fearless imagination belongs to Quixote, it is Sancho who lives in this interior, quixotic world. Sancho is not only loyal, but an enabler. Despite struggling to understand the difference between fantasy and reality, he believes in Quixote, and enters into Quixote's inner world, supporting its continued existence. These are areas that fascinate me — how fact and fiction collide and interweave; how one person becomes so immersed in the fantasy life of another and enables and supports it…

Children do this with great fluency. They use make believe to give the world symbolic meaning. But somewhere along the line most of us 'grow out' of it. Most, but not all — and, in *This is the End of the Story*, I wanted to explore the kind of enabling that requires immersion in another's fantasy. One character escapes into her own world of fantasy, determined to act as if the world is as she wants it to be. The other character supports her. Belief is Cassie's gift and I wanted to explore how this changes her and the effects of the stories she tells about herself and allows others to tell about her. She not only lets others name her — Cassie, Kat, Kitty — but goes along with her friend's insistence that she is a reincarnation of Casilda. The question becomes whether Cassie has the resources to be who she chooses for herself, especially after an act of betrayal that may be the end of the story.

6. Asserting the power of hope

As Cassie, becomes less naïve, she takes on Miriam's quixotic legacy. Don Quixote asserts that dreams are powerful; and in the second novel, *A Remedy for All Things*, Cassie, now Catherine, begins to live someone else's life in her dreams. Poetry, stories, art… these essentials keep alive the dream. They create spaces of possibility. Writing the final book in the trilogy, *For Hope is Always Born*, a key question for me was — is it ever the end of the story? As writers, surely we have to say 'no'.

Of course, as novelists, we face so many issues and, even if our narrative is set recently, one of these is how we write in the face of contested histories.

7. Weaving story between the conflicts

Going over the details of my novel set in Toledo, I revisited the museum of magic, housed in a tenth century cave that was an Islamic home during the time of Casilda. Back in the city after two years, spending time checking my memories of places, raised several questions of how to do justice to the historical threads in my writing.

Much of the novel, *For Hope is Always Born*, takes place in the present, but a significant strand goes back to Moorish Spain. It's a period that proved difficult to research. There's a great deal of writing on the broad brushstrokes and there are characters that have captured contemporary imagination, like the slightly later El Cid. But there is a paucity of detail about ordinary daily lives, particularly in English. Despite the enormous amount of historical record across centuries and locations, it's always the quotidian that is missing. Most history concerns the elites, whether of class or gender.

The tenth century home that houses the museum, with its two surviving hamsa (hand of Fatima) images beside the slender entrance pillars, guards its secrets. I could only discover that it had two-storeys, a well and courtyards.

At other points the problem was more about choosing which details to include. I read several books about Islamic advances in learning, from alchemy to botany, from geometry to the best time and way to dig wells. It's tempting as a writer to want to show off all this reading, but putting in too much detail is boring and distracting for a reader. The art is to get a sense of authenticity, to conjure the time and place with all the senses working, but not to let the skeleton of research show on the body of the narrative.

Where there were descriptions of social arrangements during this period, the accounts differed widely. Some historians view Moorish Spain as a golden age paradise with universal education; well-lit, paved streets; multicultural scholarship, religious tolerance and a high standard of living. But other historians view the Moors as barbarous invaders who destroyed an existing civilisation, stole whatever culture they had from the Visigoths and instituted a repressive regime that favoured a theocratic elite. The truth is undoubtedly much more complex than either of these extreme interpretations.

By the time of Casilda, towards the end of Moorish rule in Toledo, science, mathematics, medicine and philosophy, flourished. The status of women remains contested. It seems probable that high-ranking women could access education so I've bequeathed a broad education to Casilda.

I have no illusions that tenth century Toledo was paradise on earth. However, I'm wary of the political motivation of 'histories' that balk at the notion of cultural innovation and wealth coming from Islamic and/or black origins. What I wanted to reflect was a complex society with remarkable advances and yet many tensions and imperfections. As we weave stories, whatever the particulars of the historical period we are dealing with, we have to chart a difficult course between the real conflicts, the paucity of information and the biases and prejudices of our own time.

8. Promoting story as witness and myth

Fiction, no matter how made up, has a responsibility not to buy into extreme myths; whether they promote genocide or lead people into la-la land delusions of a perfect past. But when there is no agreement on the 'facts' and competing histories represent a range of political opinions, what is fiction to do?

I'm uneasy with fiction that masquerades as dogmatic fact, and/or is susceptible to use for scapegoating particular groups, rigging elections or poisoning our thinking. When I write novels, I'm not writing a history, but rather using a sliver of history as a point of departure for a fiction across several centuries. I want the novel to resonate with those myths that build humanity and optimism. History is not there to provide a romanticised backdrop to fiction. Nor is it there to argue that people are mere puppets of circumstance. Fiction has to take account of a more dynamic relationship between people and context. It has to make us care not only about the past, but also about how the past goes on resonating so that we can shape the future.

9. Envisaging story as imaginative reconstruction

Fiction, of course, isn't about simplistic 'facts'. It's about paradigms and perspectives. It's an imaginative reconstruction that asserts, with Cervantes, that

> The madness of the world is more insane than any fiction.

Fiction can be meticulously researched, but when the facts are hard to determine it can ask questions or float possibilities. Because novels imaginatively enter the past, both writer and reader are able to explore alternative belief, events, and politics that history might not have achieved. As novelists we contribute new ideas or ideas that never took off, but might have been in an alternative past. Fiction is about asserting that there is always another way to see things, to re-imagine life and possibility. It is the certainty, again with Cervantes, that

> Hope is always born at the same time as love.

Whatever the political mess, warmongering rhetoric or inhumane institutions of the day, in fiction what matters is humanity. The story and the facts, even if such were discoverable, don't always have to agree.

As writers, we persist in

- Offering different perspectives
- Questioning the facts
- Witnessing the personal and political
- Raising questions of tolerance
- Elucidating the human condition
- Asserting the power of hope
- Weaving stories between the conflicts
- Promoting story as myth
- Envisaging story as imaginative reconstruction

We may be 'making it up' but story writing is not without responsibility. Moreover, the way we write impacts not only outwardly, but also inwardly. Any art undertaken with commitment and seriousness becomes a metaphor for the artistic life and, I suspect, for life in general. To remain hopeful, to not become cynical and jaded, is radical, transformative, challenging and nurturing. To evolve the stories, we have to foster hope and expect great things. But we should also be open to outcomes we didn't expect. As we weave stories, we have to be willing to learn, regroup and hope again.

What is your quest?

How will unexpected outcomes along the way impact it?

The quest I'm currently on revolves around travel and writing. Each trip takes months in planning and is part of my major goals for a year, but the travel is also an aim in itself, since travel shakes up my perspective, puts me outside my familiar world and inspires me. As I travel, I expect to continue the quest whatever the outcomes. I hope to do so with a sense of expectancy and wonder. And I expect to do so by being bodiful, walking unfamiliar streets, taking in strange sights and tastes and scents and so much more. I expect to return as a different story.

Four Exercises of Chance and Place

When we write, we're opening ourselves up in an extraordinary way. Writing takes us into another space. Chance and 'the random' take us to unpredictable places and enable different narratives. Working with chance allows the writer to challenge her/his unconscious assumptions about what a piece of writing 'should be'; it also challenges the reader's unconscious assumptions. Chance leads to surprise, to revelation, to the challenge of paradox, to the springs of the imagination; it facilitates ways of finding subject, atmosphere and voice, and of fully realising the imagination into life. Using random prompts helps to break down the chaos of possibility.

1. Working with chance

So use these prompts and keep going even if you are writing the same sentence over and over, or writing what seems to be nonsense. As soon as one prompt seems to be running out, switch to the next:

- After we had crossed the…
- On the first island…
- We left behind…
- My brain gropes…
- I need…
- I refuse…

2. A Sense of Place

This description is from *The Great Gatsby* by F Scott Fitzgerald, describing a poverty stricken urban area:

> This is a valley of ashes — a fantastic farm where ashes grow like wheat into ridges and hills and grotesque gardens; where ashes take the forms of houses and chimneys and rising smoke and, finally, with a transcendent effort, of ash-grey men, who move dimly and already crumbling through the powdery air. Occasionally a line of grey cars crawls along an invisible track, gives out a ghastly creak, and comes to rest, and immediately the ash-grey men swarm up with leaden spades and stir up an impenetrable cloud, which screens their obscure operations from your sight. … The valley of ashes is bounded on one side by a small foul river, and, when the drawbridge is up to let barges through, the passengers on waiting trains can stare at the dismal scene for as long as half an hour.

You can build a sense of place in many ways: allusions to the politics, weather, music and mores of the period and place you are writing about, as well as sketches of geography. Even if you are working from the mind's eye, keep your senses open — observe, be precise. Chekhov puts it like this:

> Don't tell me the moon is shining, show me the glint of light on broken glass.

One true sentence and then the next true sentence. Every detail counts. Be wary of cluttering your writing with adjectives and adverbs. Hone them back — use them with care and precision. And cut out the qualifiers — kind of, sort of, just, very, really — they do no work. Other weasel words include — somehow, suddenly. And nothing happens 'somehow'.

People come in context. Think of a grandmother or favourite aunt — you will think of them in a place, most likely. Places tell us about character, like Gatsby's ridiculous ice-cream coloured mansion. Don't do the lazy announcement thing — 'Manchester, 1977, a dark and gloomy night in a terraced house…'

So think about a place that reflects a person. You might not mention the person at all in the writing and they don't need to make an appearance. The person can be real or fictional:

- First choose your person. Make a few notes about them, think of the type of place that would reflect that character — it might be a whole house or a room, it might be a tent or an open field, a workplace or a boat …
- Now describe the place in the present tense — make the description precise and visual, but don't forget the other senses.
- Make every line like a photographic frame — remember, 'Don't tell me the moon is shining, show me the glint of light on broken glass.'
- Keep in mind that in writing about your place, you are using it to say something indirectly about your character.

3. The Power and Pressure of Place

(The exercises which follow were developed by Seth Fortune for use during a writing residential and I'm grateful for his permission to include them here.)

How we use a sense of place to reflect atmosphere, characters and narrative arc has huge impact on the tone of our writing. In the best writing, landscape interacts with character and plot to add texture and atmosphere. It can even become a character in its own right. Broadly, we can think of place as acting in four ways, though they often overlap and in some pieces of writing place will perform several of these functions.

i. Place as mirror or mask

In Joanne Harris's *Chocolat*, Lansquernet is characterised by 'tranquillity'. It is a place where nothing happens until Vianne arrives, blown in by the wind, a metaphor for change. Location matters. We see this in Dracula's castle — the dreary, mountainous terrain that is totally isolated mirrors his isolation as a creature. Landscape and character are of a piece. Yet at other times place is less a clear mirror held up to the protagonists and more a mask for them to hide behind — Gatsby's ice cream coloured mansion filled with glitzy parties at which he often doesn't appear, is all about the surface, about attracting his obsession, but the place is the opposite of his internal landscape.

ii. Place as a psychological lever or influence

In *The Twelve Labours of Hercules*, the famous hero bows down to the cowardly and corrupt king. The setting is crucial — the king sits on his throne, but it's clear that the lesser man is the one who is physically higher up. The place is one of ostentation and intimidation, yet the subservient character is superior. It's a brilliant case of the psychological power of a place being subverted.

In other examples, we see the opposite. In Tolkien's *The Lord of the Rings*, Mordor is a place so evil that it kills nature and intimidates anyone there. And we also see this powerful psychological leverage of a place exerted in *Holy Mountain* by Alejandro Jodorowsky — the throne room is so intimidating that the thief can't function there.

iii. Place as a means to externalise the subconscious

In Ursula K Le Guin's *A Wizard of Earthsea*, the Jungian battle fought by the protagonist with his shadow self takes place at the end of the world. Ged goes beyond space in facing his shadow and, once he and his shadow are one, he finds himself in a world he has never been in before. This place is clearly as much internal as external.

And this also happens in fairy stories. In 'Red Riding Hood', for example, the forest that is full of danger; the realm of the unknown and untamed, is as much the girl's wild nature as the wolf's. In Angela Carter's retelling the forest is very much brought to the fore as Red Riding Hood's subconscious, full of darkness. Only the path is safe but staying on it represents boredom and immaturity.

iv. Place as a separate character or observer

In both literature and film, place often comes to life as a character in its own right. In Woody Allen's *Hannah and Her Sisters*, New York is a character and its architecture and shops play a part in relationships.

In your own writing, think of examples of landscape, setting and place that are integral to the story, reflect the mood or the subconscious or become characters in their own right. Then:

Take a place that appears in something you are writing currently.

Observe it and describe the place

Does the place act as a mirror or a mask? Does it exert psychological influence; externalise something going on in a character's subconscious or act as a character in its own right?

Write a further scene in which the place acts in at least one of these ways.

Next:

Let the place speak and comment on the story or character. Write a dialogue with the place — what does it want to tell your character or your persona?

And finally:

Imagine something changes, either suddenly or because of a shift in time. The change is a point of conflict in your story. How can your place reflect the conflict and changes in your narrative or poem? Write a scene that shows this, using one or more of the categories above.

4. Where Shall We Go?

In travelling while writing, we discover ourselves as much as the places we visit.

Write about places that have formed you or changed you.

Why did they have this impact? Was it to do with being impressionable, vulnerable, an insider or outsider?

As you write about each place, note how your body feels.

SECTION 4

Embodying the Writing Life

Chapter 15
From Dreams to Body

When we make too much conscious effort to solve problems, whether of creativity or life, something in the body resists. To get into creative flow, trying to force ideas can be counterproductive, destroying spontaneity. Yet we also know that time to write can be limited and we don't want to sit at our desks staring into space and feeling useless as the minutes tick away.

About eighteen months ago, I began leaving questions for my subconscious in my journal, last thing at night. Although normally I only remember dreams when I'm going through a difficult period, I began having much more vivid and memorable dreams.

In one dream I was with a group, travelling, but we had to stop in a particular place. The accommodation was one room filled with furniture. The pieces were designer, once-beautiful items, but all were old and shabby and enormous. There was hardly room to walk between the pieces of furniture and as the dream went on more and more furniture appeared, bringing a feeling of stress. There were several other dreams that involved 'baggage', in which what I was carrying weighed me down.

At the same time as having these dreams I was doing a lot of reading, thinking and journalling about my vision for the future. And that included reconsidering all the activities I was spending time on and what needed to go in order to spend more time on the things that really mattered. (For me: family, writing and travel.)

To live by design, not by default, involves not making choices reactively, but deliberately. And doing this means being willing to let go of the many nonessentials that crowd our lives. As long as we are trying to be all things to all people, denying ourselves permission to stop saying yes to every request on our time, no matter how trivial, we will continue to flounder. I know this. We all know this in our hearts and guts. And here were my dreams telling me: Get rid of stuff. Some of that stuff was physical. I cleared out my wardrobe and unused cookery books and some kitchen cupboards. But the much more important

Chapter 15: From Dreams to Body

baggage was not about becoming a minimalist, but about finding a minimalism for the soul and that needed me to re-appraise:

- work I'd taken on that was achieving nothing of benefit, but was reactive and appeasing
- overwork in general
- overthinking — I'm far too adept at taking on the worries of everyone and everything, crowding heart and mind in ways that don't help
- overeating — food is my comfort zone and it was creeping up

I needed to declutter not just wardrobes, but my life. I needed to go back to my touchstone from Henry David Thoreau:

> I went to the woods because I wished to live deliberately, to front only the essential facts of life, and see if I could not learn what it had to teach, and not, when I came to die, discover that I had not lived. I did not wish to live what was not life, living is so dear; nor did I wish to practise resignation ... I wanted to live deep and suck out all the marrow of life, to live so sturdily and Spartan-like as to put to rout all that was not life, to cut a broad swath and shave close, to drive life into a corner, and reduce it to its lowest terms ...

I needed to find simple, focussed, clear priorities. With all this running around my head, I took a weekend in solitude with my journal to look at all the ways I was using my time. I made lists and charts and calculations for everything imaginable. I looked at tasks that were taking huge amounts of time for little or no return (sometimes financial, but more importantly, emotional or intellectual). And I told myself that everything was up for grabs.

I spent the first day prevaricating, making excuses for keeping a literary competition that made no money, ate huge amounts of time, but was 'liked', for example. Then I woke up the next morning with the clear understanding that if I was going to keep making deals with myself to be a people pleaser, then I should stop having passions and quests in life. This was the breakthrough I needed. I knew that some things I felt should go from my work or from my wider life were bringing in income, but were unfulfilling and distracting in other ways. To let go of these would take courage. And it would take imagination because I still had a mortgage to pay and food to buy... But when you start to know what matters to you, when you are on a quest, then you find the way.

At exactly the right time, I read an excellent article by John Mashni. He began with a quote from George Bernard Shaw:

> The reasonable man adapts himself to the world: the unreasonable one persists in trying to adapt the world to himself. Therefore all progress depends on the unreasonable man.

John took a huge risk to change his life and to change himself. His way of life looked reasonable and right to most people — doing his duty, working hard, putting others' dreams before his own or his family, always saying yes to demands. So when he decided to leave a highly-paid job, retrain and start again, it was risky and unreasonable. But he did it and to remind himself why, he sent himself an email detailing why ignoring our passions is a terrible idea for our lives, our minds, our bodies.

So begin by recruiting your subconscious. Journal relentlessly about what matters most to you, what is essential. De-clutter your life of activities that distract you. Be unreasonable.

All around us there are people who are so busy they hardly have time to tie their shoelaces to keep from tripping up. More and more, being flat out busy to the point of exhaustion is seen as noble and amazing. Being too busy to think often gives people a sense of identity and status. But it's a false identity, and an ephemeral and bogus status. It's exhausting and it's only a matter of time before the toll on mental and physical health, on relationships and joy is felt with force. Give time to what matters and don't be embarrassed to say that you do so. We can be made to feel self-indulgent or even lazy if say we have lots of time to listen to those we love or play with our children or feel the wind blowing through the trees as we walk; plenty of time to meditate and write and read and listen to music and cook.

If we don't take ourselves this seriously, then how will we ever move our writing from dreams to page? If we don't take unreasonable steps to nurture the bodies we write from, heart, soul, mind and limbs, how will we find the flow in which there are words?

Chapter 16
Exchanging Balance for Rhythm

Writing is the perfect metaphor for life in so many ways and when it comes to finding our flow, especially so. Writing relies on rhythm rather than balance and that's a good guideline for life too. How often have you heard that your life needs balance? Particularly a 'work-life balance' (as though work is not part of life). A quick Internet search will reveal hundreds of blogs devoted to the quest for balance. We hear that balancing is an essential skill that you neglect at your peril. But is this the case? Is life a tightrope walk?

It doesn't have to be. The idea of balance assumes that there are a lot of equal calls on us and we should be treating each to the same time and attention. But life is much messier and more interesting than this. And it can be much less stressful, especially when we let go of the idea that we can or have to do everything and instead give time to those things that delight, intrigue and fulfil us. We need quests. And when we have these, work life and personal life begin to integrate as part of a whole, rather than being warring factions.

If you have work that energises you rather than drains you, the idea of striving for balance is unlikely to occur. We only crave this mythical balance when the world provides work that is stultifying or alienating. If you are a writer who has the luxury of writing, whether at evenings or in the early mornings, for weeks or even months, you may well feel ecstatic, but you won't have balance. Great artists and musicians are rarely balanced — they put as much time as possible into their art.

What exhausts us is not the prospect of a huge creative project that is complex and demanding, but that life is a succession of ticking off the next thing and the next thing that has to be done. Life is too short for 'to-do' lists and when we are in a pattern of just reacting to these lists then we soon feel overwhelmed and despondent.

Chapter 16: Exchanging Balance for Rhythm

We all have things that have to be done. We have rent or mortgages and groceries to buy and laundry to be done, but when we are immersed in each activity with attentiveness and stay in that moment instead of skittering ahead in our minds to the hundred things on the always evolving 'list' then our energy doesn't seep away but instead is nurtured. Whatever you are doing, whether it's work or preparing food, reading or spending time with someone, gardening or writing, you will be more fulfilled and less stressed if you give that thing your deep attention, savouring one thing at a time. This isn't balance, it's rhythm.

The psychologist, Mihaly Csikszentmihalyi, talks about flow as that mindspace where we lose ourselves in an activity. We're so immersed that time and space seem different. We're so 'in the zone' that the world falls away. This is anything but balanced but who would want balance compared to flow?

Being in the flow is a deep experience that exposes the myth of balance but it does require extreme commitment and focus. And for most of us there isn't only one project in life. You might want to write and write and write but you might also want to keep your relationships with family and friends intact. And even writers have to eat and do some life-maintenance. This doesn't mean you have to give equal weight to every distraction or demand that comes along but you do need to check in with yourself to keep a perspective on the things that matter. Hopefully, a limited number of areas have a call on you. In the words of Henry David Thoreau:

> Simplicity, simplicity, simplicity! I say, let your affairs be as two or three, and not a hundred or a thousand.

At the end of your life do you want to feel you've balanced it all like a complex circus trick or that you have followed your passions and skills, always open to change? This brings me back to writing as a metaphor for life. In writing rhythm is crucial, as Virginia Woolf says:

> As for the mot juste, you are quite wrong. Style is a very simple matter: It is all rhythm. Once you get that, you can't use the wrong words.

All writing has rhythm. (Poetry also has metre but rhythm is common to every piece of writing.) Think about the effect of short sentences. They set up a beat. They feel urgent. Or they halt. If they go on. And on. They drum in the head. They start to annoy. Short sentences can be effective but they soon get monotonous and choppy, so we tend to vary the rhythm. Long sentences, even complex ones with sub-clauses, as long as the sub-clauses don't start to run away from you, can give a great deal of connectedness. Whilst too many long

Chapter 16: Exchanging Balance for Rhythm

sentences can start to sound stuffy, nonetheless sentences that are both long and well-articulated give a measured pace. And short sub-clauses within the sentence can set up the rhythm of a piece.

In writing, we vary the rhythm. The form we use has an impact on the content and how it's received by the reader. In writing, sometimes we go for equilibrium. Consider the device of parataxis, which takes phrases that are all of equal weight and sets them side-by-side. This can involve linking phrases with co-ordinating conjunctions (for, and, nor, but, or, yet, so). The simplest definition of parataxis is 'just one thing after another'. Like this quote from *Bleak House* by Charles Dickens:

> Dogs, undistinguishable in mire. Horses, scarcely better — splashed to their very blinkers. Foot passengers, jostling one another's umbrellas, in a general infection of ill-temper, and losing their foothold at street corners.

As in writing, so in life. Sometimes we are holding areas in equilibrium. Sometimes life comes at us in a rush. The device of asyndeton is a sub-set of parataxis. All the phrases are of equal weight but there are no conjunctions of any kind. Like the staccato rhythm of stream of consciousness in Samuel Beckett's 'Not I' or Caesar's blunt:

> *veni, vidi, vici*

The thing about rhythm is that it changes. Rhythm, unlike balance, goes with the flow. Do you need short sentences or long? Do you need the equilibrium of phrases of equal weight slowed by conjunctions or the wild rush of stream of consciousness? Do you need to hold two areas of your life side by side or is it time to dive deep into one immersive project? The answer will change all the time and, while chasing balance is irreconcilable with that, finding rhythm isn't.

Rhythm is breath. Everything that lives, breathes. The same is true of both writing and life. If you walk in beautiful places you'll find that not only do you breathe in, breathe out, but your attention will follow the same rhythm as your pace. You'll move between looking outward and inward musing. You'll get caught up in the sights and smells and they in turn will evoke memories and emotions.

Good writing has the same kind of pulse, moving inwards to thoughts and emotions, outwards to dialogue and description. When writing has this rhythm, it constantly moves its focus, inward and outward, and it becomes much more compelling. Endless descriptions of what a character is thinking or feeling soon alienate a reader. But page after page of description with no insight into the character's inner world does the same. When there is a rhythm between the two, the story comes to life. When we get into this rhythmic flow, the writing falls into place. Of course, the rhythm in writing varies. A long out-breath of description or dialogue, a short gasp of emotion — or vice versa. At other times a steadier rhythm. Sometimes equilibrium. At other times an imbalance, an intense focus on the interior or exterior that is appropriate for the passage. As in writing, so in life. Chasing the illusion of balance drives us in circles trying to do everything at once. Forget balance, instead:

- Whatever your quest is, it's going to require more of your attention than anything else, not balance.
- Savour one thing at a time. If you're working, be present. If you're with family, don't just physically show up, attend: be in the moment.
- Let your affairs be two or three: there are so many distractions — make choices and prioritise.
- Find your rhythm and keep finding it.
- Breathe in, breathe out — flow, not balance.

Naturally, in writing as in any creative endeavour, you have to have a practice that makes the writing happen. In busy, often over-stressed lives, this can be hard to achieve, but if you commit to being a writer then the call from within won't leave you in peace until you satisfy it, until you become unreasonable and unbalanced. These are some of the ways you can achieve this, and we'll return to these in more depth throughout this book:

1. Get into flow

Experiment with what gets you into flow; the state identified by psychologist Mihaly Csikszentmihalyi, in which we are so lost in what we are doing that we forget ourselves and create. Find your cues and use them. It might be through:

- music or silence
- prefacing writing with yoga or walking
- first journalling
- meditating or visualising
- setting up an environment in a particular way

However you signal your body to settle into a state where flow can take place.

2. Protect your routines

Routines can become stale so they always need to be under review, but with that caveat, the more you find helpful routines, the more you will write. For example, a morning routine of journalling, meditation, exercise and healthy eating can set up your day so that you are in the frame of mind to write. Similarly, an evening routine that includes putting away screens at least an hour before sleep, more journalling, reading and good quality sleep sets up the next day.

3. Cultivate helpful habits

Having a time when you always write makes it a muscle memory over time. We form a habit whenever some trigger alerts the brain to go into a particular mode. It might be as simple as sitting in a particular chair or lighting a candle. The cue begins a routine, which then gives a sense of fulfilment. There are times when this can work against us. Distraction habits like constantly checking a phone may deliver a stream of small dopamine hits that mimic fulfilment, but don't lead to anything good in our lives. The best habits do something positive Healthy eating leads to better health. Exercise increases strength and suppleness. Regular writing will yield first drafts and honed drafts…

Cultivating the habits that build the routines that lead to flow requires creating triggers that will start the pattern, such as leaving your journal where it's the first thing you see in the morning and moving the phone to another room.

4. Remove distractions

Cultivating the habits that support your writing (or other quests) is strongly related to eliminating whatever might distract you, all the small stuff pulling at your attention and stopping you from doing deep work. Do you keep stopping the work to check social media or emails? Then put the phone in another room and switch off Wi-Fi on your laptop. Do you find yourself focussing on noises around the house or outside? Put on earphones, even if you are only listening to silence or white noise. Do whatever it takes to focus on the one thing you want to do.

5. Love your space

Whether you have a room of your own or a corner somewhere, make the space work for you. Make sure you are comfortable — in your skin and in your clothes; in the chair you use or the posture you adopt as you write, whether sitting or standing. If you have the luxury of a dedicated space, make it beautiful and personal, whether with objects that are meaningful to you or with minimalism that works for your aesthetic values. You are going to spend a lot of time in the space: love it.

6. Make your task challenging but attainable

If you set out to write an epic poem the first time you write poetry, you are likely to fail. If you set out to write a novel pretty much like the last one and the one before that, chances are you are going to get bored. Flow isn't about either impossibility or staying safely in your comfort zone. We get into flow when the task both engages and stretches us.

7. Start with clarity

If you don't know where you're going you will probably end up somewhere else, perhaps going round in ever decreasing circles. Your project is likely to alter and evolve as you work, but start out with at least the big picture and some over-arching goals for it and you will save yourself a lot of frustration. Writing rituals and methods are endlessly variable and fascinating but rarely random, no matter how quixotic it might look from the outside. But there's a caveat to this: having a big picture shouldn't get in the way of admitting the possibility of play.

8. Stay in the moment

Write one scene, draft one poem, complete one blog post with one idea and then the next and then the next... Flow time is always NOW.

9. Recruit your subconscious

There are times in writing when the solutions don't come, when we sit down feeling uneasy and don't find the rhythm that day or that week... Very often this happens when we are over-thinking the writing. There are many rational approaches needed in writing, especially once we are honing and editing, but at the flow stage too much thought can impede the creative rush. At such times chasing an idea too hard can make it vanish into the shadows. Conscious wrestling is inimical to flow so if it's not happening, journal about it, ask your subconscious questions, give it some ideas and let your dreams take over.

10. Try the content spew method

If you are feeling stuck, don't try to write anything good, just write. There's an anecdote, probably apocryphal, that Leonard Cohen wrote 80 verses for his famous song 'Hallelujah' before narrowing down to a couple of versions. There's a story that Janet Frame sat typing 'the quick brown fox jumps over the lazy dog' over and over so that her generous patron would hear the typewriter and think she had something to write.

Revising rubbish can be easier than writing gold dust, at least until we hit a new rhythm. Don't force, but write anyway. When you turn on a tap in an uninhabited old house the water might come out brown and full of debris for a while, but eventually it will run clear. Flow can be the same. Quality matters, but it can also emerge from quantity. Cohen didn't keep 80 verses for 'Hallelujah' and your 250,000 novel might end up as a novella. I once wrote a 120,000-word novel that ended up as a slim 80-page prose-poem narrative sequence. I couldn't have got to the flow without all the over-blown prose en route.

11. Forget the product, go with the process

There's a time for outcomes, but flow is about the joy. Not everything you do in flow will survive later tests, but that doesn't make it wasted. When you allow creativity to take over you are free to play with your writing. You begin to take risks. You begin to experiment in ways that may not work in the long term, but will certainly teach you a great deal.

12. Turn around

The word that is often translated as 'repentance' in the Bible is the Greek word, *metanoia*. It means to turn around, to do an about face and go in another direction. Routines, habits and eschewing distractions are essential for writing, but so is *metanoia*. It's so easy to find our course and then get stuck there, but to stay on track we usually need to make changes in direction from time to time, sometimes slight and sometimes radical. If a navigator sets off in a plane that doesn't course correct as it travels, the plane will not arrive at its destination. Steering a course isn't a matter of setting out on target and then forgetting

Chapter 16: Exchanging Balance for Rhythm

about any further navigation. The same is true for writing. If we become complacent then our rhythm will degrade into trundling around the same plateau.

You need fresh ideas, fresh inspiration from reading and life. Sometimes you need to entirely change direction to establish a new rhythm for the next, more challenging leg of the journey.

Interlude 5

Writing the Sun to Earth

This interlude is a chance to consider the early harvests of your creativity. It's planned to be used around the end of July to early August when the summer is ending and the seasons will soon shift again. This is the time of the last of the summer light and of fertility, though if you are in the southern hemisphere this would fall in early February and your interlude in late July would be 'Writing the Green Blade', found in Section 2.

July 31

Traditionally, this time of year in the northern hemisphere is the early harvest. The work we have done, the story we have lived, the planting and nurturing, begin to come to fruition, but this can depend on consistency, on small steps repeated. There are so many choices in life, so much to do. We can do anything, but we can't do everything. If we don't make decisions, others will make them for us. We'll find ourselves not looking forward with nostalgia for the future, but looking backwards wondering what happened. The only way to stop this is to intervene and make decisions. Choose.

In the exquisite and lucid poem, 'Stopping by Woods on a Snowy Evening', Robert Frost feels the pull of one place, but chooses to keep the promises he's already made. He has his quest. Whether it is gargantuan or quotidian we don't know, and nor does it matter. He's made the choice and he stays with it, not distracted by the beauty or all the other possibilities because he has promises to keep. What are your promises? Some of us don't have any promises to keep. For some, life has become so reactive to the next demand, and the next and the next that there is no sense of quest, no horizon of possibilities from which to choose and commit to. In some cases, this is because of appalling conditions, brutalising environments or the sheer necessity of basic survival. But for most people reading this, that's not the case. We do have choices and the time to make them is now.

Loving someone is a signal that the other person can rely on your promises and commitments. Whether the other person is a close friend, your child or your partner, promises matter. We all make mistakes. Sometimes we've half-committed to something without thinking it through or listening deeply. Sometimes life gets in the way, and usually the other person will understand and forgive, especially if letting them down isn't a continual pattern. But it's all too easy to make promises that we know will never happen, simply because it feels more comfortable to acquiesce in the moment, even though this damages the love in the longer term.

- If we make a promise in order to fob-off a child, knowing we have no intention of following through, that's passive aggression, not love.
- If we make so many promises that we are bound to run out of time and resources, that's self delusion, not love.
- If we make promises out of fear of ever saying no, that's insecurity, not love speaking.
- If we make every promise as it's asked (or demanded), that's self-sacrifice (and a total lack of creativity and problem-solving) rather than a loving response.
- If we make promises and then find we always have some outstanding and urgent reason to break it, love is being held hostage to a lack of accountability.

Every broken promise is a signal that something else was more important than that relationship. All of us fail sometimes, but promises and love go hand in hand. You have to consider why you are making the promise — is it to:

- get someone to be quiet
- appease
- avoid conflict
- self-sacrifice
- or out of love?

We're less likely to be good at keeping promises to others as acts of love (as opposed to weapons of resentful obligation) if we don't take ourselves seriously. We do ourselves and others no good if we allow our energy to

Interlude 5: Writing the Sun to Earth

be poured out in a million directions, our bodies as well as mental well-being soon show the loss. When we keep promises to ourselves, we don't only talk about dreams and pursuing a quest, we model how to live like this. It's a gift to those in our lives as well as to ourselves. A promise is a commitment that something will happen. If you keep promising yourself you will write that novel, but never start, how do you feel about yourself? If you keep promising you will exercise three times a week, but never do, what sort of self-image will you have? Breaking promises to yourself is an internal signal that you can't trust yourself. Conversely, when you keep promises to yourself:

- your thoughts, feelings and actions are coherent
- your confidence grows

You don't have to make promises so grand that you set yourself up for failure. And any promise can have as many stages as it needs. As Confucius puts it:

> It does not matter how slowly you go as long as you do not stop.

But you do have to keep the promises you make to yourself. If someone else repeatedly lets you down, how do you view them? Why should it be any different if that person is yourself? You want to write a poetry collection?

- Promise yourself you will do it.
- Then break the promise down into clear, achievable stages.
- Block out the time as sacrosanct.
- And do it.

No-one can do everything. How do you decide what to promise, whether for others or yourself? For a start, forget the endless 'to-do' lists. As we noted in chapter 16, life should be about passion and quests, not deadening and demotivating lists. When you:

- take control of how you use time
- think deeply about what is important in your life (what excites you and gives life meaning)
- build your life on values rather than demands, 'oughts' and 'shoulds'

Interlude 5: Writing the Sun to Earth

- fashion your environment to support not hinder your life

then you will know which promises are important to keep and what you should be saying no to. To make and keep promises we need love, integrity and discernment. Without these qualities we become reactive, self-sacrificing, resentful and untrustworthy. But when we act from love, integrity and discernment then our confidence, problem-solving and creativity escalate.

We are currently in the season of Harvest — the old season of Lammas in the northern hemisphere. New Year seems like a long time ago. How many resolutions have persisted? How many are beginning to bear fruit?

These are not questions to beat yourself up with, but to reset your sense of promise. We can always start again. Who you are tomorrow depends on how you act today. People who are able to make promises from love and who have a strong sense of personal integrity are not gods among (wo)men, but those with intact senses of self and imagination. We all inhabit stories, including the story of who we are. If we have a strong and imaginative self who inhabits the space between the possible and the actual, the dreamed and the lived, then we will make the right promises and keep them. The signs that we are living in the wrong story, that imagination has failed us include:

- not valuing the self (an introverted failure of imagination can become depression)
- not valuing others (an outward failure of imagination)
- not being able to discern what promises to make and keep (the playing, imagining self cut off from the deepest creative core and spark of the self)

To be a person of promise, you must nurture your imagination and yourself. Imagination allows us to fly, it ensures:

- a sense of identity and renewed self image
- autonomy within community
- deeper understanding
- listening
- alternative possibilities
- a sense of purpose and quest

Imagination helps us to become a different story.

Interlude 5: Writing the Sun to Earth

Journal exercise

What are you currently harvesting in your life as a result of past decisions and behaviours?

Is this the harvest you want?

What promises do you need to make to yourself and to your writing?

How will you keep them?

What promises do you need to make to others or the world?

How will you keep them?

Ritual

Write three promises on small pieces of paper (you can also put them in your journal): one to yourself; one to your writing; one to someone or a cause you care about. Take the three pieces of paper and bury them. Write a date (or dates) on your calendar when you will reflect back on the promises (the date/s will depend on what the promises are, how long you need…)

August 1

Yesterday we considered how promises, the small, consistent steps we take for ourselves, for our writing and for those we love, require imagination, particularly if our quests are to bear harvests. Imagination allows us to fly, it ensures:

- a sense of identity and renewed self image
- autonomy within community
- deeper understanding
- listening
- alternative possibilities
- a sense of purpose and quest

Don't forget: imagination helps us to become a different story.

Change is hard. When we are striving towards big goals, whether personal or creative, it can feel like an uphill struggle. In the short term, it can be difficult to see change taking place. And even when we do see the difference, the results can be fragile. There are several reasons why making big shifts in life can come to a halt or even slip backwards. Despite the adage that habits take only 60–70 days to establish, we all know that that they can disappear in a much shorter time. We can wipe out the habit of good nutrition in one holiday, or the ritual of daily yoga during a minor illness. Moreover, the fact of having been successful can make us complacent. After the initial euphoria we find ourselves on a plateau, feeling stuck. How do we keep the vision alive so that we keep the promises? What is it that allows passion to thrive and grow rather than wither? Part of the answer lies in knowing how the vision has become dimmed in the first place and there are plenty of possible reasons.

1. The quest was never yours

Sometimes we embark on huge projects without the goal ever having been clear. This can be because we've never listened to ourselves. It can be because we've spent a lifetime picking goals that will please others or that seem the most 'common sense'. If you've made progress but feel nothing but boredom or apathy, it's likely you've put yourself on someone else's path. It's time to start treating yourself with the respect you think others deserve. To stay vital, the vision has to be your own.

2. You've been surviving on willpower, not motivation

Willpower is finite and fickle. Sometimes we need it and summoning resolve is essential. But when we live on it, we're likely to burn out. Motivation is something completely different. If you don't desire sugary food, it isn't hard to resist. But if all you want is that doughnut then the only way to refuse it is with willpower. Sooner or later, willpower won't be enough. You'll make a deal with yourself and, five doughnuts later, despise yourself. When you begin to take yourself seriously this will change. When you take the space to think about the life you want to lead, the focus shifts from willpower to intrinsic motivation.

3. Having has stifled doing and being

If you did set out with your own quest and made it work because of your intrinsic motivation, you can still find the vision dulling. One reason is that succeeding can make us stop developing. We stop to admire the view and enjoy the rewards and some while later realise we've been standing still for a long time. Success is double-edged. As soon as we start to think we've 'made it', we're lost. Whatever we are harvesting at the moment, we need to keep the momentum in order to go on harvesting in the future. And when the benefits of success (what we 'have' as a result) loom larger than the behaviour that got us here, we're lost. Don't let the lure of success poison the creativity that ignited your initial vision. There is always more to learn, more to be.

4. The quest is too much for one person

Not all quests are solo expeditions. And even those that are might have a team in the background providing the lifeline of support. You don't have to do it all yourself. It's good to ask for help and make connections.

Whatever the reason for sometimes running out of steam, there is always the chance to start again. Harvest is a good time to appraise where you are and to:

1. Reconnect with or create your vision

If the vision was never yours in the first place, now is the time to create your own quest. We can create other stories. In the same way, we can imagine ourselves different, make daily changes until we are different. We don't have to believe we have a mission planted deep in our souls for us to discover meaning. We can create it.

2. Value consistency

Quests never end. We get to where we thought we were going and find another peak not far ahead, and then another. The death of vision is thinking we've arrived. I see this with writing all the time. A writer with tens of excellent books behind him who still hones his craft and pushes his boundaries is thrilling to work with. Not so a writer who tells you she's learned all she needs and is going to keep on churning out the same type of work.

In the film *Annie Hall*, Woody Allen's character tells 'Annie' that a relationship is like a shark. If it doesn't keep moving the shark dies. What they have on their hands, he says, is a dead shark. It's not only true of relationships. Any aspect of your life or creativity can stagnate. When that happens, what you have on your hands is a dead shark. Keep moving. Keep imagining. Small consistent steps are all it takes.

3. Say no more often

If you have a vision, not everything you're asked to do will fit into it. By all means be generous, be a giver, but continue to make choices. It's astonishing just how much of the things that claim our attention are of no importance at all or will simply take us somewhere we never intended. Whatever comes along, whether it's a pay increase or a distraction, you need to ask whether it is in accord with your vision. If the answer is no, don't say yes for the sake of short-term gain. Don't say yes to appease someone. Of course there are times when we say yes to something we're unsure of because we want to try something new or test an idea. Not everything we do fills us with enthusiasm at the outset (losing weight; starting a new form of exercise; learning a new skill). Saying yes to these expands us and we can give something a try and then review, but we generally know fairly quickly when something is a bad fit. And when your heart is sinking at the same time as you are saying 'yes' then you know it's the wrong way to go.

4. Fuel desire with clarity

The clearer your vision the more you feel motivated. Ambiguity leads nowhere. Even if all you know is what the next step should be you will be more likely to stay focused and feel the passion. If your ideas for creativity or career or fitness seem huge and amorphous, concentrate on what would move you forward now. One clear step will lead to the next... There's no compulsion to go through life imagining a vision, honing a craft, setting out the next quest. Many people drift through life and they are not all miserable. They may be asleep, but that's still a choice. That isn't how I want to live, however. We have this one priceless life with the potential for unreasonable creativity. What do you intend to do with it? How do you need to imagine and re-invent your life to make it so?

Imagination is enhanced by 'play'. Writing can benefit enormously from 'playing with language', which permits us to relax; lessens the pressure to produce a finished piece and allows us to catch the 'peripheral vision'. This sense of play can also spare us from the intervention of the personal critic who often sits frowning and muttering on our writing shoulder.

Interlude 5: Writing the Sun to Earth

Journal exercise

So JUST WRITE — each time a word or short phrase in response. Try to make each word as disconnected as possible from the last one and every 4–7 words, as randomly as possible, start a new line. (You can use occasional linking words like with, while, and, the ... and punctuation.) The prompts are:

>   a sound
>   a noun
>   a verb
>   your brain gropes for...
>   you need...
>   you refuse to ...
>   a colour
>   a type of weather
>   a verb
>   a chemical element
>   a place you love
>   a body part
>   a type of tree
>   a verb
>   a noun
>   a time of day
>   a liminal space
>   a taste
>   an emotion
>   a physical sensation
>   a type of flower
>   a season of the year
>   a verb
>   a colour
>   a type of weather
>   a natural phenomenon
>   a type of art
>   a verb
>   a sin or vice
>   an animal
>   a size
>   an emotion

· Interlude 5: Writing the Sun to Earth ·

a verb
a phrase repeated twice
a sound
a virtue
a verb
a noun
a description of temperature

Ritual

Relax and close your eyes. Concentrate on your breathing. Let it slow down. Feel your arms become heavier, warm. Feel your legs become heavier, warm. Breathe in through your nose and out through your mouth, slowly. Let your breath slow down.

There's a stream of light at your feet, it comes through your soles and travels through your body slowly, warming you — your legs, your belly, your chest, your neck, your head.

Breathe slowly.

A shaft of sunlight falls on you — it enters your head and flows down your body, your face, your neck, your shoulders, your chest, your abdomen, your thighs, your calves and into your feet.

You are as light as the sunbeam.

Breathe slowly.

Imagine yourself on a path — you come to a turn and, as you round the bend, in front of you is a place — a place you know or a new place. On one side is radiance, on another is the abyss.

Slowly, come back to the room and write the sentence:

'On one side is radiance, on another is the abyss...'

Keep writing.

August 2

We bring our whole selves to our writing. Whether we are writing poetry in another persona, a story set a thousand years ago or an article about beetles, we are in there. Who we are and how and what we write are of a piece. Thinking about harvest, about how things come to fruition, we

Interlude 5: Writing the Sun to Earth

know that it requires a combination of consistency (keeping promises to ourselves and others, giving attention and nurture to what we love and value) and letting our imagination soar so that we nurture our inner life and also let it reach out in empathy.

Keeping promises to ourselves and others, reaching deeply within and reaching out to others, builds hope and, in a world where cynicism is plentiful and fear is rife, it's not an unreasonable instinct to want to spread some joy and hope. And yet, we also know that in any life joy and despair will be mixed. Are we heading into Nietszchean territory? Nietzsche certainly thought that hardship was essential to joy. He reached this conclusion by observing the great and productive lives of some deeply unhappy and unfortunate people. But is a life of rich joy only possible for those who have known terrible suffering or torment? As writers, do we have to endure untold misery to hone and deepen our writing, to make it worthwhile? I don't think it's as simplistic as this. But there are truths here to be gleaned:

- What we certainly need is experience. We need to be courageous enough to enter the world, to have humility, to make ourselves vulnerable.
- We need to stop thinking that writing is easy and something we can learn quickly or that slick 'content' without substance can stand in the place of crafting and honing.

Many worthwhile parts of life don't come easily and yet I also want caveats. In *The Will to Power* Nietzsche writes that he wishes deep suffering on those who he cares about in order that they can prove themselves and endure.

I can't follow him to this place. Quite honestly, I want to wrap those who are my concern in warm blankets, and wish them health, nourishing lives, every shade of joy surrounded by others they delight in and who delight in them. Yes, I want my loved ones to be brave and bold and to have wide and rich experiences. Yes, I want them to have lives in which they can passionately and deeply pursue their skills and their art. But no, I will not wish my loved ones sickness and torture. Why would I need to? We all know that life is tumultuous and brings a mixture of pain and joy to all of us. And we all know that some have dire misfortune of every kind. Endurance and resilience will be found simply by living. We don't need to wish horrors on people for us to learn this.

I'm much more persuaded by Anne Lamott who considers that in such an uncertain world, what we need to give is love, not ill-wishing to make our loved ones toughen up. And yet we also know that there will be some moments of despair. If we do not cocoon ourselves and those we love; if we dare to make art or care about the planet or seek justice or value mercy and humanity, there will be periods of sadness, even of bleakness. The point is, that despair should not be courted. There is no need for any bullish call to 'bring it on'. Rather, we need to ask: how do we respond when we are ravaged by hopelessness?

To this question, the philosopher Rollo May has some intriguing and hopeful answers in his book, *Freedom and Destiny*. May sees despair not as something to seek out, but something that, when it comes to us, we use in our journey toward freedom. May begins by setting out freedom as not merely a value but as fundamental to having other values and defines freedom as how we push against and interact with our boundaries.

Freedom, for May, isn't only a 'right' but a way to live. Freedom is what we make of life and how we respond to whatever life brings. It is the choices we make even in those circumstances when we seem to have hardly any choice at all. And in those circumstances we often know despair. Faced with a terminal diagnosis, an oppressive government, planetary destruction, financial ruin, grief and a thousand other conditions of life, despair is human, but it might also be a prelude to huge creativity. When despair scoops us out and makes us question everything, then we are also ready to be reborn.

This is powerful and doesn't only apply to individual lives but to how we live as societies or connect to the planet. But where does flourishing and joy come into all this talk of despair? The best metaphor is perhaps a natural one. All through the winter nothing grows, the earth seems barren and bleak, but if there are seeds there will be new life...

Of course not all despair leads to rebirth, rejuvenation and growth. Some become so fearful and damaged that they can see nothing and no one but themselves. Some become cynical and wallow in the damage. This is not a judgement. Life can bring extraordinary suffering and it's much easier to believe that we can remake life again and again and again when we are not the ones suffering. But we also all know people who are facing a terminal diagnosis or parents who've lost children or refugees who've lost home and family and identity, who have transformed despair. Some of you are those people.

And it's also worth noting that what we are seeing and thinking about is joy, not mere happiness. Happiness and contentment are elusive and yet simpler conditions and often more passive. Joy is energetic, more related to awe and new experiences. And despair, if it doesn't grind us into submissive fear or drive us wayward into a state of cynicism, is likely to be met at some point with an energetic: No! A refusal to be crushed that leads to new possibilities.

I cannot join Nietzsche in wishing my loved ones, or indeed anyone, illness, suffering and mistreatment, but when life throws its worst, I wish them the capacity for despair that will move them to make a stand. I hope more and more of us will be people of empathy, so moved by the plight of the planet, by injustice, by suffering, that we feel it keenly and rise against it. And I hope writers will be those who notice the despair of the world and help to write the story that comes from resisting it.

There is a Zen koan of a monk who falls asleep while meditating and knocks over a candle. When he wakes, the sanctuary is on fire and a huge and precious Buddha statue just about to be burned. He wants to rescue the statue, which is enormous. The walls are too thick to burst through and the door is too narrow for the statue. Yet the answer is that the monk carries the statue through the door on his back. The too-narrow door is an illusion; a problem we've created to limit ourselves.

Journal exercise

How, when and where do you place limits on your life and your writing?

To inject freedom into our writing we need to imagine, to play, to dream, to make promises and to be open to awe and wonder, to moments of epiphany. Thinking of this, journal on these questions:

- I play as a writer whenever…
- I feel longing like carnal desire rise in my writing when…
- One of my deepest experiences of timelessness and flow as I wrote was…
- The most openness and connection I've felt as I wrote was…

Take some time to go deep into yourself — find a quiet corner if you prefer. Don't worry if you don't write straight away — centre yourself, let your breathing slow, close your eyes and recall a moment of epiphany when you have felt the boundaries between self and world dissolving. If you can't recall one, make one up. Write for 10 minutes without stopping.

Ritual

Harvest is a time of uniting the power of the sun and the fertility of the earth. It is a time for reaping the fruits of what has gone before and deciding what needs planting now. Gather or buy a bunch of flowers today. As you put them in a vase, recall your promises from the day before yesterday. For each flower think of a small step you can take towards keeping those promises so that by the time the flowers wilt, you will have dispensed with a few of the limits you place on your life.

Chapter 17
The Habits that Nurture

We began considering habits in Chapter 16 and in the last 'interlude', so let's dive into this in more depth. All kinds of things affect our creativity and designing habits for a creative environment can have a huge impact. If we don't deliberately give time each day to who we want to be, as writers and as people, then something or someone else will certainly use that time for us and we'll find ourselves older, looking back and wondering where all the time went.

To be in a creative mindset we have to dive deeply and live with purpose, whether the aim is losing weight or writing a novel. You need to use time so well that you can make this quest happen and this will require eliminating time-wasting activities and distractions. In short to live at depth, you need to optimise your time, which means:

- You need down time so that you are not fatigued.
- You need a significant amount of technology-free time. Blue-light screens interfere with sleep patterns so having time without devices before bed is good practice. When you wake up you are in a liminal state between sleep and wake that can be highly creative, so don't waste that time on emails or social media. And, through the day, a lot of social media is mindless and draining and you can answer emails in one block in the afternoon.
- You need to do something to move your body every day. Whether it's walking or yoga or a serious gym workout, sedentariness and creativity don't go together.
- You need to be reflecting in some way — journalling and/or meditating.
- You need sources of inspiration: good company and conversation, reading, art…
- You need to be awake, which requires enough good quality sleep.

Chapter 17: The Habits that Nurture

The question is, when do we do all this? Do we all need to be larks, up at 5 or 6 a.m.? There is plenty of support for the theory that a solid morning routine helps in our quests, or even makes or breaks them. In the most vociferous versions of this theory, you should begin early in the day: 6 a.m. at least. Robin Sharma, for example, leads the 5 a.m. Club, quoting a saying attributed to Benjamin Franklin:

> there will be plenty of time to sleep when you are dead.

Plenty of other lifestyle gurus are adamant that an hour lost to sleep early in the morning will ruin your day. The problem is that people come not only with all kinds of contexts, but also all kinds of bodies. I have a writing friend who is a single mother with three part-time jobs. It's ten in the evening before she is done with time with her children and household chores. So she writes from 10 p.m. to midnight every weekday. She would agree that this isn't optimum, but it keeps her writing going while fulfilling her responsibilities as a caring mother. And she's doing well with the writing.

Other people may not have life circumstances that they need to work around, but find that they are 'night-owls'; people have different chronotypes and varying circadian rhythms. Left to my own devices, I come to life in the late evening and find my brain sharp and my creativity buzzing. I'm fortunate that I run my own business, so much of the time I can work around a body that hates mornings. And there is some evidence that 'owls' can thrive as well as 'larks'. And the jury is out on whether larks are universally healthier and more successful? It was apparently Benjamin Franklin who first advocated:

> early to bed and early to rise makes a [wo]man healthy, wealthy, and wise.

But a Southampton University epidemiological study published in the *British Medical Journal* doesn't support Franklin's contention. Of the 356 larks (in bed before 11 p.m., up before 8 a.m.) and 318 owls (in bed after 11, up after 8), it was the night owls who had (marginally) larger incomes, whilst the two groups had similar cognitive functions and health levels. Another study by psychologist Richard D. Roberts of the University of Sydney and Patrick C. Kyllonen of the Air Force Research Lab, gave 420 test participants intelligence tests. The results came down marginally on the side of night owls, who had slightly better working memory and processing speeds. Similarly, Roberts and Kyllonen reported that evening-types have higher intelligence scores (though again the

Chapter 17: The Habits that Nurture

differences are marginal and it's also questionable what 'intelligence' tests actually measure).

I appreciate that for many people, rhythms are never fixed. A night owl can learn to be a lark, but if she has no pressing reasons to do so and finds herself most creative at midnight and still able to get enough sleep, then why change? It's a question I've grappled with for years. In my youth, I was able to be up early and awake late with seemingly inexhaustible energy. Post-childbirth, I switched much more to the night-owl profile and this became more extreme after a period of severe illness. I don't believe that I'm controlled by this tendency and, when I was in a period of working on weight loss a few years ago, I shifted the pattern. For around two years I was able to get up early and exercise immediately. Yet I find myself once again struggling and much more likely to be working late (and fruitfully) than early. The period when I had a more lark-like pattern was energising and motivating. but the evidence doesn't show that being a night owl is detrimental in itself. Anecdotes about 'successful people' don't tell us how many larks are finding life difficult, for example.

What I feel more confident of is that both larks and owls benefit from a life lived deliberately and that this involves designing consistent habits, around whatever schedule works for the body you are. Whatever your chronotype and whenever you decide is the optimum time to wake up, do it decisively. Don't go back to sleep or snooze. Whether it is 5 a.m. or 9 a.m., get in the zone: reach for your journal or meditate; get out of bed and move your body. Think about your quests and start your day with clarity and purpose. Then put the right food in your body and get on with your day. If you're up with the larks, your morning routine might include reading, exercise and/or working on a major goal or project. If you're a night owl you might put your exercise later in the day, read and work on a major project late into the evening. Or your pattern might be completely different. What is true for everyone is that you need to be consistent and make conscious use of your time, including:

- a regular waking time
- enough sleep of good quality
- time to reflect and plan whether through journalling, meditation or both
- movement/exercise — at least a walk every day
- good nutrition
- sources of inspiration
- recovery time & nurture

- freedom from distractions: cut out screens in the early morning and late evening; have one time for answering emails; limit social media (or eliminate it entirely)
- a time every day for your creative project

If you can develop a consistent pattern, your creativity has an environment in which to flourish. All you need then are the ideas and flow.

Chapter 18

Is This the Place?

Environment matters in so many ways to writers. When I'm writing fiction I can get lost in the people I'm writing, even begin to dream their dreams. The mysteriousness and opaqueness of others is intriguing, but so too is their context. Who we are, the stories we tell ourselves or allow others to tell about us, arise from a matrix of particular factors, amongst them time and place.

In *This is the End of the Story*, Cassie comes of age in 1970s Teesside and her context helps to shape her. The industrial landscape, the decline of employment, the cultural expectations of a class, time and place, are issues that she has to face in forming a sense of identity. Cassie shares my own background, though fictionalised. But memory is a tricky thing so I still found myself doing lots of research — songs I thought I'd heard; fashions and news items. Despite that, there was a familiarity of place that informed me and gave the writing a significant grounding. When it came to Toledo, though, another major setting in the novel, I was on very different territory.

There was no way to visit eleventh century Toledo so I had to rely on archival material and a novel I'd read as a child, *Casilda of the Rising Moon*. Books and the Internet were invaluable, but it was only after I travelled to Toledo that I felt confident of this part of the writing. When I stood in a tiny mosque that Casilda might have stood in 900 years earlier, or visited a tenth century Islamic cave-house, I felt a sense of place that I couldn't experience from books.

One of Cinnamon Press's novelists, Landeg White, who passed away at the end of 2017, was someone who knew a great deal about 'place' and the writing of place. He remarked that going to a place for in situ research was 'absolutely necessary'. He was re-reading George Eliot's *Romola* at the time, and admiring the way she took the trouble to find out things instead of making it all up. To some extent we can fictionalise places and imagine them. But if the place is essential, then we should do everything possible to visit it. It is, after all, the vital atmosphere, history, and culture that enhances the writing. Moreover, moving ourselves out of place, out of our comfort zone, pushes our boundaries. It makes us more porous to influences larger than ourselves.

In 2012, the 'Writing Britain' exhibition at the British Library captivated me. There is something powerful about an original manuscript spattered with corrections. There is something both intimate and epiphanic at once. All the books in the exhibition had a strong sense of place. I saw the hand-written last page of Stella Gibbons' *Cold Comfort Farm* and Alan Garner's *The Owl Service* (one of my favourite books from childhood). And a first edition of T S Eliot's poem, 'Little Gidding'. Kathleen Raine's Northumberland journals, in her own hand, enthralled me, especially as parts resonated with my own journals, talking about cold rural houses in winter, with no central heating and managing the logs. I came out awed, dazzled and dazed. I had entered a trance in there, among runes and spells, within the song lines of connection. When I left, the world felt too bright and sharp. This is why we write — for this extraordinary intimacy with strong magic, the reverie of words that make worlds so real our bodies feel they inhabit them as we read.

And in this enchantment, place is dominant, whether it is the 'nowhere' of utopia or the precise smells and sights of a Paris street. Writing takes us to a place — real and visceral, imagined and strange, dream or nightmare, anchored on a map or found only in the interior of a mind. Good writing takes us 'somewhere', even when the place is 'nowhere', because it is only in a place that we begin to narrativise our lives, and the lives of our characters. We tell stories to reconcile ourselves to time — to the huge events of cosmology, to the big and small and hidden events of history. And to do so we locate those stories — somewhere, someplace.

In *A Remedy For All Things*, my character, Cassie, now using her full name, Catherine, undertakes research on a writing trip to Budapest. She is tracing the footsteps of the 1930s poet, Attila József. The novel is set in Budapest in November 1993, one of the coldest winters on record. Catherine's story interweaves with that of Selene Virág, a woman who took part in the Hungarian Uprising of 1956 and was imprisoned. And Selene has her own strange connections to Attila József. I couldn't travel to the Budapest of the 30s, 50s or 90s, but I had the chance to soak up a sense of place for a month. After a launch in Paris and train rides across Europe, we arrived at Budapest's Keleti station.

Budapest was unlike anywhere we'd ever visited. Not only is the Hungarian language impenetrable, but the sense of place was different from anything I could compare it to. In the centre of a capital city, cars give way to pedestrians and stop to let people cross. People are polite and helpful — 'you're welcome' seems to be the phrase of choice in every café or shop — yet there are few smiles. The current politics of Hungary are not encouraging. One blog I read, by a Hungarian/Norwegian writer, talked about leaving due to crony capitalism,

Chapter 18: Is This the Place?

nepotism and poor working conditions. Life under Viktor Orbán's Fidesz party is replete with extreme right-wing thinking. And the major opposition party, Jobbik, is even more worrying and makes no secret of its views on 'ethnic purity'. In such an environment, Budapest is gaining a reputation as a haven for disgruntled nationalists from across the West. And the current political scene isn't the only factor in this atmosphere of melancholy.

Sadness isn't a new phenomenon in Budapest — melancholy is routinely viewed as a cultural trait. Is it due to the extraordinary isolation of the Hungarian language, so unlike any neighbouring language? Hungarian literature has certainly been slow to find translation or recognition. Is it the bleakness of the landscape, the interminable winters (captured in the writing of László Krasznahorkai and films by Béla Tarr). Hungary even has its own 'suicide song' ('Gloomy Sunday', covered by Billie Holiday) and the national anthem sings about sorrow and pity. Or is it just another stereotype? Hungary has undoubtedly suffered constant defeats; within hours of arriving in Budapest, the 'melancholy' was noticeable, but so too was a quiet hospitality that combined reserve with extraordinary graciousness.

Writing in Budapest, I became acquainted with a city full of beauty, yet teeming with ambivalence and poverty. Once grand buildings crumbled alongside others that were shiny and renovated. But I was happy to be in that place, somewhere that had known so many tears and continues to do so. There was an authenticity there and a huge amount to learn. And although I could only skim the surface in those few weeks (and later in another few weeks of return journey) it was a privilege to be able to research the novel in the place it's set. To soak up something of what shapes particular people in particular cultures, moments of history and landscapes.

I was able to write and talk to writers and archivists in Budapest, visit museums and walk the streets that my characters walked. Place and political context make a huge difference to personal stories. The stories we tell ourselves and allow others to tell about us shape us. Environment shapes character, even in fiction. So how much more does it shape us in day-to-day life?

When we exist in environments that are opposed to our quests, life is hard. For good or ill, our environments shape us to a huge extent and if we want to change then it is likely that we will have to make shifts in our environments. In short, you have to make the conditions favourable to the quest you are on. External inputs such as surroundings, people, food, music, books… shape your world view, values and beliefs. And environments that have a high expectation of us help to raise our confidence. Getting to where you want to go is not all about gritting your teeth and going at it with dogged willpower. Individualism is a lie. But neither do we need to be determinists — we can proactively shape our environments and who we chose to be. Rather than having some innate 'essence' that controls our behaviour, personality follows on from how we act. We have to be willing to be the stories and people we want to become.

1. A rhythmic environment

In Chapter 16 we looked at the notion of rhythm for the writing life. A static environment that fixes us into one way of being and working is likely to exhaust us. Creativity is demanding and intense and needs a rhythm in which we can both work and rest; create and play; get into flow and let the unconscious do its deep work. In short, it's not about one static environment, but doing activities in the most optimised places at the best times. Sometimes we need an environment that encourages us to dive deeply and push our creative boundaries, but at other times we need a place that supports nurture and rejuvenation. The optimum environment for a writer is one that allows rhythm, fully engaged, fully resting.

This may mean having a particular space for creative work that includes elements that help your particular ways of working. Do you work best with snacks or no snacks, music or silence? How will you ensure there are no media distractions? You might designate a space where or a time when no work other than your own creative projects ever takes place, for example.

2. An external environment

Getting into flow involves diving deep. We have all experienced those rare, invigorating moments of creative insight that arrive when we see the world from a new perspective. The more we are giving time to our quests, the more of these deep and often epiphanic experiences we are likely to experience. We can't fake these, but we can open the space for them by having more time away from phones and distractions to think, walk, listen to music, meditate or do nothing.

3. A cleared environment

In Chapter 15 I wrote about the dream of having too much 'baggage' and the need we all have to clear things out. This can often be emotional baggage that needs to be addressed and cleared, but it can also be physical chaos. Many of the steps we need to take in order to shape positive environments are not about adding things or activities, but about 'uncommitting' to stuff (junk, unwanted clothes...) and activities that hinder us from writing. How many emails per day do you really have to write? What hours should you actually work? How long do you in fact 'need' to spend on social media per day? Uncommitting involves eliminating a lot of non-essentials from life in order to shape the optimal environment. In particular:

- Eliminate distractions — quick dopamine fixes ultimately sap your time and energy so get rid of some apps and have times when you switch off your phone. And this doesn't only apply to phones and apps. If you want to stop drinking alcohol, don't have a cupboard full of it. If you want to give up sugar, don't have a shelf of sugar-filled junk foods. But you can fill your fridge with kombucha and your pantry with nuts instead.
- Eliminate options — once you know what you want, stressing over paths not taken is a way to stand still. Know your direction and head there. The fewer choices you have to make the more powerful your choices will be. The endless choices of modern society can often leave us feeling confused and certain that whatever we do, whatever we choose will be wrong and we'll miss out on something. Shut this down, choose and move on.
- Eliminate nay-sayers — there are people only too ready to suck all your energy out or refuse to let you change. This isn't a call to stop seeing your grandmother, but it is helpful to find ways to distance yourself from the most negative influences on your life.
- Eliminate work outside work times.

Of course, building an environment that supports your values and your writing isn't only about what we eliminate. We can enlist people who will support our efforts or even collaborate where appropriate. And we can spend time journalling and thinking deeply about what will make our environments work best for our quests and lives.

- What values do we need to live by?
- What most motivates us?
- What sort of environment best works for you and how can you shape it?

Interlude 6

Writing the Light's Balance

This interlude is a chance to reflect on equilibrium and the needs of gestation in your creativity. It's planned to be used around the Autumn Equinox as we move fully into autumn. It is a time of balance before we tip towards the dark months in the seasonal flow, though if you are in the southern hemisphere this would fall in Spring and your interlude in September would be 'Writing the Wild Flowering', found in the Section 2.

September 21

Autumn Equinox is a time when the light and the dark are of equal length, it is a time of brief balance before we tip towards the rhythmic sway that characterises most of life, in this instance towards the dark months in the seasonal flow. As we move towards winter, we enter again a period of creative gestation. This period will be all the more powerful, all the more open to awe and epiphany and to the creative leaps that will once again become green sap rising, unstoppable, next spring if we take the time to pause now; to breathe deeply, find the rhythm of kairos and dive deeply. This brief equilibrium is a moment of respite so that harmony and equanimity remain deeply embedded in our writing lives.

We need to find this equanimity. At this time of year, I begin to look towards the winter as a time of depth, digging deep into my writing practice and values. We can't do this if we fixate on being endlessly productive and busy.

We often think of the states of oppression or alienation as being those in which we have no voice, are silenced. But I sometimes wonder if a much more insidious oppression and dehumanising form of alienation assaults us when we are in constant motion and noise. When we are always busy, pre-occupied in constant shallow chatter, distracted and fragmented by the fear of missing out and constantly reacting to every email and notification, we become so exhausted that we know we're miserable but forget how to change things. I keep coming back to this idea — the need to live by kairos rather than chronos, to find kinder rhythms for life that allow us to dive deeply in order to do the creative work, which may not be masses of work, and may be the opposite of 'productivity', of seeing our art, or even our lives as 'products', but which will be meaningful.

Why rhythm matters?

The most important perspective shifts we can make for everyday life is to realise that time, like so many things, is not an absolute. Time, like any other experience, is as qualitative as it is quantitative, if not more so. We can do many practical things to find a humane pacing, to recover from all the busyness, to be less distracted and more focussed on giving our time to what matters to us. But the most important thing we can do is to live by *kairos* not *chronos*. *Kairos* is 'the right time'; it is ripeness, it is the moment of truth. It has nothing to do with being busy or reducing life to frenetic 'to-do' lists. Moreover it has nothing to do with taking time to rest and relax only so that we can make ourselves get back up and work harder and faster. *Kairos* is related to those experiences when time seems to take on a different quality. We can't force it, but the more you take moments to breathe deeply, notice the small pleasures of a day, simply inhabit your day more fully and with more attention, then the more you'll find yourself living by *kairos*.

Some *kairos* moments will be the extraordinary times of life but many are ordinary moments of attention. When I take the time to walk outside and look at the stars, then *kairos* moments come about unlooked for. One amazing day with my two-year old grandson can contain more experience than a month spent busily rushing from one to-do list to the next. We all have things that have to be done, but when we prioritise putting some *kairos* into our lives then the quality of out lives and art rises.

When we face adverse conditions, we often pause and focus on the essentials. I had two examples of this last year. The first was a minor injury to a hip joint, which made me much less active and forced me to live more slowly for a couple of months, with the result that I got much more deep work done: I thought more, wrote more, read more. And, last autumn, I cracked a rib while travelling and had to learn how to take more care and how to alter the pace of each day. I've seen this in more serious situations, when people are spending time with extremely sick loved ones. Faced with emergencies, we find the time to focus on what counts, usually those we love or those passions that we are most motivated to achieve. It's salutary and humbling to watch. When it most matters, we give time to the essentials, yet at other times we claim this is impossible. I'm not suggesting we can abandon work indefinitely, but there are always ways to make the pace of life move to kinder, more human rhythms, which will sometimes mean huge bursts of energy and natural speed, but will never mean pushing ourselves to burnout, and often begins with shifting perspective to look at what we most cherish.

Why dive deep?

At the bottom of a river, way down, is sediment. It's the fertile mulch, thick with nutrients and with the small stuff that traps toxins, controls the speed of flow and affects water quality. What we are deep within, matters. Who we are is crucial and it comes from deep, deep down. If we want to be writers who push beyond boundaries and say something meaningful, if we want to be artists of skill and imagination, we have to get down into the sediment of ourselves. This isn't an exercise in ego and narcissism but in reaching deep within in order to in turn reach out to others.

Deep work is flow and crafting. It is listening within to your vision and passions, and without, to how you can reach out to the world. It is real attention. Deep observation is how we bear care about the world as writers. Deep conversation is a way of bestowing benediction; it is a rare anointing with absolute attention to the other, which is as generous as you can get. Depth is about awe and reverence and holding the world in esteem. Being present, focussed and attentive in a world of distractions is one of the hardest and most rewarding things we can achieve.

Time is much more than *chronos*. It is the quality and depth of each fully lived, truly awake and connected moment. And we don't find those moments when we are madly rushing or letting our attention fracture against a million unimportant demands. We may not be able to add a single hour to life by worrying, to paraphrase Matthew's gospel, but the depth is in our gift. Creative people, in this sense, have much more time. When we both curate our time differently and give it intentionally, things change. To give time to what you really care about, both requires and gives an enormous shift in perspective in which we begin to listen, look and pay attention as we never have before.

We live in a world that urges us to have more, do more, be more. There's a lot of 'life advice' that urges us to produce more, to work harder

Interlude 6: Writing the Light's Balance

and faster, that glorifies results, and celebrates 'crushing it'. But if we want to feel time-rich, being busy with things that ultimately don't matter will leave our lives impoverished, whether or not we have money in the bank. What matters is not quantity, but depth.

Most of us, and perhaps especially those of us who are passionate about art and values, want to use as much time as possible in ways that open us to experiences of awe, love and beauty. We long to tell and become stories that are meaningful. We quest for relationships that are transformative, whether with the people or the earth we inhabit. This is quality of life. This is experience that is beyond measuring in 'worth'.

We're sold things all the time. If your inbox is anything like mine it will be full of spam — a million offers of products and services nobody needs. Experience is something different. Investing in ourselves, whether through courses and books, through listening to music, seeing art, adventure or travel, can be deeply fulfilling and mind-expanding. But all too often we are being sold a lifestyle that costs our lives. Do faster cars or bigger mortgages make anyone more fulfilled? Far too much of life is infected by fear: fear of missing out is everywhere. There are adverts constantly warning you that you need these 3, 5, 15, 100 products just to make it through the next month. We don't have to give them credence.

I've been doing a great deal of thinking and reading about personal development for the last few years. On the surface, the aims of many writers in this arena and my own aims have seemed to be the same. But the more I read, the more often I notice a divide between my philosophy and the one underpinning much contemporary writing. On side of this divide are the goals of results, outcomes and productivity and on the other, the quest to live a beautiful, good and meaningful life. Superficially both quests have things in common:

- developing habits and behaviours that support the quest
- developing an environment that assists and supports the journey
- valuing and giving attention to transformative relationships
- taking constant small steps in the right direction
- putting who we want to be at the centre so that we behave as the person we want to become, act 'as if' until it becomes the truth
- learning to say 'no' and eliminating distractions to focus only on what is essential
- eating slow nutritional meals
- taking care of body and soul

Interlude 6: Writing the Light's Balance

- prioritising learning and reading
- being open to failing and constantly starting again, focussing on how far we've come rather than how far we have to go

and, crucially:

- taking a lot of slow, deep recovery time

But under this surface, there is a chasm between any philosophy that revolves around becoming a better producer and product over against one that wants to savour life in all its fullness. A life in all its fullness values:

- process rather than results
- life as a work of art and ethics rather than the product of a personal brand
- profound and pivotal experiences rather than scaling dizzy heights only to see the next peak and the next ahead waiting to be 'conquered'
- living in *kairos* time as a spiritual means of inhabiting the present with attentiveness rather than as a way to experience more, faster
- not attaching to outcomes because it's the journey that matters rather than a way to come at the results from another angle
- rhythmic living, rich in experience rather than 'crushing it'
- relaxation and recovery (whether it's walking, yoga, art, meditation, music...) as ends in themselves rather than ways to equip me to be more productive
- sometimes doing nothing because it's a good thing to do rather than as a way to refresh creativity in order to become more productive.

It is good to cultivate a lack of hubris, courage, humility, generosity, openness and attentiveness. But the vital question is what motivates us to become a different story. Is it

- celebrity
- money
- living harder and faster
- establishing our brand
- increasing our productivity?

or is it to live:

- rhythmically
- in depth
- profoundly
- pursuing transformative relationships
- a good life that is a work of art for its own sake?

These paths can look the same at first or even second glance, but the underlying values, ethics and philosophy is radically different. Do you want your life to be a canvas or a poem, a legacy of profound connections — or do you want it to be a product with a bottom line?

A great deal of living with a sense of rhythmic time and greater depth is about not being afraid. Don't speed up. Don't jump at every call to fear. Excise these voices from your life by every means possible. Determine to live a life that aligns with your quest, let go of the rest and you will find that you do have the time to give to your creativity.

When we are doing something we are passionate about, time takes on a different quality. Life, David Henry Thoreau tells us, is precious. We do not want to find ourselves at the end of it having not lived, but rather to enrich life by letting alone the things that would impoverish it; to live rhythmically and deep.

Journal exercise

'The light and the dark are of equal length':
>Where are the places of equanimity and harmony in your life?
>Where are the places of stress that are out of rhythm?
>How does each of these show up in and/or affect your writing?

'*Kairos* is 'the right time'; it is ripeness, it is the moment of truth. It has nothing to do with being 'busy.'
>Journal about a moment of connection, a moment when time seemed to both slow down and yet be full, and you felt you were in the 'right time', however ordinary or extraordinary the events.

What do you need to let go of in order to have a life of greater depth?

• Interlude 6: Writing the Light's Balance •

Ritual

Today, give yourself some time to do nothing. You can sit in a park or a woodland or by a river and just be. Don't making shopping lists in your head, don't read, don't listen to music or even meditate. Simply be. Do nothing. You might listen to the birds or the sounds of the room. You might day dream or let your mind drift. Be. Later, you might like to journal about the experience of doing nothing.

September 22

The lexicon of awe is one that is both beautiful and dazzling. And when we live rhythmically, and commit to depth in our lives and writing, we experience not only more equanimity, but also more moments of profound connection and wonder. For all writers, a sense of awe is a commitment not only to aesthetic practice but to embodying this lexicon in the writing we offer to the world and in the writing lives we lead. Having a sense of awe requires us to orient towards:

- epiphany
- connection
- eternity
- mystery
- questions
- self-forgetting
- surrender
- flow
- nature
- sacredness
- reverence
- blessing
- numinosity

This is not a religious orientation, but a spiritual one. It is an attitude towards writing and the writing life that respects our connection to all life. It is about seeing spirituality not as the opposite of material life but as the opposite of an egotistical life that places the 'self' at the centre of the universe. We are inextricably linked to every life, every atom. We survive or

Interlude 6: Writing the Light's Balance

expire together.

This attitude to spirituality is similar in Jung's thinking. For him, spirituality was not about institution and dogma, but about attending to the Numinous, those moments of profound emotion when we experience flashes of awe or epiphany that don't necessarily relate to religious belief or notions of divinity.

Why is this important or relevant to writers?

The writer's task is always so much more than providing mere content. When we write, we're opening ourselves up. Writing takes us into another space. We write to explore what it is to be human, to make meaning and to connect. We write to have an impact on the world and to imagine alternatives that might provide a new myth as humanity moves forward. We write to learn, to think, to research, to dig deep inside ourselves and to make art out of everyday, ordinary moments.

So much gets lost. There are too many moments to capture them all, to always find the meaning, but some of them make it. We write for the love of stories and because it's who we are. All of this demands a stance that is life-affirming, open to huge questions and always exploratory. This is the territory of awe. When our frame of mind is one of humility, questioning, courage and generosity then we are much less likely to believe we have the answers or to write didactically and with hubris.

Writing about the need for mystery in *Against interpretation & other essays*, Susan Sontag talks about how a trend of over-interpretation kills art and reduces it to content. This could equally be applied to so much of life. How we consume story, visual art, nature, the night sky or the universe can be cold, utilitarian and destructive. But we don't have to take this route. Instead art and nature can be viewed as nourishing, life-giving and there for us to interact with rather than gobble up. Nature and art are not content to consume, but presences to engage with deeply and open our minds to. Nature and art are to be experienced. More and more we need to see and listen and attend; to feel more. This is not a call to anti-intellectualism, but a call for a style of critical engagement that doesn't trample our souls.

How do we make works of art (whether visual, or of music or literature…) that resonate with or challenge experience, that are more, rather than less, real to us? When awe is at the essence of our writing, replete with openness, flexibility and all the vulnerability and risk implied, we are ready to enter a deep state of flow as writers. This can be a state in which we become another version of ourselves, one in which we lose ourselves to the tyrannical impulse to create. Writers know this self as a tyrant we welcome and want to inhabit as much as humanly possible. When we satiate this hunger for profound flow and depth, we feel ourselves to be beyond time and space. We become self-forgetful yet feel connected to all life. We often feel we are in another universe, one in which eternity and mystery fill us with a sense of awe. We can feel at once small in the scale of the universe, yet a part of all things. We can experience dizzy exhilaration and tranquillity in the same moment.

Seeing awe as essential to the writing life, placing writing in the stream of eternity with a recognition that we are fallible, limited and don't have all the answers, brings us full circle to how connected we are to all things. The more deeply we contemplate this, the more we are in awe of life itself and full of reverence. Oliver Sacks, an extraordinary writer and scientist, saw this with remarkable clarity and with a spiritual insight that owed nothing to narrow religious adherence. In *The Island of the Colourblind*, he writes about wandering in the rain forest of Rota in a state of reverence. Resonating with Thoreau's notion that nature is itself a form of prayer, he writes movingly about his sense of mystery and awe in the face of sublime beauty that dwarfs the human scale. We are pulled into a sense of eternity and an awareness that all life is connected. As the naturalist John Muir tells us, everything is linked to everything else.

When we forget about ourselves and our egos; when we surrender to such mysteries huger than our individual thoughts; when we enter states of flow in order to take risks, create or simply be, we feel this connection. Writing in his notebook, Walt Whitman says it like this:

> After you have exhausted what there is in business, politics, conviviality, love, and so on — have found that none of these finally satisfy, or permanently wear — what remains? Nature remains; to bring out from their torpid recesses, the affinities of a man or woman with the open air, the trees, fields, the changes of seasons — the sun by day and the stars of heaven by night.

The exact nature of this sanctuary can vary from writer to writer, person to person. Some of us are most inspired by forests, others by mountains, some by seascapes, others by the night sky. For Hermann Hesse, writing in *Wandering Notes and Sketches*, it is trees that most move and shelter him. Thoreau also had a great reverence for trees, seeing them as blessings on

Interlude 6: Writing the Light's Balance

being itself and as wordless prayers.

> ... alone in distant woods or fields, in unpretending sprout lands or pastures tracked by rabbits, even on a black and, to most, cheerless day... I come to myself, I once more feel myself grandly related... I suppose that this value, in my case, is equivalent to what others get by churchgoing and prayer. I come to my solitary woodland walk as the homesick go home. It is as if I always met in those places some grand, serene, immortal, infinitely encouraging, though invisible, companion, and walked with him.

Awe connects us to all things and also gives us a home, a sanctuary not in knowing it all and pride, but in the wide mystery of life where we ask the biggest questions, knowing that often we will have to go on living with those questions. The best writers ask enormous questions and stay with them. In the poetry collection, *A Responsibility to Awe*, Rebecca Elson asks the profound question of how we face suffering and our own finitude. A gifted astronomer and post-doctoral researcher into dark matter at Cambridge University, Elson lived with cancer for several years before dying at the age of 39 in 1999. Her extraordinary collection, collated after her death, not only contains her poetry but a selection of journal entries on her writing and on life. She asks huge questions — about meaning, about why, about the randomness of early death and the enormity of mortality itself. The only thing she objects to questioning is the value of our lives and we see this absolute commitment to the value of life and to the place of awe, even in the face of death, throughout the poetry.

All writers share this responsibility to awe. We are the story-bearers, the image-weavers, the poets, myth-carriers and witnesses in a world in which narrative has extraordinary power. How then can we be anything but ready, in humility and with generosity, to listen attentively to the universe and tell the stories of connection and epiphany that we hear?

Journal exercise

Begin with the line:

> The trees, fields, the changes of seasons — the sun by day and the stars of heaven by night...

• Interlude 6: Writing the Light's Balance •

And keep writing

Ritual

(This is similar to the ritual from August 1, but with some variations and a slightly different writing prompt.)

Close your eyes. Imagine a ball of white light, your own star burning at your centre, feel its energy and light in your belly. Let it begin to sink, into your abdomen, your thighs, your calves. Feel its weight and heat in your feet, pulling you into the earth. Sink with it, through earth, through rock.

Now feel the light, your star, rising, travelling upwards again, feet tingling with it, calves tensing then relaxing as it moves to your thigh, abdomen, belly. Let it rest a moment, bright light at your centre, then feel it move into your chest, spread over your shoulders, rise into your throat, pulsing with energy, warmth, before it travels upwards, taste it in your breath, breathe more deeply, as it moves into your nose, behind your eyes, the crown of your head, where it rests, shimmering. Then it moves upwards, pulling you towards the sky.

Slowly, when you feel ready, open your eyes and as you come back to the room begin to write with: *It's a clear autumn night and…*

Keep going.

September 23

The creative life is one that calls us to dive deeply —

- into the world we observe and care about
- into the bodies we inhabit so that we never forget our creatureliness and connection to all life
- into questions of meaning that might be insoluble but demand asking
- into our interior worlds
- and deeper still into the unconscious

The call of creativity is exhilarating and profound. It speaks not to the busy, bustling ego consumed by the dictates of 'content' and 'productivity', but to the self in flow who exists outside of time and space. This self is

Interlude 6: Writing the Light's Balance

not interested in dusting or deadlines, but is in love with awe and connection. This self is dangerous. S/he has a wild self-forgetfulness prepared to live:

- with mystery in the face of our finitude
- in solitude for sufficient periods to create deeply and in flow
- courageously, taking apart every assumption in order to make something new
- in vulnerability with the ever-present chance of failure
- imaginatively, colliding ideas and adjacent possibilities
- rhythmically, following the pulse of the work rather than deadlines and fixed outcomes

The creative life is intrinsically radical, laden with values that are the antithesis of consumption and speed and a utilitarian life. But it is also a life rich in soulfulness and renewal, joy and connection. All of this requires that we feed and water the creative life and there are, of course, many ways to do this. Journalling and reading widely and voraciously are excellent ways to give our creativity power and time. And activities that relax and renew us, also give us the space to nurture our interior landscapes and allow ideas to germinate.

But to lose our sense of time and satiate a hunger for awe and epiphany, we also need an ability to fall into reverie. The best writing constantly recreates nature and experience in new images and combinations of language that transport us. When our own writing soars and resonates with our readers then we are part of enchanting others into a state of reverie. How often have you almost missed a train stop because you were 'lost' in a book? How often has a meal been late or a room left unhoovered and dusty because the next chapter or poem was just too compelling?

Images and language are strong magic. Narrative and poetry conjure and entrance us. The imagination contained in stories, writing of any genre, is, the philosopher Gaston Bachelard believes, the most comprehensive idiom of all imagination. If we are to create such spells (bearing in mind that the etymology of 'spell' is rooted in tales and myths) then we have to know the state of reverie ourselves. Images are the realm of the soul (not a religious term for Bachelard, who was a humanist) but there are two kinds, he considers in the essay, 'Water and Dreams': those that only skim the surface and others that plumb the depths of being. Entering, or rising into this state of reverie, is not quite equivalent to

Interlude 6: Writing the Light's Balance

dreaming. As Bachelard notes, in *The Poetics of Reverie*, a reverie is hard to put into words, something also noted by William James. Yet Bachelard did consider that we can translate reverie into writing that dives into every sense and emotion.

In a state of flow memories and perceptions combine in new ways, we reach for the oneiric material of dreams and archetypes and allow imagination to reach deeply within. In this state, we hardly remember our own names. In this state we are not good company, but require solitude. In this solitude, soaring at great heights or diving into profound depths, extraordinary creativity takes over. Paradoxically, this state of mind, whilst requiring solitude, is far from being a state of disconnection. We feel the subjectivity of the world and all that is in it. Self-forgetful but connected to all life, what takes place is both deconstruction and construction. Imagination is a game of taking risks with old images, breaking and remaking them, combining them differently and surprisingly. Writing from reverie turns our works into invitations to extraordinary journeys. 'Come and breathe in these new images… Travel with these images to places you have never been…' the writing beckons, as we write it and as our readers engage with it.

This, of course, requires a good deal of upheaval. It invites our minds and souls to be mobile and supple, to be willing to fracture old ideas and images, live with doubt and negative capability and sojourn with mystery and risk. Changes will occur which might be catastrophic unless we are brave and flexible and humble enough to traverse the explosive imaginative power of reverie. But the promise is equally compelling: the openness and newness is utterly captivating. We are back again with that wild self-forgetting that is at the heart of our connection to all things and to joy. The pursuit of happiness can be an elusive goal, a creature likely to disappear in the hunting. Yet writers know how powerful the sense of fulfilment and deep joy can be when we are so far inside our creative flow that the world falls away.

Whilst this is powerful and heady material, it is not fanciful. Writers do not enter a state of reverie as an act of escapism; the imaginative language of heights and depths, the soaring sensation of otherness are always grounded and connected. In John Linton's *The Notebook of Malte Laurids Brigge*, he talks about how Rilke insisted that writers must immerse themselves in life — in nature, in many places, in objects — in order to be able to write a line.

How often has the universe suddenly answered. O my

things, how we have talked!

For a reverie to recur and make a difference, it must have substance. The inner world has to interact with the external world; a complex interaction in which the writer is herself re-written and transformed. We are changed by the stories we write. We embody our writing.

Journal exercise

'O my things, how we have talked!' (Rilke)

Choose an object — something precious to you. Make some notes on it using all your senses.

Why did you choose it? What is it about this object that makes you respond?

What stories begin to emerge?

What symbols or images come to mind?

Repeat this with another object, but this time not a precious object, choose something fleeting that catches your attention, perhaps something from outside.

Write a piece of prose or a poem that brings together the two objects.

This is an exercise in adjacent possibility (see Chapter 20), which is when two ideas get together to innovate; the kernel of one idea married to another to make something new. Keep the piece concrete — no qualifiers, sparing use of adjectives and adverbs, lots of strong verbs and nouns. Think of William Carlos Williams' aim to have 'no ideas but in things'.

Ritual

Find another object — something that inspires you, that is beautiful or brings memories or resonates with you in some deep sense and bring it into your writing space. Try to use it as a starting point for journalling over the next few days or just as a focus point before you begin writing.

Chapter 19
Tending the Creature

Writers can be cerebral creatures. By its nature, writing is sedentary and we spend a lot of time in our heads. But when the writing loses all sense of embodiment it becomes remote and ineffective. When we instead embody our writing it takes experience and offers it to the reader in ways that resonate. Our bodies matter. Despite being someone who will get so far into my own head I forget to move or go to the bathroom when deep in flow, I also know that his has an impact on my writing, however subtle. When I write after doing yoga, adopt a better posture and get up between sections to stretch or walk, the writing changes.

So how do we become more holistic as writers? We first have to replace the dualistic model of what it means to be human. The Cartesian split between body and soul, object and subject, self and world, doesn't serve us. We have to stop thinking of ourselves as discrete parts which we can separate. I *am* my body. My brain *is* matter. Ideas and mind are not even mine alone, let alone some kind of opposite of 'flesh and body'.

Throughout history many eminent scientists have glimpsed the fact that we are connected, not separate minds in discrete boxes. This includes Nobel physicist Erwin Schrödinger who was adamant that there is only one mind, and the distinguished physicist David Bohm has asserted this in similar vein. And whatever our model of consciousness, I am not two separate and opposite 'things'. That's not to say that we can't have meaningful conversations about 'soul' and 'spirituality' (whether as metaphors or as part of belief systems), but it is to assert that we are physical systems with emergent properties of thinking, values, consciousness. It is to assert that there is no ghost in the machine, but rather one integrated and exquisite animal with language and thought.

If we stop thinking of ourselves as compartmentalised pieces, some of which we can neglect, then holism is inevitable. So too is writing that is more embodied and a writing life that integrates the whole person. Which makes it beholden on every artist to attend to the body.

Chapter 19: Tending the Creature

I recently read the book, *The Body Keeps the Score*, by Bessel van der Kolk. It's a detailed and fascinating account of his work as a psychiatrist with people who've suffered extreme trauma. The post-traumatic stress disorders of his patients have arisen from extreme violence, abuse and involvement in wars. Many of the stories are harrowing and many of the patients appeared to be beyond help. Kolk also discusses less extreme trauma that nonetheless goes on having lifelong effects. People who are socially isolated and suffer childhood neglect, for example, can build patterns of feeling numb and never taking any pleasure from life in order to protect themselves from feeling future trauma.

Yet, far from resorting to extreme medication with antipsychotics, Kolk works on restoring the balance between our rational and emotional reactions. He is critical of many conventional treatments, exposing terrifying statistics, for example half a million US children and teens were prescribed antipsychotic drugs in the year he was writing. And between 2000 and 2007, the number of privately insured 2 to 5-year-olds on antipsychotics doubled. He is clear about how devastating PTSD or even less severe trauma and stress is for all health indicators, citing an extensive list of physical ills arising from emotional and mental suffering.

His treatments are innovative. Kolk argues for integrating trauma by turning it into a bad memory. This is the opposite of the usual Cognitive Behaviour Therapy, which makes patients relive trauma in therapy. Kolk concentrates on limbic system therapy, retraining the arousal system using breathing exercises, chanting and movement. And he maintains that ten weeks of yoga markedly reduces PTSD. Kolk also uses a range of other body-based therapies, like somatic experiencing to examine how thoughts and emotions register in the body. For example anxiety might be a crushing sensation in the chest that changes when breathing alters. He assists patients to access physical and emotional support from within relationships and uses rhythm, movement and touch (through massage) to help people feel intact, safe and protected, as well as utilising EMDR (Eye Movement Desensitisation and Reprogramming), similar to REM in sleep, as this lowers depression, activates creativity and simulates memory and trauma resolution.

Aside from being a fascinating, if hard-going, book, Kolk's work has widespread application. All of us have bodies that keep the score of our personal journeys. Writers, who —

- elucidate the human condition
- make deep connections
- detect the patterns of events and name them
- bring to light things that might otherwise remain hidden

Chapter 19: Tending the Creature

need to attend to the body, need to tell the stories rather than letting them knot us and misshape us. In the words of Macbeth:

> Give sorrow words; the grief that does not speak knits up the
> o'er wrought heart and bids it break.

Simply breathing well gives us a better heart rate and makes us less vulnerable to illnesses. Movement, particularly yoga and massage, make us more aware of ourselves as the soft bodied animal from which our writing comes. And walking, getting into the physical world, makes a world of difference to health and longevity, as well as creativity. Writers not only need an integrated view of self, but also need to attend to those selves with compassion. There are many ways to tend to the creatures we are, but some recur across the practice of multiple writers:

Walk and interact

From Thoreau to Nietzsche, Whitman to Mary Oliver, the list of writers who recommend walking is extensive. We need to get outside and walk. We need to lose ourselves in the senses. You may want to stop and take out the notebook you always carry and name what your senses bring you. You may want to go into detail, concentrate on a sensation or object or make notes on the emotions or stories that begin to emerge. Or you may simply want to experience the rhythm of your pace, the sensations unfiltered by words. Interaction with the natural world is transformative. We become more aware of ourselves as bodies, more appreciative of the world.

Reclaim nostalgia

As we noted earlier, the etymology of the word 'nostalgia' is from 'homecoming' and 'ache'. The body is our primary home and some of us are so out of step with our physicality that we forget this and need to return. All the grief and pain we experience doesn't simply get buried in the unconscious. It becomes toxic waste dumped for the body to deal with. We have to open this up, dig deep into ourselves in order to connect with others. And we do this by writing from the senses, from authentic, embodied human experience.

Direct your energy

Holistic as we are, it can be useful to direct our attention to the variety of sensation that body and brain give rise to. When we write from sensations, listen to the emotions and consider what interests, intrigues and fascinates us then the writing becomes whole and more lucid. Writing takes a great deal of energy so then we need to guard that energy fiercely.

Love your creatureliness

Too often, writers have a poor record when it comes to self-care. The drunken or drugged poet is a stereotype. Being dislocated from the body can lead to negligence or abuse. Perhaps we have bodies already keeping the score of traumatic memories, even if not as extreme as the PTSD Kolk writes about, but we have to redress the balance.

- Do we ask what our body wants or do we ignore and repress signs of discomfort, pain and illness?
- How will the mind and spirit continue to soar if the home is tumbling down?
- Do we fail to eat or even not go to the bathroom because we're 'too busy'?

Only when we see ourselves as body, do we begin to inhabit the present moment.

Nine Exercises in Coming Home

The etymology of the word 'nostalgia' is from two Greek words — 'homecoming' and 'ache'. It's about acute homesickness. When we begin to embody our writing, our concept of home becomes at once complex and simple. Home is the world we inhabit, connected to all things. Home is the body we live in and experience this connection through. Home can be the place we began life from or the pack on our back as we wander, but it always has the sense of security, belonging and being centred.

In the last section, the exercises looked at sense of place and how place can function in various ways within our writing, including as a character in its own right. In particular, 'home' is not only place, but the hearth-place, whether that's a portable stove in a tent or an Aga in a farmhouse kitchen. Home is elemental and existential. It is sanctuary and an extension of persona, but also feeds back into that persona. So these writing and journalling exercises move from the person to the place, both of which are home.

1. Asking the subconscious

As I previously mentioned, for a while now, I've been leaving questions for my subconscious in my journal last thing at night, which has resulted in more vivid and memorable dreams. Dreams are not just fanciful, but ways in which our unconscious and inner life communicates with the conscious. This exercise is based on a technique from Jungian analyst, Robert A Johnson, and I'd recommend his book, *Inner Work: Using dreams and active imagination for personal growth*.

i. The evening before doing this exercise, ask your subconscious a question

As soon as you wake up, journal about a dream. When you have an outline of the dream, take each of the images (an image might be a person, an object, a conversation, a colour, a place…) and for each one make a list of associations (this isn't a chain of associations — each association should be directly linked related to the image). You might prefer to do it as a series of diagrams radiating from the image.

Each image relates to your inner life. Not all the associations will 'click', but highlight those that jump out for you, that seem most relevant. If you dreamt about a loyal dog, what part of you is like that? If you dreamt of someone you dislike, what part of you is like that person? If you dreamt of a huge house stuffed with furniture, what associations do you get from that and how do these associations relate to your inner world, traits you have or are repressing, values and attributes in your life? Don't look for standardised interpretations. The important work is what is unique to you. From all of the associations, attributes, values, notions of what kind of personalities you have within, that you value or denigrate, how do you interpret the dream? Don't look for a ready-made interpretation and don't interpret until you have mined all the possibilities.

When you feel ready, ask yourself what the single most important insight of the dream is. If the dream seems to have multiple interpretations, write them all out — the physical act of writing will help you see which one 'clicks'. It's likely to be the interpretation that arouses the most energy and feelings or gives you one of those moments of insight — 'aha!' The right interpretation may be the one with some small clue that rings true (like a good literary plot device).

ii. Insight can remain abstract and easily not be integrated into life so journal about what you are going to do about your dream

The message might be to take more time to write; to be more grateful; to uncommit from activities that are draining you… Whatever it is, devise a small step towards doing it. Don't feel you have to declutter your whole house in a day. It might be a simple act like sending someone a card to show your appreciation of them. Check back with your journal about how you are making the abstract physical from time to time.

2. Minimalism for the soul

What are your essentials? Think about what most relaxes you; the activities or experiences that most excite and energise you; the people and values you most care about.

How are you prioritising those activities, experiences and people (including yourself) in your life? (Or not?)

What's the one step you can take today in that direction and how will you build on that each day?

3. Clearance to be unreasonable

There's a huge rise in minimalism and it's understandable. In a world of mass production and over-consumption, 'stuff' can start to weigh us down, even sicken us. Personally, I like the comfort of objects — books and ceramics, a vase of flowers, a beautiful Welsh blanket, but we all have things that we need to let go of, and these are not always physical, though sometimes this is a good place to start. When you start to realise, or let yourself admit, what most matters to you, it's an avalanche. And once you are on a quest, then you will find the way.

Imagine yourself taking an action that you know would help you live more in alignment with who you want to be and your goals. No matter how unreasonable it seems write as though the decision has been made, no matter how small or large, easy or terrifying this decision is. So:

i. Write about what happens next

How do you feel in retrospect? Are you excited, calm, ecstatic, filled with regret?

What is your next small step today?

ii. In what way do you need to be unreasonable to clear space in your life for your passions and growth?

Write a letter to yourself about why you need to remember to be unreasonable.

4. Dreaming, perchance to live

When we get clear about what matters, the conscious and unconscious start to work together to nudge us along the path we need to take. Remember to:

- Recruit your subconscious
- Journal relentlessly about what matters most to you
- De-clutter your life of activities that distract you from the who you want to be
- Be unreasonable
- Remember that 'No' is a complete sentence

Then write about:

What do you need to say no to in order to say yes to life?

What routines, habits and rhythm does your life need now in order to be the writer and person you want to become?

5. Your mark on the clay of the universe

To embody our writing and find our flow, we need less encumbrance, more space to breathe deeply and soar with imagination. To embody our writing, we have to know what matters. So journal on these questions, for your writing and for your life:

- What values do you need to live by? (Try to limit yourself to 6–10)
- What most motivates you?
- What sort of environment best works for you and how can you shape it?

6. You, the creature

What do you, the creature, love and need?

How do you embody your writing?

7. What ails you?

As I explored in Interlude 2, we all have bodies that keep the score of our personal journeys. In order to attend to our bodies we need to reach out to others and allow the stories of healing to arise. In the story of Parzival and the Fisher King, the healing comes simply by asking the question, 'What ails you?' The healing isn't about having the answers or solutions, but taking the time to see the other and care; to pay attention.

It takes a lot of courage to face our own pain or to dare to let someone else stop telling you 'they're just fine' and share their depths. It takes courage and a huge amount of kindness, which is a rare form of bravery and connection.

This is bold, embodied journalling:

What ails you?

Who else do you need to ask that question of and how will you listen?

8. The reclamation yard of the soul

This exercise was contributed by the brilliant poet, Lizzie Fincham. Lizzie led us through it at a masterclass workshop based at our home in North Wales.

She starts her workshops by asking one member of the group to get up and open the door so that our esteemed ancestors will bring us stories.

> First, describe the most far-flung or remote place you have ever been. Use all the senses.
>
> Second, describe *this* house, which is a house only briefly glimpsed, yet it's never left your imagination. Fill in every detail, even those you have to invent.

Third, describe *that* house, which is for you the ur-house, your original home however you conceive it (it might be your grandparents' rather than parents' home; it might be a best friend's home that provided sanctuary, but it goes a long way back in your story…)

Now imagine you are travelling with a friend. It's the end of a long, hot afternoon and you come across an Aladdin's cave emporium or yard full of antiques and junk. Your friend agrees you can run in and take a look but there is no legal parking and the owner is about to shut up shop. Inside, two objects catch your soul and you run from one to the other, the owner grumpily closing things down around you and your friend's anxious face outside worried about being double parked. Describe the objects. You can only take one. Which and why?

How do each of these places and objects figure in the reclamation yard of your soul and how do they resonate with one another?

9. Write yourself home

Remember, invent, dream — bring the night sky into your bedroom and the wild into your hearth. Be imaginative and interpret this in any way you want:

Write yourself home.

SECTION 5
WRITING THE SOUL

Chapter 20
Of Purpose, Quest and Craft

The notion that we are here for some pre-ordained purpose is a pervasive one. We're sold the idea that all we have to do is discover this one thing hidden deep in our souls to know why we exist. But the secret of 'what we are on earth for' is often elusive or turns out to be so general it becomes meaningless. Too often 'finding your purpose' seems to go hand in hand with generic slogans. And slogans don't translate into motivation or enable us to live intentional lives. How do we actually go about living 'to bring peace to the world' or 'to radiate light'? And if we were born to fulfil some god-given, determined goal, how come it's not obvious and clear? Why do we need to search for something that we are born for? I remain unconvinced that I or anyone else has been 'put here' to fulfil some need in the universe. So is life meaningless? Does it not matter one jot how we live and whether we are purposeful? Quite the contrary. This life is everything we have, it matters completely. But that doesn't mean we are puppets put here for some hidden purpose. Each of us makes meaning by the stories we tells about ourselves and the world.

Sometimes the stories we tell about ourselves and the world are not healthy. We tell ourselves we're not good enough, don't know the right people… Sometimes our stories can limit us. At their worst, we retell stories that make us more fearful. I grew up in a household where the saying, 'It's not for the likes of us' was more frequent than meals. ('It' being anything good in life, from holidays to hope.) Even when I moved to university, I carried those limiting stories with me. And later I had someone in my life whose mantra was: 'It can't be done'. And yet we know that neither people nor stories are set in stone. Stories communicate values, share mores and understanding, but they are still only stories. We can create other stories. In the same way, we can imagine ourselves different, make daily changes until we are different. We don't have to believe we have a mission planted deep in our souls for us to discover meaning. We can create purpose. So how do we go about it?

Creating purpose isn't an elite activity. Everyone can do it, but writers are particularly well placed, especially through journalling. Thoreau, quoted earlier, talks about going to the woods 'to live deliberately'. I don't live in woods, but at the foot of a mountain. It's rural, but not as remote as it seems. It's only a click away from the World Wide Web and a short drive to larger places. But, in this sanctuary, journalling creates a space where I can make sense of life. It's the place where I can be both realistic and optimistic or work towards crafting a story. It's the space where I can experiment, work out my values, discover my goals and create a vision for the future. Wherever we are, we can live deliberately and think deeply about passion and purpose. What is it that you love to do? What are you good at? What do you think the world needs? Where do those answers intersect?

I love new places, immersing myself in somewhere unknown. I love words and to write — novels, poetry, daily journalling. I sometimes believe I don't know what I'm thinking until I've written it down. When I'm writing, I'm in another space, lost in the trance of it. What are my skills? I'm a creative person who sees both the minutiae and structure in writing so I work well as an editor. I'm an enabler, a teacher and a performer. I'm organised, can hold a lot of disparate information in my head and I'm good at solving logistical problems. So running a small press and being a writer, editor and mentor work for me. How do I perceive the world? We live in a time when there is crushing pressure to conform. Too often the lowest common denominator grabs the most attention. There is too much mindless consumerism and way too much distraction. We sleepwalk into political and environmental disasters and there is fear of difference. We don't deal well with 'the other'. And yet there is also extraordinary generosity, resilience and honesty in the world. There is so much that gives hope, a great deal to celebrate. There are oases of imagination and courage. The world needs the right stories to survive.

So, I write writing courses and books and teach online and face to face to challenge the idea that our options are limited. And I travel to constantly renew that sense that life is bigger than we sometimes allow it to be. The novels I aspire to write are those that move and challenge readers. By this, I'm not talking about books that preach and browbeat. Rather, writing that is humane and extraordinary, that is never mediocre or bland. I recently read Anne Michaels' poetry collection, *All We Saw*, and it's a perfect example. The writing is exquisite. It's personal and poignant with stunning flashes of subtle insight. It makes a difference to have read it. I want to publish and write books that, like Michaels' work, believe in life without sentimentality and put a marker down for hope.

What do you love? What are your skills? How do you see the world and what it needs? Where do your responses overlap? Now set about creating your purpose.

Once you have a sense of purpose (and it's not set in stone, we are always becoming new stories) it will set you on your quest.

In the last section, we noted that 'to-do' lists can often be deadening and demotivating, whereas when we shift to living in the present and doing what is needful with complete attention, whether it's our highest passion or cleaning the bathroom, we are more motivated. We all have things we have to do and some of those things are routine and don't set the world on fire. But in addition to learning to live more in the present so that the routine things don't drain us, we can also limit those things that take far too much time and energy to little point.

1. Think about your use of time

We thought about this at length in Chapter 5, considering the mindset of the writer. Look at it again. Revisit the journalling exercise. Constantly ask yourself: What could I eliminate? What could I automate or streamline? What could I delegate? How can I put routine tasks into limited time blocks to give myself time? How can I say 'no' more often? (Something we talked about at length in Chapter 3). We all have the same amount of time each day, but how we use it makes the difference.

2. Think about why certain activities are important to you

We all have different goals, activities that are more 'quest' than 'to do'. It's sad that the pace of life often relegates these to the 'add-ons' that we hardly have any time for. But the more passionate we are about these things, the less we will find excuses for not doing them. We don't need huge reserves of willpower to do the things we love and usually we know what our passions are, but sometimes life becomes so stressful or muddled that we lose the sense of this. If this happens try journalling to dig into your motivation. This is a technique I learned from Benjamin Hardy:

> Think about what it is you want. Write it down and then ask yourself this simple question: 'What about _____ is important to me?'

If your goal is to work from home, then ask yourself the question: 'What about "working from home" is important to me?' Your answer might be something like, 'to have a more flexible schedule'.

You then put that answer into the previous question.

It's good to go at least 7 questions deep into this exercise.

Don't over think it. Let the answers come and move on and you'll find your thinking is much clearer than you imagined.

For me:

- Writing is the most meaningful and transformative activity I undertake. It's fundamental to how I reflect on life and connect with others. Becoming a different story is my life's work.
- Travel puts me in unfamiliar places and situations. This in turn stimulates creativity, writing, thought and deeper work.
- Family (including an extended family of close friends) makes my world make sense. These are the people who confirm for me that generosity is the way to live.

If we are clear about what matters most and why these things matter, we are more likely to live life as an exciting quest rather than a tedious to do list.

3. Think about building your life on values rather than 'oughts'

When we face a long list of things we have to do, resistance sets in. Life becomes drudgery sustained by a diminishing supply of willpower. Even if we manage to achieve everything on the list, we're not likely to take much pleasure or pride from it. When we manage our time by eliminating, streamlining, delegating, sharing, time blocking and saying no, we find we have 'more time'. When we know what we are passionate about and why, we release energy that is much more effective than willpower. And when we act from our deepest values rather than 'oughts' imposed on us from outside, then this energy increases beyond our imagining.

Living from values gives us this bigger vision, which comes from intrinsic motivation rather than from something imposed on us. As with goals, we will each have different value sets. I found the system attributed to Benjamin

Franklin useful — choosing thirteen key virtues and thinking about one each week through a year. But as the year progressed I found that some of the virtues didn't resonate with me as deeply as I thought they would and that there were important qualities that didn't appear on the list so, in the second year of doing this, I concentrated on a smaller list of more interconnected values that are more integrally linked to my passions and quest. Constantly refining our stories is, after all, one of the main aims of this book, so don't get stuck in a system that isn't helping you.

4. Think about taking time out

When you know how you want to live and why; when you are discovering and refining the values your life rests on, life becomes a quest rather than a mundane list of demands on your time. This is exhilarating and motivating and it demands that we redirect our energy to what matters to us. How do we do this?

i. We need to take space to think

I periodically reread Virginia Woolf's *A Room of One's Own* — it's an important text and the idea that we need a dedicated space in which to write is essential. I'm lucky to have a dedicated writing room in which to work. It has 26 years of past journals, all the books I've bought but still need to read, important texts that have informed my current thinking and my collection of poetry books. If you can't take a whole room, find a desk, a corner, a favourite table in a café, any space that you can call your own and where you can think and write.

ii. We need to create a mindset that helps us to focus

Whatever your daily commitments, journalling morning and evening can make all the difference. Five minutes of writing about how you envisage your future. Five minutes of reflecting on how you have used your time, lived your values, makes an enormous impact on how you see the world and interact with it. Take time every day to affirm and reflect and watch your world change. We have already considered the power of journalling in Chapter 10 and it's worth re-iterating that it's much more useful to think about your gains — how far you have already come — than about the gaps — how far you still have to go.

iii. We need time in other environments

Environment is crucial to our perspective. This is why travel is so important to me. It puts me into unfamiliar places and stimulates creativity, writing, thought and deeper work. If you can't leave the country, go for a long walk; swap houses with a friend for a week. Do something that shifts your perspective and in the unfamiliar situation you will find yourself having new thoughts.

When you begin to make these changes you'll find life is no longer a mundane to-do list, but a quest of your own making. But that doesn't mean the quest will be fast and your dreams will be delivered tomorrow. Quests trump a life of drudgery, but they are not quick and easy. You are setting out on the path of meaningful creativity, but it will require commitment, work and that you embody your passion, heart, mind and soul. Simply dreaming won't get you there. So how do we behave on the quest?

1. Be generous

As you set out on the quest, asking 'What can I give?' rather than 'What can I get?' is a better route. The fantasy-route is one paved with craving. We all want things, whether emotional, spiritual or material, but organising our lives around what the world can give us tends to lead to wanting more. It's not the way of satisfaction, deep work and meaning. The myth is that living our passion, whether pre-determined or self-discovered, we find the elixir of happiness while making millions. The reality is that a life built on dreams can sour. When we reverse the order, ask what we can give to the world, the passion is congruent with the sense of connection. And when we think like this, we become soulful writers who also know that work is involved.

Whenever we stop giving it's because we have entered into a state of fear and small-minded living. There's a wealth of research on how giving reduces stress or benefits health, but we don't need to reduce generosity to a crude transaction to know that it's simply the right way to go. Yes, generosity always returns to you, but it may not always do so in the ways you expect. That's not the point. Rather, quite simply, an intentional life of quest should be a generous one.

2. Push your skills

When we ask not only what we are good at, but how we can get better, we stretch our abilities. Deliberate practice and pushing our boundaries increases the flow of creativity. When we focus on our craft and on what we can give to the world, we develop a level of congruence, generosity and clarity that will stretch, challenge and delight us. What it won't do is allow our egos to run riot.

3. Make connections

A meaningful and fulfilling work life requires particular types of connection. The biologist Stephen Kauffman coined the metaphor of the 'adjacent possible' from his work on evolution. It is the space beyond the edge of current thinking where the collision of ideas (often from different areas) results in innovation. It's the space in which new ideas are possible and viable.

New ideas often arise from putting together existing ideas in new ways. The more we make connections, the more inventive our thinking. I've been teaching writing for the last twelve years and delivering mentoring for the last six, but as I work on a new project I find myself going back to draw on things I learnt in other fields. It's exciting to make such connections. The synergy of ideas from writing, education theory and theological metaphors is powerful. But it's also deep and deliberate work. And very often, we have to rely on an element of serendipity. If you are reading widely and giving your unconscious time to play with ideas, rather than constantly hunting them down and trying to force ideas to come, they will emerge.

And it's not only in the arena of ideas that we need to connect. We also need to make connections with people. People who always depend on others and give little or nothing are draining. But people who appear to need nothing, who go it alone, face a different sort of challenge. Sooner or later life throws a problem into the mix that demands we ask for help. If we've done nothing to build connections then being independent might seem less attractive at this point. In the same way that the collision of disparate ideas can result in innovation, when people connect and collaborate they are more than the sum of the parts. Collaboration enables us to be generous and outward-looking. It also builds a network of people who will help when needed. Being interdependent is far better than being either dependent or independent. Find other creative people or people you love being with, online, at occasional courses, locally or globally, but make the connections deep.

And we need to connect with the nature that we are part of. When we see ourselves as part of the flow of all life, we push beyond ego and our creativity soars.

4. Small experiments, tiny steps

You don't have to do it all at once. Instead of thinking 'overnight sensation', think about building knowledge and skill with patience. Try out small but important projects that make you create new value. Go for small steps. The Japanese concept of *kaizen* is a fascinating one. It developed as a way of making change to organisations and workplaces, but the thinking is useful for individuals. It involves tiny, incremental steps for constant and continuous improvement. There are days when it's an effort to write in our journal that we made the bed today or smiled at someone. That's fine. The increments build up. Every tiny gain creates momentum and affirms that we are keeping the promises we've made to ourselves; that we are keeping the faith.

5. Be extraordinary

When you focus on skills, put in the work, try things out, take tiny step after tiny step, learn from the results and make deep connections, you become extraordinary. When what you do is excellent and deep; when what you do makes a difference, people will gather around it. The numbers don't matter. It's about impact, whether for one person or a million, and whether you know it or not.

While I was writing this chapter the extraordinary poet and human being, W S Merwin, died. In one of his amazing poems, 'Berryman' Merwin explored the difficult but ego-busting, soulful truth that we often never know how good our work is or what effect it had. 'Success' is always double-edged. As soon as we start to think we've 'made it', we're lost. And when the benefits of success (what we 'have' as a result) loom larger than the behaviour that got us there, we're lost. The ego, full of hubris, hates not knowing how important our work is. But the soul, which is all about being connected and doing beautiful work whatever the outcome, thrills to it. Be extraordinary, then let it go.

Chapter 21

Who Will Make the Quest?

Writing the soul flows from setting our purpose, entering on the quest and being prepared to do the work along the way, one step at a time. This changes us; we become a different story. But whenever we make a quest of the soul, we will encounter lures along the way, siren calls that will lead us elsewhere, distractions that will dull the vision. To keep the vision alive and keep the promise you have made to yourself, you need to be the person who will make this quest and this can involve a lot of soul-searching, a lot of digging inside ourselves. So in this chapter, we'll consider this person, thinking about the baggage we all carry; the lures to become a brand instead of a person; the need for generosity, but not self-sacrifice and the ways in which we can embody and ensoul our values.

Anyone who thinks s/he has no shadow is likely to be living in delusion. To push the metaphor, in everyday life someone without shadow would have to be not simply thin, but transparent, without substance. Even a slender pole casts a shadow. We all have baggage, none of us is finished and perfect. Even the most contented of us has hurts from childhood or from society's prejudices and many of these wounds are repressed. There's a bit of Dr Jekyll and Mr Hyde in everyone; the 'nicer than nice' outer person concealing the dark. Maintaining this inner baggage takes a great deal of energy. And we find our buttons are easily pushed by people (real and fictional) who seem to have no problem expressing the traits we've schooled ourselves to repress. Those of us who have become overly compliant and unassertive may find ourselves disliking and distrusting people who are confident, for example. Alternatively, we may gravitate towards people who exemplify a shadow we are hiding, or even project that shadow onto those we are in relationships with.

Repressing our shadow sides is exhausting but letting the shadow run riot isn't a solution. So we are faced with the conundrum of whether we go on repressing our baggage or begin to express it, which might result in behaviour

Chapter 21: Who Will Make the Quest?

that is immature and destructive. What can we do instead? In *A Little Book on the Human Shadow*, the poet, Robert Bly, recommends meditating. In meditation we can allow repressed emotions to arise without throwing tantrums. Alternatively we might dialogue with our shadow, a form of active imagination, a technique recommended by Robert A Johnson in *Inner Work: Using Dreams and Active Imagination for Personal Growth*. We can encounter shadow in play — playing with it as a role or through creative activities; Bly also recommends simply walking, with all your senses open to the world and travelling, which puts us into the role of the outsider.

Of course, most obviously writers can dig into this baggage with words. We can journal, write poetry, write fiction, write articles, create… Writing takes us deep into the human condition and the more we shine a light on this, the more our own shadows will be worked on too. We can't constantly retreat from the shadow without consequences to our lives and to what we write, as Rilke expresses in 'Already the ripening berries are red':

> Already the ripening berries are red,
> and the gold asters hardly breathe in their beds.
> The man who is not rich now as summer goes
> will wait and wait and never be himself.
>
> The man who cannot quietly close his eyes
> certain that there is vision after vision
> inside, simply waiting until nighttime
> to arise all around him in the darkness —
> he is an old man, it's all over for him.
>
> Nothing else will come, no more days will open;
> and everything that does happen will cheat him,
> even you my God. And you are like a stone
> that draws him daily deeper into the depths.

The novel, *A Remedy for All Things*, is a book replete with shadow, both national and individual. To write it, I had to allow the darkness to rise up to consciousness. It is a book that invites hope, evolving identities and a new future, but along the way it grapples with political oppression, imprisonment, brutality, mental illness, suicide, loss… It demanded of me not only that I do a great deal of reading and research and plotting and planning, but that I got involved with the material. The story of *A Remedy for All Things* inhabited me.

I launched the book in Budapest. It felt appropriate to travel there via trains to Paris and Munich, in the season of All Hallows-All Souls-All Saints, when traditionally we think of those who've gone before us and those we've lost; when the everyday world seems to thin and the past reaches out to us. Unless we return with the shadow, not in a bag kicking and screaming, but integrated, we will go on perpetrating atrocities, producing the conditions that break individuals. And I am aware that I couldn't write the shadow without the journalling I do. The space where all the reflecting and writing begins to emerge into consciousness and be made bodily; the space where the energy of the shadow is eaten and nourishes the soul, feeds the next story.

But it isn't only our own baggage that whispers to us that the quest is useless. Sometimes it's the voices of the world that tell us, not that we can't do it, but that we have to force ourselves into conventions that crush the soul. Writers have to play a part in getting their work into the world, but in the eagerness to see our books find readers, it's tempting to overwhelm the writing with promotion. Does every author have to blog, spend hours on Facebook, run a website, tweet, be active on LinkedIn, Instagram and Pinterest, secure literary festival engagements, organise a reading tour and get promotional flyers printed, preferably before breakfast? Some of those activities might be useful or apposite for an individual writer. Blogging and building an email list of interested readers feel like the right fit for me, for instance. But the more worrying concept that underpins our anxiety about needing to be everywhere, doing everything, is that each of us ought to be styling ourselves as a 'personal brand'. This thinking makes not only what we write just another consumer product, but also makes the writer into a 'product'. So what's wrong with that?

Writers want to find readers. Even given that a lot of what we write never makes it into the public domain (journals, notebooks, aborted stories and poems…) somewhere along the line we may want people to engage with our words. Writers work with a reader in mind and communicate things that matter to them. If things go well, the end of a particular writing project might be a beautifully produced book that you want the world to know about. The book is a product and if you care about it you will promote it. The hope is that you can do so without getting distracted from your main purpose: being a writer. This might mean getting some expert help. Or it might entail finding ways to support your book that don't overwhelm you. It shouldn't mean that *you*, the writer, become a 'personal brand' and this is why:

1. We don't respond well to anything that has an agenda for us

Writing to John Hamilton Reynolds in 1818, Keats noted:

Chapter 21: Who Will Make the Quest?

> We hate poetry that has a palpable design upon us — and if we do not agree, seems to put its hand in its breeches pocket. Poetry should be great and unobtrusive, a thing which enters into one's soul, and does not startle or amaze with itself, but with its subject.

What is true of our writing is true of writers. We resist writers who do nothing but try to sell to us. That's not to say we should never try to sell, but no one likes to be sold to constantly. When writers are more 'brand' than 'person', they become both unattractive and counterproductive.

2. Authenticity speaks louder than sales pitch

If you don't love your book and care about it getting into the world, it's likely no one else will either. That doesn't mean you have to be in permanent marketing mode. Passion communicates itself. If you love what you are writing, care about what it stands for, write well and communicate well, the authenticity will shine through. At its simplest, promoting writing demands a transparency to the work that is infectious. You don't come across as genuine by being a brand. Rather, people soon tire of someone who hustles them, suspecting that a person who packages herself is little more than:

> a poor player
> That struts and frets his hour upon the stage
> And then is heard no more. It is a tale
> Told by an idiot, full of sound and fury,
> Signifying nothing.
> (Shakespeare, *Macbeth*, Act 5, Scene 5)

3. You're a person, not a commodity

Being a personal brand is about creating yourself as a 'package' that gives a particular impression. It's a static image that limits you and needs to be constantly maintained. Of course, we all present ourselves in a myriad of ways; the story of the self is fluid and we have many roles. But the notion of the brand has an 'acted persona' at its heart. It creates an image that appears 'on stage' but which may not be congruent with our values or our writing. What matters most in establishing a brand identity is self-promotion. The self becomes a commodity and not necessarily an honest one.

4. You're an individual, not a thing

A brand is an object that is perceived in a certain way; not simply the product in itself, but a whole complex of product, logo, promises, expectations and lifestyle allusions. That's not my definition of a writer. A brand can also be a mark left on property — it's a mark of ownership; a practice associated with cattle or slavery. A branded item is a commodity bought and sold. That's definitely not my definition of a writer. Don't be a brand, be yourself — be honest, be passionate, have values you are zealous about and want to share, tell the world what you do and keep your soul. Don't become a brand, become a different story.

The more we work with our shadows, the more we ignore the distractions to become a brand or commodify our creativity, the more generous we are likely to become. But the quality I return to most often and which seems to me to be the most fundamental is generosity. I'm not talking about having pots of money to give away, though that might be a factor for some, but something deeper. We can be generous whether we are wealthy or in financial poverty. The point is the giving, whether it's of time, skills or resources. But if we are always giving, doesn't this lead to self-sacrificing? How can we be writers who say 'no' to protect our writing and yet be givers?

Self-sacrifice isn't about caring. What we give to demonstrates what we care about, but what we merely 'give in' to shows a lack of self-respect and creativity. Sometimes we fail to find a solution with another person, whether it's a child or a colleague. Sometimes life gets in the way and we compromise or simply put the other person's needs first. It happens. But when we end up self-sacrificing on a regular basis it's a negative signal for many reasons.

1. Self-sacrificing cuts creativity dead

If you've spent hours trying to find a solution to no avail and you're too exhausted to go on, giving in might seem like the only way to cut your losses. But if you give up early in a negotiation, then you abort the problem solving skills you and the other person might have employed.

2. Self-sacrificing is a path to bad feeling

Regular self-sacrificing builds resentment. A person who always gives in might seem 'fine' about it, but over time this kind of self-negation eats away at us. It poisons the atmosphere of being solution-oriented. Chronic self-sacrificers often become passive aggressive manipulators. They might say they 'don't mind' what the other person decides and claim to be happy to go along with anything, but at the same time, they often put others in the position of having to guess at their needs rather than being open and honest about them.

3. Self-sacrificing is a sign of fear

Fear paralyses us. Living out of fear keeps us living small, timid lives that are so much less than their potential. People who always self-sacrifice are likely to be people-pleasers who live in terror that not doing what someone else wants will result in the other person not liking them or getting angry. But no matter what you do, not everyone in your life will like you. You are not responsible for controlling other people's tempers. Moreover, a life completely devoid of conflict is likely to be one in which issues are being repressed. And that way all kinds of suffering lies as we discussed when considering the shadow.

4. Self-sacrificing puts others in your debt

When you renege on your self-care and needs and make it obvious that you are doing so, the other person owes you. The other person has to be 'nice' to you because you gave them what they wanted. The other person has to like you, never be angry with you and feel grateful, because it's only 'fair' when you've done so much for them... Self-sacrificing in this way is neither rational nor realistic. If you give so much of yourself that there is no room for others to give in return, they are likely to feel less comfortable around you. They are likely to feel undervalued because there is nothing left for them to contribute. And far from never feeling angry with you, people can feel they are being dumped with a lot of emotional baggage by self-sacrificers.

Collaboration always trumps sacrifice. Unschooling my children taught me that at all stages of life, self-sacrificing is a route to bad feeling. It sabotages creativity. We have to take ourselves seriously if we are going to do the same for others. Hillel the Elder is reputed to have put it like this:

> If I am not for myself, who will be for me?
> If I am only for myself, what am I?

When we collaborate with others, everyone can give and take. We can offer our creativity to whatever problem or issue we are sharing and act without fear and without feeling indebted. Collaboration benefits our creative thinking; sense of self-worth and usefulness; optimism and learning. And collaboration doesn't preclude those occasion when the other person simply needs to ask for something, whether it's physical resources; attention; information or time.

Giving isn't about negating ourselves out of fear of conflict or because we're too lazy to spend the time finding a solution. Generosity, unlike self-sacrifice, is not about exploitation or using giving to manipulate others but about a shared bond that we want to honour. It might be a remote bond, as when we give to a cause that is far away from our own lives, but resonates with our common humanity. Or it might be a direct bond with someone important to us. At its best generosity is about empathy, compassion and a delight in the value of others.

And, like all good qualities, generosity creates win-win situations. The generous are apparently more healthy and certainly more satisfied with life. If self-sacrifice comes from a fearful mindset, generosity is the opposite. I recently observed someone who finds it hard to give. She pales at the thought of letting go of small amounts of money — it's visible — a look of distress, hunched shoulders, tension. She's afraid of 'not having' and it makes her stressed and unhappy. Generosity, on the other hand, acknowledges that resources are fluid. In the words of Shakespeare in *Romeo and Juliet*:

> My bounty is as boundless as the sea,
> My love as deep. The more I give to thee,
> The more I have, for both are infinite.

Instead of having a mindset in which everything is scarce:

- there isn't enough time to give any away
- I can't afford to help, I'm not rich
- I don't want to listen, I've got my own problems
- generosity reassures us that
- time is about how you decide to spend it — we experience it as qualitatively 'more' when we make deep connections
- there is always something we can give
- giving attention builds bonds and is more likely to make other people listen to you in turn

Generosity is crucial to a culture of creativity. Being closed to others or self-sacrificing are bo th ways to kill creativity while generosity does the opposite. This is vital for writers or other artists. A great deal of the time, we create alone. But we rely on others to edit our work, review our novels or articles, read what

Chapter 21: Who Will Make the Quest?

we've put into the world. We need communities of positive critics and engaged readers. We need to value the creative work of others as much as we want our own to be valued. I'm fortunate to belong to an extended community in which so many authors are givers. Their generosity is humbling and salutary. Generosity is a largeness in the way we think, live and create.

- It assumes that life is good and plentiful.
- It is a refusal to live by fear.
- Generosity is good for your emotional and physical well-being.
- It's an act of hope and optimism.
- It's collaborative.
- And it's creative.

None of us need to be self-sacrificers, but we can all be givers.

As we continue our writing quests, we'll need to draw on many virtues and values to keep the promise we've made to ourselves. As I mentioned in Chapter 20, I've been experimenting with how I integrate virtues into my writing life. 'Virtue' is a word we don't hear a great deal. There's an anachronistic ring to it. It can also sound smug. A problem with over-focussing on self-improvement is that it can make us seem remote, self-satisfied and self-centred. An irony if we're setting out to be kinder or more patient. But rather than focussing on how 'I' can be more virtuous we can simply take small steps to do something that makes a difference. The first step toward virtue is to act as if you have that quality. Who we are is fluid. We don't come written in stone. Humans are adaptable. The environment we live in makes a huge difference, as do the choices we make. There are things we have little or no influence over in life, but we have the capacity to change, to become the person we want to be. One of the joys of being a storyteller is that it's not only about fiction, I can also write myself. But it has to go further than narrativising — my journal is a good place to plan and reflect, but it also has to translate into action.

When I spent a year journalling about and trying to put into action thirteen virtues, inspired by Benjamin Franklin, who chose 13 virtues and focussed on one each week. I liked the idea of revisiting each quality and these are the virtues that emerged for me over several journalling sessions:

1. Generosity

We discussed this above. For me, it's a deep and joyful mindset that allows us to be enabling, empowering and encouraging without taking away the self-respect of others. And when we are generous we feel more optimistic, lighter, more rooted and connected.

2. Abundance

When I was in ministry I once failed to get a job I was interviewing for because when asked for my favourite quote from the Gospels, I didn't give a verse on converting the 'heathen', but replied:

I came to give life, life in all its fullness.

I don't have a religious faith now, but that quote is one of many that stay with me. Life is short and precious. To live from a sense of fullness is an act of hope and a blow against despair.

3. Consistency

There's no point being generous one day and mean the next. We are much better making tiny steps, one day at a time, to build consistency. Consistency has a bad press. Oscar Wilde called it the 'hallmark of the unimaginative' and Ralph Waldo Emerson called it the 'hobgoblin of little minds'. So this one needs a caveat. I'm not talking about inflexibility or refusing to be adaptable. Change is crucial. Change is a sign of life. But there is a value in others knowing that we mean what we say, that our promises are trustworthy. And there's a value in keeping the promises we make to ourselves. And the things we persist with shape us.

4. Faith

Just as abundance builds on generosity, so faith builds on consistency. You don't need to believe in an unchanging essence at the core of every person to keep faith with yourself and humanity. Rather, as Sartre proposed, we can take responsibility to shape our life and actions. Faith is another blow against despair.

5. Attentiveness

It's not enough to show up, you have to focus. If you are playing with your children in the park, you can't be texting on your phone or taking work calls. If you are listening to a friend who is going through hard times, you have to commit to truly listening. If you are working on a creative project, you have to push the boundaries of your skills and give it all of your attention. Attentiveness is about being where we are without reserve. It's about the moment. When we are not paying attention, things go wrong.

6. Letting Go

In a busy noisy world we can only pay attention to the few things that deserve our undivided attention if we let go of all the distractions that keep us fractured. There are so many things we don't need, but especially:

- negative thoughts that mire us in the past
- limiting beliefs about ourselves and others that make life smaller
- the distraction of constant technology (unplug for a period each day, a longer period each week or month)
- masses of stuff — I'm not a minimalist, but when my environment is full of clutter it starts to overwhelm

7. Creativity

To write, to cook, to make, to give meaning to a space, a day or a moment, to have a vision — these are lifeblood.

8. Gratitude

The deep sense that life is valuable and the ability to mark it and celebrate it is transformative. When we acknowledge how much good we have in life, we become more open and flexible. Sometimes life is dark and challenging, but people who experience thankfulness also tend to have more empathy and emotional resilience. The universe gets a lot wrong but, whatever the context, how we respond always makes a huge difference.

9. Courage

A couple of years ago I went to a conference on crowdfunding. Another conference was going on in the same building with an inventive filmmaker who is adamant that we can all break through limiting beliefs. He demonstrated this by giving the members of his class the chance to walk barefoot on broken glass. And he came into our conference to ask if anyone wanted to join in. It was an extraordinary and powerful experience.

So many of us do courageous things all the time but don't notice how brave we are. We travel, give birth, start new careers in strange places, resolve not to stay in jobs that are crushing our spirits. Walking on glass wasn't the most courageous thing I've done, but it focussed my attention on this quality. Courage is foundational. If you are going to be grateful, it will take courage. If you want to create, it requires courage.

10. Openness

This might also be 'flexibility' or 'adaptability'. To be open to new places, truth, people and experiences. To be open to life takes courage, creativity and faith. It makes life richer. It's a quality highly-prized by Rainer Maria Rilke:

> … only someone who is ready for everything, who doesn't exclude any experience, even the most incomprehensible, will live the relationship with another person as something alive and will himself sound the depths of his own being.

11. Humility

This is not Uriah Heep's variety of humbleness, which exists to draw attention to itself. Humility is at home with quiet, strong self-esteem. When we're comfortable in our skin we don't need self-aggrandisement. Humility shouldn't be about ego. It's a hard quality to focus on. The act of thinking about it tends to distract from the aim. But it is possible to have a week thinking about others in your life, giving them some of that precious and undivided attention.

12. Humour

There are urban rumours that children laugh around three-hundred times a day whilst adults might laugh less than twenty times. Even if this is false, we can all

Chapter 21: Who Will Make the Quest?

use a bit of levity. Humour goes hand in hand with civilised society because it's a way of speaking the truth.

13. Passion

Is passion a virtue? It should be.

- to live deliberately with purpose and belief
- to care about justice and dreams
- to be proactive, not reactive
- to live each day awake and on fire

I go back to Thoreau:

> I went to the woods because I wished to live deliberately, to front only the essential facts of life…

Life is a gift, which brings me full circle — whatever else, be generous…

And finally —

What would your 13 qualities be?

Would it be useful to focus on each one for a week during the next year? I found after a year, I wanted to make changes and narrow the focus, but it was a great place to start.

Interlude 7

Writing the Darkness

This interlude is a chance to take time to think about our needs for flow, silence and solitude. It's planned to be used around the end of October to early November when the trees are becoming bare; the light is shortening and soon it will be winter. If you are in the southern hemisphere this would fall in late April to early May and your interlude in October/November would be 'Writing the Bright Fire', found in the Section 3.

October 31

Writing takes extraordinary persistence and concentration. We have to give it an extraordinary level of attentiveness, which is so deep that it becomes almost prayer-like, a kind of consecration. Aldous Huxley, borrowing from William Blake, described it as the moment the doors of perception open; James Joyce called it epiphany. There is a sense of touching the Numinous when we get into flow as writers, or in any art. In *A Sense of the Mysterious*, Alan Lightman describes the state of flow as a mixture of excitement and weightlessness, a state of exhilaration that is 'without ego'. When we find ourselves in flow we can be overtaken by huge bursts of creativity that pour out of us in such a way that when we look back we wonder who the writer was. We find ourselves reaching for images, compressing emotion into language, constructing sentences that lead one to another with ease and elegance. As we attend deeply, unaware of anything else, we make meaning.

Some writers can do this anywhere and some of us can do it in unexpected places some of the time. I've had experiences of being so far inside what I'm writing that a whole train carriage can slip away from my immediate consciousness and I'm in danger of missing even the most familiar of stops. But to have sustained, deep periods of flow often requires solitude and many notable writers, such as Susan Sontag, agree. Some writers are deeply lonely. Virginia Woolf wrote poignantly about a gnawing sense of loneliness, not in solitude, but in company. And in his (recorded) acceptance speech of the Nobel Prize for Literature, Ernest Hemingway talked about the loneliness of the writing life. But flow is not this sense of suffering, whether alone or with others. Rather, it is a sense of entering another state of mind. This is an extract from my journal about one of those flow states:

> It's midnight and the house is cool and quiet. I tiptoe to my desk and begin writing the scene that won't let my mind rest. I lose all sense of time, the fact that I have meetings in the morning or people arriving who will expect clean bed linen. At that moment, all I care about is a maze deep in the countryside of Roscommon and the young woman whose life revolves around it. This is all that exists. The scene emerges and I'm exhilarated and exhausted, but not guilty. This is my quest, my heartbeat and soul. This, above all, is what I am responsible for. Perhaps I'll ask my guest to make the bed with me tomorrow. It will be fine. I've kept my promise to my art.

Flow in solitude can feel risky. It leaves us wide open with only our own resources to fall back on, but it is also a fertile state, where we can become self-forgetful and make surprising leaps of imagination and creativity. Whilst allowing us to forget ourselves as much our distractions, solitude also allows us to develop a distinctive voice as writers. In *Daybreak: Thoughts on the Prejudices of Morality*, Nietzsche talked about needing solitude to write so he could really think as himself. And Eugène Delacroix counselled writers to 'Seek solitude'. Elizabeth Bishop was also a proponent of solitude for honing the creative voice, as was the artist, Louise Bourgeois. And writing about solitude as the ground of imagination Keats claimed:

> ... my Solitude is sublime. ... The roaring of the wind is my wife and the Stars through the window pane are my Children.

Solitude —

- frees us of distractions, especially if we are willing to turn off our phones

- allows us to find and maintain a state of flow
- allows us to develop distinctive voices as writers, which is not to say any of us are 'self-made' or without influence, but that we also need to step back to see what our contribution might be
- makes us confront ourselves and then forget ourselves so that we return to the world as a different story

Most of all, solitude is about renewing our connections — to the world and to others. It is not an act of running away, but of grounding ourselves. When we embrace solitude, the self-forgetting of flow puts us beyond the clutches of pride. We more often emerge with work that we hardly feel we can take credit for. We tap into something living rather than become individualistic creators. Similarly, solitude puts us beyond despair. In the cacophony of everyday life we can so easily become jaded and exhausted. In this state we do poor work and get increasingly despairing. Solitude offers another way.

Journal exercise

What are your experiences of solitude?

How does it differ from loneliness?

What inner voices do you need to listen to?

What are they saying? Write a piece of prose or poetry in which the natural world and your world flow into one another.

Ritual

Find a time to be completely alone today or as soon as practical. What happens when you are alone?

Write a piece that begins: 'This is why I go into solitude…'

November 1

Our finitude is a constant source of fear, yet it is also one of the things that give life meaning; the brevity and preciousness of life go hand in hand. In this short span, not only of individual lives, but of our species, we often yearn for more, we long for eternity, for infinity. The ache for something that is permanent is a subject the physicist and novelist Alan Lightman has written about extensively. Why is it that we want absolutes and fixed certainties in a universe that is mutable? Perhaps the longing for the infinite is a yearning for meaning, that we mistake permanence for significance and value. But we can find meaning without an appeal to eternity as Camus shows in *The Myth of Sisyphus*.

Choosing life is an act of making meaning and when we make a mark on the clay of the universe, we enact that meaning, particularly through art and narrative. Life is precious and fragile. We get one chance to make it count. Significance is not about living forever or infinity, it can be small marks on the page of time. And neither is significance about money or fame or Twitter followers. What matters is facing our finitude without despair, making small but profound differences. Our one precious, fragile life can be an act of being defined by others or an act of creation; what Camus calls his 'revolt, freedom and passion'. The latter is brave, but it's also an uncertain road. We have to be open to outcomes we had never imagined, to going into the dark. We have to have the courage to extend our boundaries of the self into unknown territory. We have to be prepared to let go, to lose ourselves in creativity, to make ourselves vulnerable to what life offers, to allow ourselves to be surprised and to take more delight in the path than in any fixed outcome. When we choose to throw off the stories we've been told and set out with warm and generous hearts, epiphany, even if it doesn't look as we'd expected it to, awaits. And when, as writers, we wield language and story with courage and generosity, then we have the mightiest tool for wrestling meaning from reality.

Journal exercise

As a writer, what language will you use, what story will measure your life?

How does finitude affect how you write and who you are?

In what ways does your writing and your life express your own revolt, freedom and passion?

How can you leave the door to the unknown open in your life and your writing?

• INTERLUDE 7: WRITING THE DARKNESS •

Ritual

Write a story or a poem that deals with notions of mortality and/or 'the unreasonable silence of the world.'

November 2

How do we face fear, particularly when that fear is about our art and creativity? In a letter to his brother Theo, Vincent Van Gogh writes about fear: fear of the blank canvas, but also of the 'infinitely meaningless, discouraging blank side' that life can face us with, and which can only be countered when a person 'steps in and does something.'

In one of many extraordinarily poignant letters, Van Gogh raises the question of how we face the terror of creating at the point when there is nothing, but also opens up wider existential questions of fear. It brings us back to the point that courage is foundational, especially if you want to create.

We all get stuck in patterns that don't help us to live up to this strength, passion and courage. Too often, what we feel we know about ourselves is not our strengths but our weaknesses. I'm much more keenly aware that I struggle with mornings than that I write in deep flow late at night, for example. Or we goad ourselves on with willpower — to diet, to exercise, to write 1,000 words a day, then fail and feel helpless and lacking in both capacity and fervour. But we can change. Breaking patterns involves not conformity to what it takes to be 'successful' (however that is defined) but digging into what motivates, delights and inspires us. There are times when breaking patterns does not require huge shifts fuelled by diminishing reserves of willpower but small, consistent steps that compound into huge transformation. Changing habits can work like this.

But, of course, some changes are enormous and radical. They involve such comprehensive breaks with what has gone before that it would be strange if they did not scare us. The opening of Dante's Inferno is one of those terrifying moments of paradigm shift:

> Midway upon the journey of our life
> I found myself within a forest dark,
> for the straightforward pathway had been lost

· Interlude 7: Writing the Darkness ·

As in life, so in writing. We have to be prepared to look at the blank page, the well-worn path and to 'violate' it. It is terrifying and it's so much cosier to hide in our excuses, to believe we are incapable or have no alternative or that it's our 'nature' not to be able to change. This is fear talking and so often fear works by being amorphous. Fear is vague, it's the material of what 'might be', of poorly formed yet ubiquitous imaginings. Fear is not what will happen but the worst thing that could happen. It is dire anticipation, as Mark Twain is alleged to have put it:

> There has been much tragedy in my life. At least half of it actually happened.

And yet the blank canvas or the path of life lost in the dark forest also represent the chance to make something new. This is going to take focus and energy. It is likely it will involve some extremes of emotion but it is also the way to create and the way towards a life that is richer and deeper. It will certainly involve confronting whatever terrifies us, whether it's a blank page or leaving a long-dead marriage; whether it's a huge creative challenge or moving across the globe. We live in fear of so many things: failing, having nothing to say, what others will think of us, what we think of ourselves, loss and grief… and yet we also know we do not have to live cowed by fear. The page or the screen may stare back at us blankly. The huge decision sits in the pit of our stomach, waiting. It is both terror and our moment of chance. Think of the beginning of Creation in the Judeo-Christian tradition.

> the earth was a formless void and darkness covered the face
> of the deep
> (Genesis 1:2)

In Jewish Kabbalah the *Chalal Panui* or empty space is the primordial vacuum in which the infinite God creates a finite universe and it this that explains how God is able to be both present within and absent from in the world. Even God faces the blank page. Creation begins by first making that space and only then by marking it. The origin of any act of creation is not the initial mark but a kind of self-forgetting, a withdrawal of ego so there is space for whatever comes next. After this comes the mark, the act of breaking, changing and transforming, which in turn marks us as finite but also free. It's hardly surprising that we feel fear and yet perhaps the more afraid we are the surer we should be that we're engaged in something transformative. Whether the fear is of the empty page or living alone or

Interlude 7: Writing the Darkness

leaving a secure but soul-crushing job, it can be as motivating and stimulating as it is paralysing but only if we trust ourselves.

Too often we hide instead. We might hide behind excuses or increasingly unlikely anticipated scenarios. Or we might put barriers between ourselves and the creative act, the act of marking or changing that feels radical. In *The Courage to Create,* Rollo May talks about how tools and mechanisms (technology) can act as barriers between ourselves and our unconscious world to stave off fear. Whether your hiding place is an app; a conviction that you don't have the skill or can't learn it; a worry that you don't have the time; or a thousand and one other voices that rise up in us, keeping us small, the only time to start, the only time to make the mark that breaks into the terrifying blank space, is now. We can change.

Journal exercise

What story do you want to write? What story do you want to become?

What are your hiding places, or the voices that prevent you from starting or continuing?

What scares you about your own creativity?

'We have to be prepared to look at the blank page, the well-worn path and 'violate' it.' (Van Gogh) What does this mean to you in your writing?

Where do you need to make space, clear some emptiness and voids for the creativity to flow in to?

Ritual

This is a time of lessening light, of going into the places of darkness and solitude in order to germinate the seeds of creativity, not as negativity or from fear, but in order to wait on ideas and give ideas the time and nurture they need. It is to sit by the fireside and remember, to tell stories of those who have paved the way and of what might be.

What story do you want to remember? What story do you want to leave in legacy? Write them.

INTERLUDE 7: WRITING THE DARKNESS

November 3

We have confronted our need for solitude, perhaps especially powerful at this season when the world seems to withdraw and there is migration and hibernation. We have faced our own finitude and the fear of the blank page, which is redolent with existential metaphor. And now we are going to take a journey. Traditionally this was a time when the veils between worlds were thought to thin. The transcendent, for good or ill, leaks into the imminent. Whatever our faith position or absence of religious belief, we are all affected by the light dimming, by shorter days and longer nights, by cold and shadows and the metaphors for our writing are rich.

Writers and thinkers who are enlarging the imagination and asking profound questions of direction and myth are deeply aware of the power of story. To develop a personal myth, a way to live in the world as writers, involves all of who we are and want to become. It involves finding the Numinous in the everyday and fully inhabiting our bodies to be present to each moment so that we can observe scenes and objects, and make emotional links that will allow story to emerge; the story we are writing and the story of self.

In *Negotiating with the Dead*, Margaret Atwood concludes that in writing story we make mythic journeys. We go into the Underworld, taking our offerings and return with treasures. When we write story (including poetry or nonfiction) we are not just working on the book or the project, we are writing ourselves. Writing and life resonate. We both write our inner world into the outer world and offer an embodied experience that speaks some truth. We participate and emerge changed. All writers must 'negotiate with the dead', with our influences and forbears. Atwood notes that both prose writers and poets use the metaphor of going into the dark to retrieve their stories. She develops this into going into the Underworld where the dead have the stories that writers want. Writers plumb the darkness to bring back treasures.

Sitting in Pohárszék, our favourite café in Budapest, on the last day of November a year ago, before leaving for a night train to Munich, I gazed up at an elegant apartment block opposite. The late nineteenth century building has a beautiful doorway; a huge arch of glass covered in wrought iron. At the top of the building, someone was switching on lights in an apartment that spread across four elegant windows. The only view was of beautiful globe light fittings and the amber glow of the lights. Yet in that moment, I'd invented a whole life within that flat. What is it about looking in at other people's lives? This was the merest glimpse: lights on a freezing

Interlude 7: Writing the Darkness

evening in winter from which I conjured comfortable sofas and fluffy blankets, stimulating books and soothing music. I summoned a life of elegance; cultured, intellectually rich and harmonious, all from a few lights and shadows. In Venice a couple of months earlier, out walking with my husband, we'd glimpsed an apartment overlooking a canal and bridge. The walls were richly coloured. There was a cat in the window. Tiny details. Yet enough for us to picture a bohemian life, artistic and joyous.

Looking in is particularly alluring at night. The contrast between the evening dark and the lit room draws eye and imagination. A stacked bookcase, a deep indigo wall, a plum velvet curtain, a candle or a cat and we can conceive whole lives; often replete with qualities we're yearning for. In my mind these lives are always filled with intelligent conversation at lively dinner parties, endless time for baking bread, tranquil evenings reading and creative endeavours. What is at work in these flights of fancy?

We are story-makers. We go to the past and negotiate with the dead, but we also go to the other unknowns, to lives in different places or languages, to other cultures, genders or even worlds. We are, quite simply, a story-making species and the dark time of the year is an excellent time for telling tales. Stories not only give us words for our own experiences, but for extrapolating to other experiences, for imagining. Storytelling is a tool for knowing who we are and what we want and how we relate. Storytelling helps us to see what we value. In a world awash with information, it's story that touches on truth, on what counts in life, on what makes a life. Looking in and making a story about the lives we hardly glimpse is pure fiction and deep reflection. We're not spying on people, but sifting for metaphors and connections that tell us about life in general and who we are and want to be. If the story we invent is one we also aspire to live, one we admire, then by 'looking in' we also have a moment of transcendence. As we look in and conjure a world, we expand our vision. Making up stories from the merest fragments is not mere fantasy, but a way of shifting perspective, inhabiting a larger world and diving deep into imagination.

In finding this moment of transcendence and letting the imagination play in the realm of 'not ourselves', we also touch another profound aspect of how we constantly stay in flux rather than ever imagining we have arrived. At its best, looking in and imagining lives of charm and grace is not soul-rotting envy or mind-numbing fancifulness but is an act of hope and expectation. Looking into that top floor apartment on a cold November night, on the verge of a long journey with overnight travel and early morning changes, I was the outsider.

The metaphor of my imaginative flight was a powerful one. I was the traveller and foreigner looking in on those who belonged, who were settled and at ease. But on the other side of the glass, perhaps there was someone looking down from that cosy window and thinking: *Those people are on an exciting adventure while I am stuck in one place, going through the same routines, always looking at the same view from this place I've grown too accustomed to. Ah, to travel and see new things, it must be a life of intellectual richness and invigorating encounters.*

There is more to this than the dismissive cliché of the grass being greener on the other side. There is more to this than simply being perverse and never satisfied. In winter, we long for summer. We think about hot skies and green places to walk by streams. In summer, we yearn for winter, dreaming of log fires and curling up with hot chocolate and a book to lose ourselves in. We certainly don't want to be always dissatisfied or never able to delight in the moment. We absolutely do not want to write our current lives off as shoddy and not enough. But without going down these paths, these imaginative cravings can tell us something about the need for harmony in our lives.

All this imagining and aspiration, all this longing for one thing and then another — for summer then winter, for being settled then travelling — is a way of hand-writing our lives. As writers we know that our work needs rhythm and harmony. The sounds we use in each sentence have to support what is being said and give the piece harmony. In prose as well as poetry, every syllable we use has resonances and how we link these resonances is what gives a piece of writing harmony. Consonants stop the airflow and create boundaries. Vowels are open and needed to make a syllable (certainly in English). They are the movement of a word combined with breath. Syllables hold the sounds together. The same is true in writing as in life. We love the day because we have the night to contrast it with and vice versa. I love to travel. On that journey back from Budapest the dated little sleeper couchette was magical. Falling asleep to the rhythm of wheels on the track and the soft tinkling of the metal hangers in the compartment was strange yet lovely.

I don't think I had any deep sleep on that train. I drifted in and out and, for a while, sat watching fields of snow and snow-laden trees speeding by, somewhere in Austria. The journey was enchanting even when the next train was 're-organised' and I had to persuade the Deutsche Bahn staff to let us onto an earlier train so we wouldn't miss our connection from Stuttgart to Paris. On a gorgeous morning, the first day of December, we passed beautiful villages in Germany, the sun low and watery, too heavy with winter to climb any higher than the trees. The sky was pale; blush-grey and whisper blue, clouds touching the houses with winter-breath, the fields

• Interlude 7: Writing the Darkness •

were frost speckled and the roofs steep, ready for snow.

I love to travel. But I also love returning home and having months when I don't leave the area where I live. To be among familiar books and objects. To cook in my own kitchen. To ease into the rhythms of our quirky house perched on a hillside in North Wales, is a deep pleasure. The winter can be a time to hunker down, to look inward, to use the dark nights to write and think. But it is part of a seasonal flow of energy and rhythms. Valuing the other times does not have to be a way of not dwelling richly in the present moment. It is not a way of being ungrateful for this life, now. Instead it can be:

- a way to spin stories that feed imagination and life
- a remembrance of a wider or alternative vision
- a way of discovering our hopes and expectations

Journal exercise

For Atwood the 'forbears' to be negotiated with include such writers as Dante, Homer, Shakespeare, Alice Munro, Virgil, Borges and Emily Dickinson and Adrienne Rich.

Who do you need to negotiate with? Why and how?

Write an imaginative piece going into the darkness. Who do you meet there?

Have a conversation or several conversations. What story do you return with?

Ritual

All Hallows is a time of waning sun, and finding our way into the dark before we emerge again next spring. Light candles today for the writers and anyone who has influenced you to write. Take some time to be quiet, alone and to feel grateful.

Chapter 22
Beyond Ego to Connection

Creativity can be as fascinating as it is elusive. On one level, it's something we can dissect and study, giving ourselves a structure in which to create or inspiring ourselves with the examples of great creatives. It's a good starting point, but we also need to dive deeper, and then deeper still because, when we open ourselves to the possibility of going beyond 'self', creativity is no longer a technique but a spiritual practice.

Creativity goes through stages. We begin with research and planning. At this point we're thinking with language and information-based. But then comes incubation. At some point we have to stop over-thinking the idea we're pursuing or even stop thinking about it at all. We have to be willing to look away so that the creative project can germinate, perhaps working on another idea or going between several ideas that might, at some stage, begin to give rise to connections we'll never see if we push too hard. This leads to illumination, not something we can fake or force, when there are moments of epiphany. And finally there is confirmation, when we try out the insight or allow it to find its form. Of course, on any given day we'll have all kinds of ideas and projects in different stages, sometimes sparking off one another to lead in unexpected directions.

Stories and poems begin as seeds that we ruminate on before giving the idea over to the unconscious. The meditation continues while the writer is engaged in other occupations. And then comes the first draft, which might sometimes be written at speed, letting it all pour out. And finally comes revision, anything from minor changes and honing, to radical rewrites. And often repeatedly: revision, revision, revision.

Along the way there is flow, the deeper pull of creativity, in which we move from bliss to forgetting where we are. We feel intense heat one moment and nothing the next. We forget the headache we felt earlier or to put another log on the fire. All we know is the next word and the next. We are in some mystical space, floating, creating. Some writers or artists have particular rituals that assist them into the state of flow. But however we find it, this is the gateway to a deep place where creativity and spirituality begin to merge. In flow, time becomes liquid and dreamlike. Trying to force an experience in which we deeply inhabit our creative flow, so that we cease to think about food or comfort or time, is doomed. But opening ourselves to the dissolution of the personal ego primes us for flow; for experiences that might be described as mystical or that alter our perspective.

The more we get out of our own way, the more we cultivate our connections, to others, to the nature that we are part of, to the night sky and the ocean, the more we are likely to experience a sense of continuity with all life and with the universe, a continuity in which we create unselfconsciously, as children do. The key to changing your mind and creating more deeply could well be the ability to let go of ego, at least for a while. We do this through connection and also through stepping back from all the ways we learned to name and categorise the world. For a child a tree is not the word 'tree' standing in for experience, neatly categorised and understood, to such an extent that we no longer see the tree in any meaningful way. Rather a tree is the feel of bark, perhaps even its taste, the challenge to climb, the scrunch of leaves, the scents and mystery of it all. The tree is a thing that relates to every sense, not a word that allows us to sum something up and move on to the next thing. Mystery is everywhere.

Inevitably, as adults, we name objects and experiences so that we can function in a complex world. But for children, as for visionaries like the poet, William Blake, 'the doors of perception' are wide open. A leaf, an insect, the light through the branches, enter consciousness without the filters of language and categories and schema. Writing about this from the perspective of a scientist investigating the use of psychedelics in *How to Change Your Mind*, Michael Pollan notes how, as adults, our responses to the world too often become rote and predictable. Whilst habits can enhance our creativity by giving us the framework in which to write, they can also become constricting if we lose flexibility and openness. Habits are both useful tools and ways to not live in the present moment because we are constantly looking at past data to infer what will happen next. We are rarely surprised.

In contrast, we forget ourselves and dissolve the ego, at least temporarily, when we focus on our connection to all things, and when we allow ourselves to encounter the world more directly and playfully. And we become less anxious, more available to surprise when we challenge habits that might be stultifying rather than enhancing our creativity. One way to do this is to introduce new experiences, ones in which, like children, we don't have all the categories and answers at our fingertips. Experiences like travel, seeing new art, losing ourselves in nature, immerse us in the present and so are more conducive to flow and creativity. Faced with new experiences that we don't have all the language for, we experience wonder.

And feeling wonder in turn deepens our sense of connection. We begin to see the Numinous in life. At this point, creativity and flow are deeply spiritual, which is not to say they are otherworldly. Whatever faith or none we might espouse, I'm convinced, like Pollan, that it is not the material world that is the antonym of the spiritual, but rather it is ego, and the hubris that accompanies it, that is spirituality's opposite. When we pare back ego for a moment, whether through encountering great art or music, being awed by a sunset or a newborn baby or through meditation or travelling to somewhere that interferes with our ability to predict what will happen next, we are both more vulnerable and more open to epiphany and deep experiences.

For Pollan the epiphany comes through using psychedelics but many others reach the same depth of experience in a host of ways. The philosopher Simone Weil, for example, had a deeply mystical experience from reciting George Herbert's poem 'Love III', and it was after this that she wrote:

> Attention, taken to its highest degree, is the same thing as
> prayer.

Others achieve this sense of unity and the feeling that there is more to consciousness than the self, through meditation while some, like the writer Nathaniel Hawthorne, find it in the liminal state between being awake and asleep. What they all share is the transcendence of the self. It is something akin to Keats's 'negative capability', when we can live with doubt and it allows us to take in the sense of subjectivity in all things, not only other people but all of nature. It is in this transcendence of ego that we come full circle to the links between self-forgetfulness, connection to all things and creativity. As a writer, diving deeply into flow; being vulnerable to new experiences and willing to encounter the universe with the wonder and playfulness of a child, are vital. And in a world in the midst of a mass extinction, in which writers are recording the struggle for survival that all life is engaged in, connection has never been so urgent.

Chapter 23

The Alchemy of Your Writing Life

Stories are powerful. We don't simply tell stories, we inhabit them. Since language began, we've been storytelling animals. Every time and culture has dominant stories that shape us, whether they are stories from religion, ideology or the market-place. Sometimes these stories have such a grip that it's hard to see beyond them, yet alternative stories can change the world, as Walter Benjamin insists in *The Storyteller: tales out of loneliness:*

Amongst the dominant stories of our age are several that are leading us down blind alleys or into destruction. In her retelling of the Ragnarok myth, A S Byatt portrays the gods as stupid, selfish and short-sighted. They deserve to die. They can see the end of the world coming, yet they do nothing about it. It's a powerful warning of ecological disaster, but it could also be a story of soured relationships with others or with the self. It's a call to change and, like all good stories, wakes us up.

So how do stories change the world?

1. Story makes sense of the world and those we share it with

The neuroscientist and novelist, Keith Oatley, has noted that in terms of how the brain responds when we're reading, the simulation of reality is so vivid that it's as though we are within the world of the novel. The researcher, Uri Hasson, backs this up, noting that people who read a lot not only tend to have better understanding of others, but that those hearing the same story have the same brain reactions. This isn't merely about a response to spoken language. Stories with their words changed prompt the same brain patterns in scans. In stories, we dig deep into archetypes and in so doing we bridge the personal and the universal. We recognise ourselves as connected with the world we inhabit, an intrinsic part rather than something 'other'. In other words, story increases empathy and builds shared experience.

2. Story helps us interpret the past and shape the future

In addition to helping us interpret the world and building community, stories are tools for self-reflection. Look at any fairy story or traditional tale and you will find an embedded fragment of advice for living. Within the metaphors we find deep truths and lessons that bear revisiting at various stages of life. Stories are both what happen to us and how we make sense of what happens to us.

3. Story tells the truth

From Homer to Chaucer; from Shakespeare to Margaret Atwood, we find truth, as we read stories. We learn about the depths and heights of human nature; the impact of war, ideology, technology… all the world is in story. And presented in a way that gets under the skin.

4. Stories untangle the mess and give us hope

But stories don't simply lay the universe before us so that we feel it, viscerally. Story also offers a way through when we've made a mess or life seems unbearable. The stories of ancient Greece and the stories of refugees today are equally mirrors of experience. This is why stories can last for thousands of years. The horrors of Sophocles' *Ajax* are still being played out today. And by the same token, ancient stories of love and hope, go on resonating and giving voice to current experience. Stories are vital to well being From Greek myth to Dante's *Inferno*, from folk tales to contemporary novels, stories give meaning, structure and healing with which to negotiate the world.

5. Stories challenge one another

Story can change and save lives. Story is magical and transformative. But story, like so much, is both a culture we inhabit and a tool. And as with any culture, it can degenerate. Hitler was a first-rate storyteller. The stories he wove were evil and the results so horrifying that the world is still resonating to the harm caused.

Chapter 23: The Alchemy of Your Writing Life

Transformation isn't always for the good and neither is the slow slide away from stories that have stood the test of time. I'm not a Luddite or Golden Age thinker, but there are an increasing number of voices raised in concern at the dominant stories of our age. Perhaps the single most powerful story that shapes our lives is that of consumption. It's so pervasive that we hardly even notice it. It's encultured and shapes our environment.

If stories are powerful, and they are; if stories shape societies, and they do, then we need to choose our stories with care. We need stories of hope, kindness and community, old and new, that challenge false and toxic stories.

6. Stories expand our thinking and feeling

It's not enough for a story to be compelling. Moreover, baldly didactic stories that make too blunt a point rarely endure. Storytellers tell the tales. It's up to the listeners to find those that resonate, to make and live the meanings. The best stories don't persuade, rather they expand our ability to think and feel. And this in turn is transformative. Stories, if they are functioning healthily, are not instruction manuals or propaganda yet they change our hearts and thinking subtly and deeply because they are of the soul.

7. Stories give us wisdom rather than information

Walter Benjamin saw the decline of storytelling as inextricably linked with the rise in information, which is fast and ephemeral, unlike story, which persists across time. We live in an age that wants immediacy. Ready-made information fills the void left by contemplative wisdom. Yet we remain hungry. Information is not the same as knowledge, much less wisdom. Stories take us back to the wisdom.

8. Stories assert our embodiment

We are part of the universe. A false story that we've grown accustomed to is that of dualism. We make distinctions between mind and body as though disembodied mind could make sense. We oppose ourselves to the natural world as 'other'. In contrast, the philosopher, Husserl, offered another story, that of the lived body as the crucible of experience. Subsequently, Merleau-Ponty built on this thinking by asserting that experience and the world are coterminous in the sense that we access the world through the senses. Distinctions between body and mind or body and world are arbitrary. When we start to experience the world through our senses, not only cerebrally, the stories we tell, the stories we become, change. Writers mould the stuff of experience.

9. Stories are fundamental to change

Stories are not only what we tell, they are the medium in which we exist. They are culture and ideology, myth and magic, toxic or transformative, decline or hope. Stories define communities, expand our thinking and feeling and give us direction and belonging. If you doubt that stories change the world, look at any holocaust, or consider the impact of the *Bible* or the *Quran*. Whether for our individual journeys, our communities or the world, we can be a different story and make the magic happen.

There are, then, many reasons why narrative is vital, why writing is an extraordinary and powerful calling, none more so than the fact that story shapes our lives. How we perceive the world and therefore how we act in the world is intrinsically bound up with what we believe about the nature of reality, the values at the core of our lives, the stories we tell about the world and ourselves. In short, we live in myth. The landscape we live in is not only physical but also narrative. What kind of stories do you live in?

Sadly, many of us live in an increasingly impoverished, degraded or misleading storyscape. Whether we are tired of hearing the story of MORE MORE MORE or the ubiquitous story the (most often male) hero, we need new stories or we need to mine ancient ones with subtlety and attentiveness. The enormous challenges of our time can sometimes take us to the very limits of our capacity to respond meaningfully, yet there are stories that deal with falls from grace and redemption; stories of staying constant and enduring without the aid of magical intervention or superpowers; stories of quests that demand strong and compassionate maturity.

Whilst some writers draw us back to traditional stories, other writers, like Thomas Berry, suggest that the world needs new stories in which we understand humanity as intrinsically linked to the planet and the universe, not separate from it. And, with a similar sense of urgency, thinkers like D Stephenson Bond warn us that contemporary society has fallen out of myth. Bond suggests that the dominant stories of society have become intolerable and we increasingly feel 'unstoried', alienated and rootless.

Myth gives us a sense of meaning because we have a living relationship with the stories we inhabit. We live inside particular contexts and when our subjective consciousness and the mythological consciousness work together all is well. Myth tells us the principles to live by. But when the environment changes and the cultural myths that have sustained us no longer resonate, we end up with mythologies that fail to nourish, or even do harm as we can see in the way that symbol is debased into propaganda in the swastika of Nazi Germany, for instance.

When myth dies there are earth tremors. After all, myth is multigenerational and enormous; it has contained people, perhaps over centuries, and its death is bound to bring social turmoil until new sustaining myths arise. Myth and meaning are of a piece. Story makes sense of who we are, as individuals and as a society. If our society's myths fail us we are forced back into personal myth-making to give sense and narrative to life.

Myths tap into symbols, which in turn are potent living things at a deep level of consciousness. For anything to stand as a symbol for something else, it has to not only carry the image of the other but also the energy of what it points to. Symbols have intensity. As the theologian, Paul Tillich, points out, a symbol is much deeper than a sign; it not only points beyond self but also participates in what it points to. To be alive, myth and symbol must stir the imagination, must grip and fascinate us. The fire of myth is powerful, yet in a period of political uncertainty, rapid technological development and ecological threat, the content of shared myth is often in question.

Symbols can emerge in the space between the unconscious and the conscious. For many of us, the stories that emerge in dreams are where we encounter potent symbols that invite us to dive deeper into imagination. It's in dreams that we may touch on archetypes from the unconscious and so encounter myth. In dreams, actual life and potential life are held together under great tension and the symbols we encounter there can show the way to psychological development.

We cannot return home by the way we came. When the old myths fail and the interim myths of greed and superpowers are exposed as hollow, we need extraordinary new myths that are as imaginative as they are true. When the myths around us fail we have to be among the courageous who leave the failing symbols behind as we head into the unknown in search of new stories to live by. We live in myth when our lives have meaning and intention; when our life is an unfolding story. And meaning always requires an act of imagination.

This means that we cannot wander around the world half-asleep. To do so makes us prey to pseudo-science and snake oil salesmen. On the other hand, we need enough trust, imagination and flexibility to make new meanings, arrive at new symbols. This is the space of the soul, where we can dwell in a myth without losing sight that it is a myth, where we can play with meaning in ways that nourish and enrich the world. Soul space is both internal and universal.

The psychologist Carl Jung would say that this is the oldest layer of the mind, where ego drops away. This is the arena of the collective unconscious — the impersonal patterns of organisation that shape human experience. Deep within this experience is the living otherness, the 'Not-I' that lies at the heart of our subjective experience. In the Biblical story of Jacob wrestling in his dream, this 'Not-I' may be an angel or divinity. In the encounter, Jacob is wounded and renamed. He asks what the name of the other is and, although the answer is evasive, he learns who he is and his life is changed as a result.

The world needs story. The world is in search of myth and of a new mythological consciousness. Writing and story have never been so urgent. We are living in times of wrestling and wounding. As light dawns we need a story that asks who we wrestle with, recognises the other within and redefines who we are, who we want to become. Those of us who take writing seriously are a small part in making narrative meaning of life. It's a task of awe, responsibility and alchemy.

C G Jung talked about 'religion' not as an institution and dogma, but as an attitude and way of apprehending reality. For Jung religion is about meticulously attending to the Numinous. 'Numinous' was a word invented by the theologian Rudolph Otto in his book, *Das Heilige*. We experience it as profound emotion, rather than through willpower. And it connects the self to experiences of awe, holiness, otherness, mystery and cultural symbols. (Though this doesn't have to imply belief in a personal divinity.)

Times when there is drought of meaning give rise to psychological unease and to distortions of culture. They give rise to fanaticism and fundamentalism. They give rise to cultures in which we relate only to certain aspects of ourselves and the world. We relate only to the functional and rational at the expense of imagination and internal life (or vice versa). Jung considered that at this point we have to begin relating to our environment through the cracks in the culture. Individuals have to find ways to make new myths that, perhaps over generations, will lead to cultural renewal as well as giving individual meaning.

Finding personal myth is both urgent and difficult. Living in the cracks when the old myths no longer function is fraught with possibility of error. We have to remain tentative and we need to leave a trail of breadcrumbs to find our way back if we discover we've taken several wrong turns. Two things call to us through the forest: imagination and story.

Imagination is much deeper than fantasy. It is the whole question of 'How do I live?' This is a mythological question because it's about how we relate our inner life to culture and environment and when the prevailing myths are failing

Chapter 23: The Alchemy of Your Writing Life

or decadent then we have to proceed cautiously, testing what gives health and what makes us ail. Another metaphor is finding a path in an overgrown forest when there are paths leading in every conceivable direction. Finding the direction takes deep imagination. Imagining the path is an act of renewal, empathy and courage. It's not an ego trip, but connects us to the Numinous, to intense and humbling experiences of awe. Imagining the path is an act of invention in which we become a different story.

Where do we find the inspiration for this enormous act of imagination and courage?

Stories are everywhere. We grow up in stories. We constantly narrativise our lives. Stories are in the air, like sculpture is in stone. For writers, originality is about what we weave from the ideas we find around us in the world; how we process experience and the ideas which are all around us. Whether we are writing fantasy or social realism, a dystopia or a poem, writers, as mythmakers, are always concerned with the truths of the lives we live, the lives we observe and the lives of those who have gone before us. Every writer stands on the shoulders of every other preceding writer. We use each other's ideas and skills, plots and secrets. Writing can be a lonely business, but literature and myth are communal enterprises and nothing we write arrives *ex nihilo*. In Interlude 7 we acknowledged that much of our material comes from the dark. We learn from the dead. 'There is nothing new under the sun' the writer of Ecclesiastes tells us.

And the inspiration to find the myths and stories that nourish is also in the origins of language itself. For Virginia Woolf, beneath memory, words, imagination and experience there is rhythm. The words we use as writers have to go deep enough in to move in this rhythm:

> Style is a very simple matter: it is all rhythm. Once you get that, you can't use the wrong words. But on the other hand here am I sitting after half the morning, crammed with ideas, and visions, and so on, and can't dislodge them, for lack of the right rhythm. Now this is very profound, what rhythm is, and goes far deeper than words. A sight, an emotion, creates this wave in the mind, long before it makes words to fit it; and in writing (such is my present belief) one has to recapture this, and set this working (which has nothing apparently to do with words) and then, as it breaks and tumbles in the mind, it makes words to fit it. But no doubt I shall think differently next year.

Chapter 23: The Alchemy of Your Writing Life

Woolf's wave in the mind is fragile and elusive. If we try to grasp it before the wave breaks we miss the words, but if we attend to it, inspiration comes. Using the experiences that are all around us, diving deep into the dark to bring back the treasures of the underworld and being present to the rhythms of language, emotion and of humanity, takes us into the trance that is writing, from where we offer the makings of myth. Creativity is fragile, tangled and exploratory, as William Blake understands:

> I give you the end of a golden string
> Only wind it into a ball
> It will lead you in at Heaven's gate
> Built in Jerusalem's wall

We find inspiration

- in the air, in the stories that surround us
- in the dark, by daring to dive deep and by going to the underworld to bring back the treasures of the dead
- in the rhythm of every sight or emotion that is deeper than words, that we attune to without grasping
- in the golden string that we wind as we explore
- in the timelessness of flow, where we lose ourselves and open ourselves
- and in the surprising parts of ourselves that surface as we do deep work

Stories are powerful. We don't simply tell stories, we inhabit them. Stories are who we are and our home.

Six Exercises in Soul-writing

1. A map of your creative soul

You are more creative than you imagine. I see myself as a writer, but as a child I drew and sewed. In my teens I did poetry eisteddfods and acted in amateur dramatics and, briefly, played piano and made my own clothes. Later I learnt medieval dance and jazz ballet and took up patchwork quilting and then got into baking and cooking. And, as a young mother, I learnt papermaking and a host of artistic techniques that I could do projects around with my children. I sang in a choir and took up yoga.

Day to day I forget much of this. Or I simply don't think of cooking and yoga as 'creative'. But they are and all of us are much more creative than we often realise.

So take a double page of your journal or a big sheet of paper and draw a time line path across the middle. It can be straight or meandering. Now add lots of branching paths. On each path put a creative activity you've done, even if it was drawing stick figures when you were five. Use lots of colours and many paths. Some of those paths trail away, some you are still on — take the ones that are part of your current creativity and wiggle them back onto the main path — how colourful is that path? How much more creative are you than you generally allow?

2. Writing your quest

In Greek myth, the young woman, Psyche, is too beautiful for the goddess Aphrodite to bear. So Aphrodite commands her son, Cupid, to shoot an arrow into a monster to make the monster fall in love with Psyche. Instead he falls in love with her himself, a secret he must keep from the gods in case Aphrodite should find out. He marries Psyche but makes sure even she doesn't know who he is or even what he looks like. She assumes her unseen husband is the monster set on her by Aphrodite, though he is a tender lover at night. Her jealous sisters urge her to look at her husband as he sleeps. Psyche lights a candle, hoping to catch a glimpse of his face. But a drop of wax falls on her husband. He wakes and realises his identity is no longer a secret. Cupid flees and Psyche wanders, constantly searching for him. Along the way, she endures a series of trials, unaware of Cupid's presence helping her. The last trial involves a journey to the Underworld to retrieve a box from Persephone, containing some of her beauty, to give to Aphrodite. But Psyche opens the box and is overcome by Stygian sleep. Cupid finally comes to her rescue and pleads their case with the gods, resulting in their marriage and a rare happy ending.

Folk stories and literature abound with quest stories: from the Holy Grail to the search for love. And quests are not only for story characters, heroes and gods. We've thought a lot about quests throughout this book and this is an opportunity to ruminate on your next steps on the path.

Once again, take a double page of your journal or a big sheet of paper and draw a path. At the end of your path draw or write your Holy Grail. What does your soul love? What are you heading towards?

Along the path draw some obstacles — boulders, raging rivers, muggers, wild animals or thick undergrowth too dense to see a way through. Give your obstacles names: Not Enough Time; Burn-out; Self-doubt... Whatever you see potentially getting in your way, name it and put it on the path.

How are you going to negotiate each of these obstacles? I'm not going to talk about weapons or vanquishing. Who needs the language of war in their soul work? But you might want to think about new habits or small steps that could help. It might be that there's a way round that you can take. For example instead of doubting your abilities and bemoaning an apparent lack, you could take the longer but more fruitful road of improving your skills or learning something new.

When you have finished, take out a calendar or download a free printable calendar and put the steps for negotiating the obstacles into the calendar. It doesn't matter how small the steps are, but make them real and keep them. Each day put a cross through when you've taken your steps. A big X. Each day as the Xs build up they form a chain — and the longer and more unbroken the chain, the more your momentum will build.

3. Finding the still small voice

In the exercises at the end of Section 4 we thought about ways of using the subconscious to aid our journeys and we considered ways to clear out what is not serving our writing lives and the people we want to become. We've also recognised that we are embodied creatures, connected to all life. The tension between our still centre and how we connect is at the heart of the last interlude in the concluding section of this book but it has something to do with having the right filters.

We live in a noisy world. That's not always a bad thing. There's a lot of music in that noise so long as what we are hearing is harmony rather than cacophony. But to find the harmony we have to know what not to listen to. As George Eliot writes:

> If we had a keen vision and feeling of all ordinary human life, it would be like hearing the grass grow and the squirrel's heart beat, and we should die of that roar that lies on the other side of silence.

We have to know what to filter or we will simply be overwhelmed. There's a dramatic story in the *Book of Kings* of a prophet, Elijah, running for his life at a time when the world seems to be turning upside down. He hides in a cave, trying to hear the voice of his God. (It might, for others, be an inner voice of intuition.) God passes by and a strong wind tears into the mountain, shattering rocks:

> but the Lord was not in the wind.

Afterwards there is an earthquake:

> but the Lord was not in the earthquake.

And then a fire:

> but the Lord was not in the fire.

Finally there is 'a still small voice'.

> And Elijah hides his face as he goes to the entrance of the cave, knowing this is the voice of God.

Listening to many voices, especially in harmony, motivates and stimulates us. But we also have to know when to listen to the one quiet voice within that is saying something different. And we have to know when not to listen at all, when to completely unhook and take time in solitude and silence. In the Biblical story, the still small voice asks:

> What are you doing here, Elijah?

Sometimes we need a small voice inside to ask us that question. To prompt us to retreat, for a small time or for a longer time, so that we can come back to the noise equipped with discernment, able to hear the harmonies.

Take some time in quiet with your journal. Think about your quests, the demands on you and locate that still, small voice within, asking: What are you doing here?

What is your reply?

4. Creating a personal myth

A personal myth is the way we live in the world as writers, it is the story of who we are and who we want to become. It involves finding the Numinous in the everyday and fully inhabiting our bodies to be present to each moment so that we can observe scenes and objects, and make emotional links that will allow story to emerge; the story we are writing, the story of self and the story of the connection of all things.

The first part of this exercise is based on a workshop led by the poet, David Gilbert, for a group of writers gathered around my kitchen table:

> Think of meditating. As we quiet our minds and slow our breaths, inevitably our minds wander. Instead of fighting this and telling ourselves we're doing this wrong, we can simply notice the thought or sensation and bring our attention gently back to the breath. We need that same kindness as we write.
>
> So simply quieten your mind, focus on your breath, bring your focus back with gentle kindness as you continue to breathe and centre yourself and after a while begin to write, with that same kindness, starting from the phrase:

> I took a wrong turn...
>
> As you write, imagine you come to a place you hadn't expected. Describe it.
>
> In the distance, you see a creature. The creature approaches you. What kind of creature is this and what does s/he want to tell you about your journey?

We take wrong turns, but every day is new and, with imagination and story, we can track back or find a new path.

Imagine trying to find a path in an overgrown forest where small paths lead in every conceivable direction.

> Stand still within your imaginary forest. Take a deep breath and choose a path.
>
> Finding direction is an act of imagination, restoration and resolution.
>
> Write about your path.

Where do we find the inspiration for this enormous act of imagination and courage?

There are stories all around us. Among the decaying myths are amazing stories of hope, courage and generosity. In Chapter 23 we noted that we find inspiration and stories:

- in the air, in the stories that surround us
- in the dark, by daring to dive deep and by going to the underworld to bring back the treasures of the dead
- in the rhythm of every sight or emotion that is deeper than words, that we attune to without grasping
- in the golden string that we wind as we explore
- in the timelessness of flow, where we lose ourselves and open ourselves
- and in the surprising parts of ourselves that surface as we do deep work

What are the myths (old or new) that sustain you and why?

For me this would include several children's books like Antoine de Saint-

Exupéry's *The Little Prince* or anything by Tove Jansson. It would include the stories of activists like Rachel Carson and a huge range of literature and poetry from Margaret Atwood to Ursula Le Guin; from John Berger to Mary Oliver, from Michael Ondaatje to Anne Michaels.

How can you be part of these sustaining and life-affirming myths?

What in your own writing touches on myth? (It doesn't have to be fantasy elements, it doesn't have to be prose or a particular genre, but it might be themes of our place in the environment; deep connections; the balance of the shadow and the light...

5. Facing the Numinous

The theologian Rudolph Otto, who developed the concept of the Numinous, considers that the Numinous has three characteristics. It is *Mysterium tremendum et fascinans* (awe-inspiring mystery).

Mysterium is outside our comprehension, the Wholly Other that fills us with wonder and awe.

This mystery is in turn '*tremendum*', a word that contains a sense of being completely overwhelmed by the vastness of the Other, leading to feeling tiny in the awesome scale of things and even to terror in the face of one's creatureliness in comparison to such majesty and ineffable power.

Yet the mystery is also '*fascinans*', irresistibly attractive, glorious and compelling; overflowing with blessing and the beauty of transcendence.

Depending on one's faith (or not) the Numinous is the profound mystery of divinity or of existence itself.

What in life fills you with wonder and awe?

Write an account of vastness or terror in prose or poetry. It can be real or fictional or something between.

When do you feel overwhelmed by the vastness of everything?

When have you experienced beauty or transcendence? Write about the emotions and sensations of it. Write in prose or poetry, remember or invent...

What does the Numinous mean to you, in your life and in your writing?

6. Rhythm down deep

> Matter is spirit moving slowly enough to be seen.
> ((attributed to) Pierre Teilhard de Chardin)

This is my manifesto for writing and for life:

> To live in a more humane rhythm, embracing the need to miss out on things that never mattered anyway in order to value the quality of art and life over quantity and to allow for experiences of *kairos* (moments of truth, epiphany and connection) as well as *chronos*.

To quest for

- rhythm: realising 'balance' is a myth that opposes work-life, light-shade, fast-slow, when each activity, each section of the path, has a particular rhythm
- depth: realising that who we are is crucial to the stories we tell and become so we have to be prepared to dive into the sediment of ourselves and learn to change without condemning ourselves because we only become radically generous and attentive to others when we treat ourselves with some consideration
- profound and pivotal experiences over scaling dizzy heights, particularly through connecting with family and friends and through travel
- process and becoming over outcomes
- congruence of thought, emotion and action

To create

- stories with soul that witness to humanity
- transformative relationships
- a life built on the values of
    - attentiveness
    - humility
    - courage
    - vulnerability
    - compassion
    - generosity

What is your manifesto for writing and for life?

How did you arrive at this story?

How fully are you living it?

What is the next step to take?

Conclusion

Writing Your Story

Interlude 8

Finding the Still Point of Your Story

This interlude is a chance to take a longer period of time in the run up to Christmas to think about how we prioritise the writing life at period that is often a demanding time of year. It's planned to be used through December and into January in deep winter. If you are in the southern hemisphere this won't be winter and you might want to do the short Summer Solstice course 'Writing the Soaring Sun' around the third week of December, found in the Section 3. However, you will hopefully find a great deal of the material in this interlude is pertinent over the five weeks of December to January 6, despite the difference is season.

All of us write, to greater or lesser extents, to explore what it means to be human and how we make meaning. When the natural world is dying back, growth is heading underground, the temperatures fall and the light diminishes, writers often feel an urge to go within. Whatever your personal beliefs and whatever you write or aspire to write, the pull towards deep reflection and recharging our creativity often has a seasonal rhythm to it.

Yet at the same time, the world is gearing up not to support your deep thinking, your longing to give time to creativity, or your desire to recalibrate your writing quests as you turn towards another year, but to convince you to eat more, drink more, party harder and buy more. On top of that, we all have the ongoing things that keep us busy — whether it's work or young children or elders that need care or commitments we've made, or a mad combination of things that all want a piece of us. Writing is never easy, but your intrinsic motivation and your ability to curate your time and give it to your art can come under particular pressure at this time of the year.

This is not to denigrate the need for taking time out for joy or celebration. The long tradition of marking the year with periods of both fasting and feasting is not only time-honoured but reinforces deep social bonds. Festivals of light appear in many religious practices, from Solstice celebrations to Christmas, from Diwali to Chanukah. They not only share the human narratives of finding celebration in the midst of the darkness and of turning back to the light, but all revolve around stories. The myths that connect particular groups to places, events, traditions, and shared cultural references are powerful in all of these festivals.

So the question for writers becomes how to participate in the myths that resonate with us and/or help us feel deep belonging, whilst also not buying into the myths that would leave us frazzled, exhausted, possibly more out of sorts with those we love than if we hadn't seen them during this season, and facing the new year feeling enervated and ragged rather than energised and refreshed? How do we use winter to go within when there are so many calls on our time, many of them legitimate? There isn't one simple answer to this question. But part of it is by giving a short time each day, through Advent, Christmas into the New Year to Epiphany, to find some solitude, reflection and ways to respond to the season with intention, rather than getting swept along by it. This interlude is one small way to help us find a new rhythm with this pivotal time of the year, feeding our writing lives along the way. Each day there will be thoughts about Advent or the run up to New Year and how we set quests as well as a writing element and a 'ritual' as in the previous interludes.

December 1

We're not sure when Advent calendars started, perhaps as homemade artefacts in Germany in the early nineteenth century, but the idea of counting down to a major event gradually took hold and many people now use calendars regardless of whether Christmas is within their faith tradition or is simply seen as a major family holiday.

As I was writing this, a card company sent me an advert for calendars that would 'spread joy'; I had another from a chocolate company. A quick look online confirms the link between calendars and buying in our culture — there's a dizzying array of calendars with different 'luxury' beauty and bath products for each day, others with an assortment of different gins, candles, perfume, teas, beer, or a even new pair of socks for each day, as well as sweets and toys.

Feeling overwhelmed? The beginning of December is a good point to step

• Interlude 8: Finding the Still Point of Your Story •

back and think about what matters. How do you want to spend this month and the holiday season? Who do you want to spend it with?

The Advent season and working through the calendar traditionally encompasses important themes for any writer — patience, expectation and hope of change run through it. This is how the theologian Dietrich Bonhoeffer, an anti-Nazi campaigner and pacifist, executed just two weeks before the concentration camp he was held in was liberated, puts it:

> The celebration of Advent is possible only to those who are troubled in soul, who know themselves to be poor and imperfect, and who look forward to something greater to come.

Journal exercise

Do you use an Advent calendar or have memories of opening one, perhaps as a child or with children? What are its associations for you, if any?

What part do patience, expectation and hope play in your writing and in your life?

Are you happy with this?

Are there ways you want this to change?

In what ways (in your writing or life) do you look forward to something greater to come?

Ritual

Block out some time every day this month and the first couple of days of January, as a gift to yourself this winter season, and use it for some small act of self-compassion each day (reading a chapter of a book after journalling; sitting and looking at the stars for ten minutes before you go to bed…).

December 2

When I was writing, today fell on the first Sunday in Advent in the Christian tradition. It's a time associated with lighting candles, sometimes daily, sometimes one for each Sunday, with a final one on Christmas day. Although I don't belong to a faith group, years of liturgy and theology have left me with strong and positive associations with some of the narratives and rituals of faith, many of which have become as much cultural as religious, so we still light a candle each Sunday, during the main meal, as a countdown.

Today, I'm also thinking about Chanukah, the Jewish festival of light that has a powerful narrative of overcoming oppression and of a light that (miraculously) lasted eight days despite there being only sufficient oil for one day. (The year I wrote this course, it began on December 2, but it varies across December as it is part of a lunar calendar, falling on 25 Kislev.) If you light Advent or Chanukah candles or use candles as part of ritual (whether related to religious beliefs, wider spirituality or simply to set an ethos), think about what the lighting means to you.

This is a time when we move towards the shortest day and the longest night. When the natural light goes, it is profoundly disquieting. This is Virginia Woolf, writing in her diary about an eclipse:

> We had fallen. It was extinct. There was no colour. The earth was dead. That was the astonishing moment; and the next when as if a ball had rebounded the cloud took colour on itself again, only a sparky ethereal colour and so the light came back. I had very strongly the feeling as the light went out of some vast obeisance; something kneeling down and suddenly raised up when the colours came. They came back astonishingly lightly and quickly and beautifully in the valley and over the hills — at first with a miraculous glittering and ethereality, later normally almost, but with a great sense of relief. It was like recovery. We had been much worse than we had expected. We had seen the world dead. This was within the power of nature.

The metaphors of light and darkness are powerful because they go to the roots of our survival.

• Interlude 8: Finding the Still Point of Your Story •

Journal exercise

Where in your writing and your life do you find darkness and light?

Are there ways you want this to change?

Ritual

Spend some time in quiet and darkness. Then light a candle, just a single flame. Sit with it, breathe, focus on the light and think for a while before you switch on lights or light more candles.

December 3

This is a time of year bursting with rituals. We will think about some of these in more detail as we go through the month: from Christmas trees to food, from decorations to cards, from gifts to how time is spent.

Think about the rituals of your family, your faith group (if you belong to one), your friendship group, your workplace as holidays approach, everything from what food you will eat on Christmas day, to when and whether you put up a tree, the works' 'do' if it's applicable, or your friends' expectation that you'll want to get drunk with them on New Year's Eve, to what colour candles you might light or not on Christmas Eve, or whether you have mistletoe hung up anywhere…

Journal exercise

Make a list of every conceivable ritual you might be expected to be involved in, or you might expect others to take part in with you, or you do for yourself.

Which ones are meaningful and why?

Which ones fill you with dismay and why?

Are there 'traditions' you feel obliged to take part in that you want or need to disengage from?

How are you going to do this?

· INTERLUDE 8: FINDING THE STILL POINT OF YOUR STORY ·

Are there traditions that, even if you might pause over them, you feel are important to who you are/your family or other culture?

How do you honour those?

Ritual

Write yourself a promise:

a promise of at least one way in which you are not going to buy into or collude with a tradition/pattern of behaviour/expectation that you normally just go along with; a promise of one way in which you will wholeheartedly honour a tradition that is part of your family/culture/group.

December 4

Advent is a time of preparation and anticipation that was traditionally associated (like Lent) with fasting, though this now seems very far away from the image of December in popular western culture. This isn't a call for you to fast during December but, today, think about what needs less in your life in order for you to give time to writing and to be the writer and person you want to become.

If this month is one that is going to get busier for you as Christmas approaches, think of what you need to eliminate. Even if you spend Christmas alone, think about what distracts you from spending deep time with yourself.

Henry David Thoreau talks about how it is when we are both alone and still that we begin to converse with ourselves, to face whatever is inside:

> The really diligent student in one of the crowded hives of Cambridge College is as solitary as a dervish in the desert. The farmer can work alone in the field or the woods all day, hoeing or chopping, and not feel lonesome, because he is employed; but when he comes home at night he cannot sit down in a room alone, at the mercy of his thoughts, but must be where he can 'see the folks', and recreate, and, as he thinks, remunerate himself for his day's solitude; and hence he wonders how the student can sit alone in the

house all night and most of the day without ennui and 'the blues'; but he does not realize that the student, though in the house, is still at work in his field, and chopping in his woods, as the farmer in his, and in turn seeks the same recreation and society that the latter does, though it may be a more condensed form of it.

Journal exercise

What do you need less of at this time of the year?

What do you need to let go of in order to be the writer and person you want to be and in order to make this season a time of renewal and deep connection rather than frenzy and stress?

It might be stress or family drama. It might be watching yourself enter particular roles in relationships that you don't want to continue but continue anyway rather than give offence. It might be spending too much or over-eating or drinking or going with the lowest common denominator to watch something awful on TV when you'd rather be reading or writing. It might, for some, be spending too much time alone and avoiding others…

If you want to change any pattern that involves other people, how will you do this, even in small and subtle ways?

Ritual

What do you need less of at this time of year? Write it down — now find a way to safely burn the paper as a sign of what you are letting go.

December 5

Advent is associated with longing for new possibilities. Even if the narrative of how the world is saved by the birth of a child in difficult circumstances is not part of your belief system, it's still an effective metaphor and myth.

In Kathleen Raine's extraordinary 'Northumberland Sequence (IV)' there is a strong sense of how we contain in ourselves a range of powerful emotions that are nonetheless vulnerable. A new-born child is the promise of the future, yet utterly demanding and also completely dependent. A new-born elicits in us boundless hope yet provokes, equally, endless fear for the future. As the line in the Christmas carol, 'O Little Town of Bethlehem', puts it:

> the hopes and fears of all the years are met in thee tonight

Mid-winter can be a time of going deeply within, not to stoke the ego but to face the shadows, to make peace with the past, near and far, to consider its legacy, to interrogate what we need to do to move into the future and to face both fears and hopes. All of this, it seems to me, is contained in Raine's poem, 'Northumbrian Sequence IV' in which she develops a litany of those things we must let in to our lives — wind, rain, the natural elements even when they storm and threaten, but also what they evoke in us — fear, pain, grief for those we've lost and for the lives we thought we might live but never have... The poem calls us to face the darkness and sorrow we each carry, including the mysterious enormity of the universe itself (or of deity if that is your tradition). As the piece progresses Raine shifts into a voice that might be Mary, wondering how one frail person can take in and give birth to the impulse at the heart of all creation; how she can let in the child. It's also reminiscent of the Celtic story of Mabon, a sun god born from the mother goddess, Modron, he is stolen when he's three-days old and it takes a quest of three months and the wisdom of animals such as the salmon to find him so that he is reborn again at the Solstice, when the days gradually lengthen again. In both traditions there is the theme of birth and the power and fragility of the child within.

Yesterday, we thought about what we need to let go of in order to connect deeply, write authentically, and use the short dark days of winter to slough off whatever might be holding us back. Today, think about what you need to let in.

Journal exercise

What are the emotions or experiences you need to sit with, pay attention to, give yourself time. For Raine, these are huge and conflicting — fear, pain, desire, loneliness, love, those we've lost, nature, power and peace... You can't expect to encompass so much in one short journalling exercise, but you can begin to notice what is surfacing and what you need to allow space for.

Interlude 8: Finding the Still Point of Your Story

Journal about these things.

Ritual

And over this month, give yourself a gift — time to return and sit with these emotions and thoughts with compassion.

December 6

Gifts aren't always obvious or material. Sometimes, spending time with someone is an enormous gift. Sometimes it may be material, but simple, or it might be a mixture of time and skills with a material element. Last year, as a birthday gift, my younger son sanded and varnished the living room floor and a staircase while I was away writing. This year he's doing another staircase and a hallway, plus painting the hallway. It's a huge investment of time and skill.

Today is Saint Nicholas's Day, one of the figures behind the myths of Father Christmas or Santa Claus. His story is one of material generosity, providing three bags of gold for a poor family with three daughters who had no dowry, so couldn't marry, hence the notion of gifts appearing overnight from an unseen benefactor.

There can be real excitement in giving things and huge anticipation in opening a gift bought with love and chosen with care. But how often does this degrade into a desperate tick list to get an increasing number of people 'something that will do' within a groaning budget? And how often do we feel that our efforts aren't enough, even when we've vastly overspent? How do we celebrate, resist becoming miserly Scrooge-figures, and yet redress the balance in the face of rampant consumerism and adverts that make our 'lifestyles' feel shoddy, lack-lustre or downright impoverished?

We can certainly steel ourselves to resist the advertising and think deeply about the types of gifts we buy for those close to us.

We can also remember that Saint Nicholas's gift-giving was an act of kindness from a stranger. Perhaps not all of our generosity should be to those closest to us, even if it's a matter of donating to a food bank or taking clothes to a charity shop?

But, as writers, another way to rethink gifts might lie in an alternative origin story for Father Christmas. In the nomadic Siberian Evenki culture, in which healthy reindeer herds represent survival, the shaman, the one

Interlude 8: Finding the Still Point of Your Story

who knows the spirits, provides a model for giving story as gift. The shamans, whose reindeer could reputedly fly, used psycho-active Fly Agaric mushrooms to aid their own flights. The mushrooms, which grow under particular evergreens, are toxic in their raw state, so would be dried in socks hung over fires.

Shamanic journeys to the otherworld not only involved mushrooms, but also made use of a tradition of bringing an evergreen tree into the yurt to symbolise the World Tree. They would see their spirits as flying to the otherworld, the tree mediating their journey as they flew through the chimney hole at the top of the yurt. At the top of the World Tree, representing the Upper World of the cosmos, was the North Star, another connection with a Christmas tradition. The shaman's spirit would return through the same chimney, bringing the gift of life-giving knowledge and story to the group.

You don't need psycho-active substances to know the power of story and myth. Stories carry the 'Numinous'. As a writer, you can offer this gift during the long winter months. It might be reading stories to others or telling stories by heart. It might be sharing family or community stories around a table, or having a time for family or friends when people share a favourite story, song or poem.

Journal exercise

The shamanic Santa Claus returns in mid-winter with the life-giving story that the sun will return. What story can you offer?

Can you think of ways you can use your gifts as a writer as a gift to those who spend time with this season?

Ritual

Take some time today to write about your own story as it relates to the winter.

December 7

Recently I read an account of someone learning how to use a potter's wheel. What is most difficult for new potters is centring the clay on the

Interlude 8: Finding the Still Point of Your Story

fast-spinning wheel. The clay never lands on the midpoint and it never lands in an even shape, yet both conditions are necessary if something of use and beauty — a bowl, a mug, a jar — is going to result.

The novice potter has to learn to nudge the lump with exactly the right pressure and direction, whilst keeping her hands and the clay moist and the speed just right. It often fails. The pressure isn't right, the wheel spins too fast or slow, the clay is dry and cracks, or too wet and sags into a globby mess. It's a superb metaphor for finding our own centres. The potter, Patricia Pearce talks about sensing the still point in the centre of the clay even before she begins. Imagine it for yourself and see if you can detect that still point that is already there, present, waiting for you in the centre of your being. Even in the midst of commercial flurry, family pressures and office parties, there is a persistent stillness to this time of year. The natural world is stripped back, the palette of the season is cooler, more limited.

Journal exercise

When life is busy, how do you find your still point?

When do you feel a sense of the infinite breaking through into your everyday life?

What one thing can you do today to give yourself an experience of stillness or of the infinite?

How can you build experiences like this into your days throughout this month, even in small ways?

Ritual

Today, try to take a walk alone, even if it's just round the block. Notice what is noisy, what is still. Breathe deeply. Really attend to what you are seeing and hearing, what the air tastes like, the temperature. Later, journal about this spot from which you are viewing the universe.

December 8

The last few days, we've dived deep — thinking about what we need to let go of and what we need to let in, thinking about hopes and fears and about the ways in which we find still points and touch the infinite. If we are to retain any of the magic of this season, whether we keep Solstice or Christmas, Diwali or Chanukah, or a more secular festival of lights that is still imbued with story, then we need to return to those deep wells of narrative within. But we also have to be present in the world. Part of the magic of this season is how we make connections.

So often we have wonderful ideals about spending meaningful time with friends or family, of spending time walking in nature and feeling renewed, of communicating in a significant way with those we don't see often but still hold in our hearts. And yet all too often we end up feeling fractious and out of sorts. Meaningful time becomes slight misunderstandings that build into unspoken resentments and significant communication becomes the rush to write a pile of Christmas cards as quickly as possible, perhaps stuffing them with a badly printed round-robin which we apologise for, explaining that it's all we had time to send…

Just like us, our family and friends crave a little appreciation. When tension rises or we're running stressed, to be able to stop and find the good in those around us can transform the atmosphere. Everyone needs to be appreciated.

This doesn't mean you should put up with abuse or go along with expectations that leave you uneasy, but is simply to point out that countering a tense situation with complaint and criticism will only wind up the bad feeling. You can be appreciative without being a doormat.

Journal exercise

Journal about how you will alter some element of the usual dynamics this holiday season, whether it's how you fall into a particular role at a family gathering or how you send Christmas cards. Think about one thing you can change with grace and appreciation, without self-sacrifice.

Ritual

Send someone a message — it could be a Christmas card — but make it personal and significant.

As an extra:

If you normally send a lot of Christmas cards that are bulk written, hone your list. Limit yourself to 10 really personal messages that connect. If others will 'expect' a card, think about ways to handle this — send them an email and let them know you made a donation instead or send an e-card. How many people can you connect with deeply at one time?

December 9

Every year at the beginning of Advent I put out a set of little olive wood figures. They were a gift to my oldest son from his godmother, brought back from Palestine, and, although I wouldn't describe myself as Christian, Christianity's stories and liturgy are deeply embedded in me and integral to the journey I've made. And the figures are part of our family story: a story of birth and hope in winter, a story of caring for the vulnerable… and a story about how, every Advent, my children, all adults now — and now aided and abetted by partners — stealthily re-arrange my beautifully laid out tableau (no baby till late on Christmas Eve, no kings until Epiphany) to balance sheep precariously on shepherds and make unlikely circus towers out of Mary, Joseph, a donkey, perhaps a cow…

We all have stories. And we all are stories. There are stories that we once told over and over; there are stories we've read that have never left us; there are stories of family events, including our own nativities, perhaps complete with pictures of us as babies and young children; memories, routines, anecdotes and sayings that are part of a particular family or group's texture and culture, that signal to us that we are where we belong.

As writers, we not only deal in story and how story is moulded (even if that comes through poetry) but we also, like all of humanity, live in story; the big myths of our culture, the personal stories of life and belonging, the media stories that bombard us, the story we construct of who we are.

Journal exercise

What stories do you have the strongest memories of in relation to this time of the year?

What are the stories or anecdotes that signal that you belong (it doesn't have to be to a family, it might be an interest group, a faith group, your local reading group, the street you live in…)

· Interlude 8: Finding the Still Point of Your Story ·

What story do you believe about yourself that you would like to change?

Ritual

Make the commitment to this change in your story. Now share it. Telling someone you trust that you are going to shift this bit of your story will make you more likely to keep the promise to yourself — ask them to check back with you after an agreed length of time.

December 10

For children, festivals like Christmas can be magical. They have the ability to lose themselves in the story, to see another world in a string of fairy lights and to burst with anticipation. As we get older we often feel we've lost some of this, that we're a bit more jaded and tired, or that the commercial frenzy and spectacle has distanced us from depth and meaning.

Young children live not so much in *chronos* (chronological time) as in *kairos* (the right time). The more you take time to breathe deeply and notice small pleasures, the more you'll find yourself doing the same. Moments build into hours, into days and into lives. A good life is not about having more but about experiencing more deeply. This is something we might do well to repeat to ourselves every day, but perhaps most especially during a holiday season that has been hijacked by the rhetoric of 'more and more': The life of the spirit requires less and less; time is plenty and its passage rich.

Journal exercise

What are your childhood memories of times that seemed most magical?

What is it that makes a day good for you now?

When are you most likely to feel that time expands?

What one thing can you do today to give yourself time for a simple pleasure?

Ritual

Whatever you just identified as a way to expand time, do it today — whether it's telling someone you love them, sitting with a hot drink and a good book for an hour, going for a walk…

December 11

Far from being a time of decorated trees and glittering lights, sentimental Christmas songs playing in every shop beckoning you to 'buy this', 'and this' and… the theology of Advent is darker. It anticipates not only the coming of a child who saves the world, but also looking forward to the 'last things': death, judgment, hell and heaven. This doesn't need to be a call to gloom and doom. In the darkness of winter when we are sending greetings to, or spending time with, those we care for, it is good to pause and give time to remembering those who were with us for past winter seasons and who've now passed on. Life is precious, and it is a privilege to remember those we've loved and lost and to savour having known them, recognising that we are all mortal. This is not morbid but a life-affirming reminder that now matters, that how we live our days is how we live our lives. Change and transitoriness, despite their associations with grief, are ultimately what give life value. Timelessness is lifeless and stagnant, whereas transitoriness makes life supremely precious. If there was no beginning, no end, there would be no progress, no movement forward, no creativity.

Journal exercise

Journal about two things: you are thankful for someone in your past who gave you some of their precious time, and how you will give time during this season to a particular person.

Ritual

Light a candle today in memory of the person you remembered in your journalling.

December 12

Great writers write the truth. This is not to say that they don't write fiction, but at its best fiction encompasses 'truthful lies'. Fiction is a way to dig into the truth in ways that simple 'fact' can never attain. Earlier this month, we looked at the stories behind Santa Claus and we've also considered ways in which children enter into the magic of Christmas. One of the constant questions that arise about this aspect of the mythology around Christmas is how we spin the myth for children without lying in such a way that there is a sudden sense of betrayal. Yet we know as writers that there are ways of telling stories that are profoundly true without suggesting that there is an actual analogue in everyday life. We don't have to tell children a story and insist there is in fact a jolly fat man in a red suit who watches them all year, knows everything and comes down the chimney after landing his sleigh on the roof. Parents know how to convey stories to children that are both truth and fiction without having to break the spell and point it out. There needs to be no discontinuity as their children articulate for themselves that Father Christmas is not 'real'. Children are not too stupid to know the difference between a 'fact' and a poetic truth, especially if they are accustomed to being told the truth on important issues.

Journal exercise

In what ways does your writing explore 'truth of a different kind'?

What are the most important 'truthful lies' for you?

Ritual

Revisit a favourite myth — it might be a fairy story, or ''Twas The Night Before Christmas' (perhaps written by Clement Clarke Moore?) or... read it, savour it, and feel the power of a truthful lie.

December 13

The festival of Saint Lucia or Lucy is largely kept in Nordic and Scandinavian countries, Italy, the Balkans and Hungary. It is based on the story of a third century saint and martyr who carried food to the Christians hiding from persecution in the catacombs, wearing a wreath of candles so she could see her way while having both hands free to carry food. The celebrations often involve processions with girls wearing wreaths of candles and revolve around having enough light for the winter. In Croatia and Hungary, wheat grains are planted and will begin to sprout by Christmas day, signs of birth and nourishment. The song of her coming, used in Scandinavia but likely to be of Neapolitan origin, runs:

> The night treads heavily
> around yards and dwellings
> In places unreached by sun,
> the shadows brood
>
> Into our dark house she comes,
> bearing lighted candles,
> Saint Lucia, Saint Lucia.

There's also a darker tradition, particularly in Norway and Sweden, of Lussinatta. Lussi is a more Lucifer-like figure or female leader of a wild hunt, merciless to anyone who is out at night or even indoors but not sufficiently prepared for Yuletide. Giving food and preparations are the watchwords of this day, whether from light-bearing Saint Lucy or the demon-like Lussi.

Sharing the light and sharing food are at the heart of this season. But the notion of having everything done by yesterday, the pressure of to-do lists and perfectionism and fearing 'not being ready' is probably something that afflicts many of us even without the existence of a rampaging angry demon in the dark. Many of us are experts at playing the part of Lussi for ourselves in the dark hours, anxious that everything should be just right, while, by day, we want to be perfect, like the all-giving Saint Lucy, even at the cost of martyrdom.

Hospitality, feeding others, offering life and nutrition, are rewarding traditions, but we have to find ways to incorporate them into our lives that are about grace, not sacrifice; joyful sharing, not fear of not doing or being enough.

Journal exercise

In what ways is this time of the year stressful for you?

• Interlude 8: Finding the Still Point of Your Story •

How can you quiet those fears?

What light- and life-riches do you have that you can share this winter?

What are all the ways in which your writing and your life are abundant?

Ritual

Share a simple meal with someone important to you today. Linger over it. If you live alone or this isn't practical, call or write to someone you care about and toast them with a glass of wine or cup of hot chocolate or…

December 14

Food is a major theme of this season. Whether it's the potato latkes of Chanukah or a Christmas turkey (or goose or…), there are certain foods that tell you not only where you are, but what season you are in and who you are with. In our household on Christmas Day, there is always asparagus and quail's egg soup, there is always a chestnut roulade for the vegetarians and dauphinois potatoes (with leeks) for everyone. We wake up to orange or blueberry muffins, and, as we gather on Christmas Eve, there are quiches: mushroom; broccoli, courgette and tomato and salmon. On Boxing Day there is smoked salmon and eggs, leftovers and cheeses. We always have paella (with vegetarian chorizo) on New Year's Eve.

A couple of years ago, a friend (and poet) with a difficult family, described to me how she and her partner made an alternative Christmas, disapproved of by her wider family and especially by a more conformist sister, with a meal of raw salmon gravlax and a long walk. It's so tempting with Christmas food to feel that 'more is more' and that even more is still not enough. If we are people used to providing for others, being hospitable, ensuring that nothing ever runs out, this season can become stressful. But it's likely that the only person feeling that there is never enough will be you. And those you love will feel more than satiated.

The concept of 'enough' is an important one in a season prone to excess. It's salutary and sad to meet people who have so much but who clearly never feel a sense that they have 'enough'. When I was studying A-level Religious Studies and Philosophy at the end of the '70s, my teacher (an ex-Methodist minister) would end every lesson with the saying:

· Interlude 8: Finding the Still Point of Your Story ·

'Sufficient to the day are the evils thereof.' In other words, 'enough'. He didn't know it, but he planted in me the seed that there is such a thing as 'enough'.

Journal exercise

If you are the person providing the Christmas meal, for yourself or for a couple or more... how will you bring to the table the concept of 'enough'? And if you are accepting hospitality, how will you draw your own line of 'enough'?

What are your experiences of trying too hard or pushing yourself beyond what is 'enough'?

Whether in food or gifts or spending or how you use your time during the holiday season, what will be 'enough'?

How will you find a balance this year between giving and providing, so that you are generous whilst giving yourself and your writing time?

Ritual

Today, find your point of 'enough' and when you have reached it, do something that completely relaxes you.

December 15

Smelling and thinking are remarkably similar. Both are acts of perception, and both link us to memories. The cells we use for our sense of smell are neurons that carry first hand information from the outside world. Smell is vital. A whiff of a certain odour can transport us to childhood or a particular place or day or hour. The scent of a bonfire on a sharp autumn day; the aroma of hot milk, the tang of salt on the wind... All kinds of olfactory treasures spark memory and the winter season is full of them.

Journal exercise

What are the scents of the season for you? Roasting meat? Chestnuts?

Mulled wine? The spices of Christmas cakes? Oranges?

What memories do these scents evoke?

What do you want this season to smell of? And how will you make it so?

Ritual

Do something today that will leave a strong scent — it might be burning incense or a candle, it might be baking bread or lighting a real fire or filling a room with greenery…

December 16

As we've seen, many writers have noticed the strong connection between walking and writing. There is something about the rhythm, as well as the mixture of acute observation and letting ourselves become present to the moment, that is inspirational. Walking is rhythm that takes over mind and body. Winter can be an excellent time for walking, giving it distinctive features. In 'A Winter Walk' (from *Excursions*) Thoreau writes beautifully about the nature of winter:

> … while the earth has slumbered, all the air has been alive with feathery flakes descending, as if some northern Ceres reigned, showering her silvery grain over all the fields.
>
> We sleep, and at length awake to the still reality of a winter morning. The snow lies warm as cotton or down upon the window-sill; the broadened sash and frosted panes admit a dim and private light, which enhances the snug cheer within.
>
> […]
>
> There is a slumbering subterranean fire in nature which never goes out, and which no cold can chill … What fire could ever equal the sunshine of a winter's day, when the meadow mice come out by the wallsides, and the chicadee

lisps in the defiles of the wood?

Journal exercise

Do you walk regularly?

Where do you walk? Are you able to get into nature?

Write about a walk that stands out in your memory.

Ritual

Whatever the weather, take a walk today. Walk slowly. Let your mind roam but gradually try to let the chatter fall away — presents that need wrapping, or buying; cooking or cleaning to do; work that is bothering you; a conflict in your life… let them arise and then quiet them.

Be in the moment. Take in the place you are walking in. Open your senses to it. Be still. And walk some more.

December 17

During the winter a lot of nature dies back, so things that remain green become powerful metaphors for the journey through the darker, shorter days. In his illustrated poem, 'The Cultivation of Christmas Trees', T S Eliot talks about how we can retain the spirit of wonder into adulthood. This spirit is certainly helped by participating in simple traditions that make us focus on the rhythms of life and which add meaningful metaphors to those rhythms.

The history of putting up trees in public spaces or bringing fir trees indoors for this season is long and disputed and there are antecedents like the Mediaeval Mystery Plays' wooden Paradise Trees, paraded on December 24 to remember Adam and Eve in the Garden of Eden. There are stories of miracles, like that of St Boniface cutting down an oak being apparently used in connection with a human sacrifice and a fir springing up in its place, or of the Christ-child visiting a poor family incognito and leaving a fir branch as a gift of thanks for their hospitality, and associations with the tradition of yule logs, particularly through the trees of Riga and

Tallinn in the 15th and 16th centuries, which were danced around, then cut down and burnt. Trees decorated with food and candles are certainly known by the 18th century, as Goethe's description in his 1774 novel, *Die Leiden des jungen Werther*, shows.

More widely, bringing in greenery goes back a long way, certainly to the Roman festival of Saturnalia, which was originally on December 17 but gradually expanded across several days. After the harvests and in honour of the winter sowing, and the god, Saturn, it was a festival when social norms were relaxed or even overturned (a household king might be chosen on the basis of who found a coin in a cake and servants and slaves took full part and were often served by masters). It was a time of feasting, music, and gifts (often candles), all of which made their way into Christmas traditions by the 4th century.

Holly was a symbol of the god Saturn and decorating with greenery was part of the festivities. Holly is also associated with protection and so was placed around windows and doors. Mistletoe has links with both Norse and Druid traditions as a protection from storms and evil. In the Norse myth associated with Balder, mistletoe was the only thing he wasn't protected from, so he was killed with an arrow of mistletoe. The tears his mother, the goddess Frigga, became the white berries that brought her son back to life and so the plant is blessed and becomes a symbol of peace and of bestowing kisses.

Greenery is full of life. Green foods nourish us and, surprisingly, we share 99% of our DNA with the lettuce. We really are deeply connected to all things.

Journal exercise

Evergreens dignify the cold, dark months. And 'greening' is a wonderful way to think about the creative life germinating within us.

What are your memories and/or associations of Christmas trees, wreaths and seasonal greenery?

Do you decorate with greenery in this season?

Is it just another task/tired tradition or can you relocate the wonder in it?

In what ways is your writing alive and green and in what ways does it need greening?

· Interlude 8: Finding the Still Point of Your Story ·

Ritual

If you normally put up a Christmas tree, it might already be up and decorated, or you may have a family tradition of doing it on a specific day (for some, Christmas Eve) but if not, consider putting it up today. Alternatively, gather some greenery and make a feature of it somewhere in your home, perhaps near where you write.

December 18

Yesterday we thought a bit about Christmas trees and the greenery of holly and mistletoe and other evergreens. But what about other decorations? Do you hang fairy lights? If you have a tree, is it elegantly sparse or cluttered with a cornucopia of ornaments from the kitsch to the folksy? Are there paper streamers, strings of cards, Advent calendars, candles…? Or do you eschew the whole lot of it?

In our house, we put up a big tree. It has to be large enough to take years of ornaments, each of them a memory. Many were made by my children over many years of home educating. Others were bought at particular times, often chosen by the children as they were growing up. There are clay stars and angels, hand-painted by small hands; beautiful cut glass baubles or icicles; wooden reindeer and Santa Claus; felt Christmas trees and snowmen; *papier maché* painted globes and a whole lot more. There's a pinecone wreath that goes on the door that was made by someone in my parish nearly thirty years ago. There's the olive wood nativity set my now-grown children and their partners will arrange into ever more acrobatic and bizarre installations, and a big shamanic-looking Santa (in green) from a woodworker in Prague.

None of these objects are valuable, many could be written off as 'tat', but they are physical reminders of times, places and events. I hold a paper origami robin made a quarter of a century ago and I'm transported. It's not the only way I could access those memories but, together, they reinforce a particular experience of Christmas. Of course, objects don't only evoke good memories. For some, getting out a box of decorations might signal old resentments, family conflicts and disappointments. Or they might just feel like dead weight, sentimentality, and a lot of fuss to put up and take down again.

Journal exercise

Do you have traditions around decorating your home over the holiday season?

Do those traditions delight you or leave you cold... or something else?

Are there ways you'd like to change these traditions?

In your imagination, conjure the perfect Christmas scene (by your own lights, which might be radically unlike what anyone else would imagine) and write yourself into it.

Ritual

Make some small change in your environment today — anything from removing an object you dislike or which evokes negative memories, to putting a vase of flowers somewhere; from clearing out a cluttered cupboard, to making yourself a corner with a collection of objects that you love.

December 19

In 'A Winter Walk' in *Excursions*, Henry David Thoreau, remarks:

> In winter we lead a more inward life. Our hearts are warm and cheery, like cottages under drifts, whose windows and doors are half concealed, but from whose chimneys the smoke cheerfully ascends.

Winter is a great time for imagination. When we are not working or socialising, we tend to be more inward-looking during this season. It's the same throughout nature. Some animals hibernate or semi-hibernate, deciduous trees shed their foliage to conserve energy for new growth and, deep underground, growth is happening in the dark.

Winter is a powerful metaphor as well as the season we're currently in. When we pause to consider politics, ecological disaster, fake news, the inequalities of the planet or the suffering of friends, life can seem like perpetual winter in which the season becomes associated with gloom, barrenness, death and absence. And yet, not only does the sun always return but it is also carried within, especially in how we choose to live our days. Moreover, it's possible to recast the metaphors of winter as something much more life-affirming. Many people love winter. It is a season of extraordinary, pared down beauty. There is something stark yet honest about the bare trees and the pale skies. The light changes, the days are short but allow for evenings full of firelight and fairy lights. There may be snowfall and there is increasing anticipation of Christmas. And in the shades of white and grey, the particular light, there is a sense of mystery and peace.

There is also something fascinating about a season that strips away so many things — warmth, greenery, even moderation as temperatures plummet. We are taken to extremities in the way that ice wine is made sweeter by being placed under the stress of bitter cold, even freezing. Sometimes, as writers, we need a certain kind of pressure. In botany the term 'vernalisation' refers to seeds that only germinate and subsequently thrive in spring because they have been through a severe winter.

This happens too, in life. The spring is a miracle because we know what winter is like and how we have just survived it. Shade is essential to light; we need both the sharps and the flats. And this love of winter, and going into ourselves in this season, isn't only about privation and cold. As Rilke illustrates in his *Letters to a Young Woman* (written to Lisa Heise) tending the 'inner garden' is vital.

Journal exercise

In what ways do you go inwards in the winter?

How do you feel about the season of winter, the cold, the short days? Are the associations negative, positive or a mixture?

What are the stresses of this season for you and how does this show in your writing?

What are the nourishments of this season? For writing and for life?

Do you feel vernalisation in your writing?

Where do you find peace and mysteriousness in this season and how do these flow into your writing life?

• Interlude 8: Finding the Still Point of Your Story •

Ritual

Comfort foods and ruminative, inward days go together. Today, take some time to carefully prepare and savour something that comforts your body. Perhaps hot chocolate or raw cacao in almond milk, or a thick vegetable soup or... For me, it would be hot porridge made with organic oats, almond milk and nutmeg, and topped with berries, seeds and a smear of local honey. Take time cooking and take time eating.

December 20

This time of the year has distinct musical associations. The tradition of wassailing, that was associated with Twelfth Night, involved going house to house, swapping drink from the wassail bowl in return for gifts or, historically, calling on the lord of the manor to sing and offer blessing in return for hospitality. Carolling has largely replaced this tradition with Advent and Christmas carols, though carols, originally circle dances going back to the 12th century, didn't always have religious significance. Carols like 'Make we joy now in this fest' (Seldon manuscript, c.1450), with its verses and choruses interleaved, is a great example of the round dance structure in the music.

Some carols were part of Mediaeval mystery plays. The Coventry Carol, for example, goes back to at least the 14th century — it's a carol of haunting sadness in its references to Herod slaughtering the innocents in his raging search to find the baby king that might oust him. Carols were originally in Latin, like the Gregorian plainchant, '*Verbum caro*', but became popular after the Reformation when there was a big push to translate and write carols in vernacular English. Now we find ourselves surrounded by the same popular, and largely secular, Christmas songs on loop in every store or café we visit from late November onwards, until we want to pull the speakers out of the wall rather than hear Slade sing 'Merry Christmas Everybody' one more time.

Winter also has a host of other musical associations, from operas like Puccini's *La Bohème*, set in a snow-laden Paris, to Rimsky-Korsakov's tragic *The Snow Maiden*; ballets like Tchaikovsky's *The Nutcracker*, Korngold's *Der Schneemann*, or the more strange 'Ballet of the Snowflakes' (from Offenbach's very odd opera, *Le voyage dans la lune*); song cycles like Schubert's dark *Winterreise*, or Liszt's much lighter Weihnachtsbaum, dedicated to his granddaughter and containing pieces such as 'O Holy Night', 'Adeste Fideles' and 'Evening Bells', and piano pieces like Debussy's 'The Snow is Dancing' and *Des pas sur la neige*. There are symphonies, too, such as Peter Maxwell Davies's Symphony No. 8 'Antarctic Symphony' or Tchaikovsky's Symphony No. 1 'Winter Dreams', or Rachmaninov's choral symphony, 'The Bells', as well as waltzes, like 'The Skaters' Waltz' by Émile Waldteufel (*Les Patineurs*), and polkas, like '*Winterlust* Polka' by Josef Strauss, and of course there's J S Bach's Christmas Oratorio.

Nietzsche tells us:

> Without music life would be a mistake.

Journal exercise

Do you use music when you write?

If you play music while you write, does it shift with the season or is it more related to particular pieces or musical genres?

What music do you associate with December? Are these associations positive or otherwise?

Write a piece about a memory that you link with music — prose or a prose poem or poem.

Ritual

Choose a piece of music to listen to today that makes you think of winter or Christmas. Sit and listen to it carefully, with attention.

December 21

The Winter Solstice is a time brimming with associations, images and archetypes. It includes themes of solitude and deep contemplation, mindfulness of the narrative of death and (eventually) rebirth. At the solstices the sun stands still and the Winter Solstice is the beginning of the astronomical winter. At this time of the year, the tilt of the planet and our

Interlude 8: Finding the Still Point of Your Story

elliptical orbit around the sun conspire to make the shortest day (in the Northern hemisphere). In the night sky, Orion is bright. The year is coming to an end, the light poised — before it begins to lengthen again by tiny increments.

Traditions associated with Solstice are somewhat murky, but the Yule log appears to go back to Norse and Saxon cultures. This is Bede, writing in the 8th century:

> They began the year with December 25, the day we now celebrate as Christmas; and the very night to which we attach special sanctity they designated by the heathen mothers' night — a name bestowed, I suspect, on account of the ceremonies they performed while watching this night through. (*De temporum ratione*)

These ceremonies included burning a Yule log. In many places the log was huge enough to burn through twelve days (so might be a whole tree), with the leftover ash kept to light the next year's log and attributed with many protective qualities. In other places (like France), the log was burnt in pieces over the twelve days, and in the West Country in the UK would be a bunch of ash twigs. However it was practised, the burning represents death and new life, the coming of the sun again, and traditionally logs should be foraged or given as gifts rather than bought.

As the year turns, a lot comes our way — families and relationships (whether wonderfully supportive or not) take huge emotional energy, as do friendships; we face illnesses, sometimes life-threatening or stripping away the quality of life, in ourselves and others; we balance work and the fast pace of modern living with needs for an inner life and a creative life; we have domestic concerns and a thousand-and-one other things competing for just a bit of us until sometimes we realise there isn't one bit left over for the next thing, but still have to keep going. Even if life is going extraordinarily well and we feel continually blessed, there can still be a pace to this that we need to rest from.

The Solstice is a good day to step back, even if only for an hour or two, and give yourself time to think in stillness and quiet; a time for spiritual nourishment (whatever 'spirituality' might mean to you). Going inward in retreat is not a rejection of the world and responsibilities and love, but a way of storing energy for whatever life throws at it — think of it as your stash of squirrel nuts for the winter. It's also a way of giving yourself the space to digest emotions, to absorb and contemplate what is going on in your life at the moment and how you want to move forward — by doing this deep considering we become more considerate, less likely to be reactive or to project our shadow parts onto others.

Transforming ourselves within is continual work, but this is a day to mark this work, which is rich and fertile. Change begins deep inside. What often prevents change is that we remain trapped in limiting conceptions of ourselves. These conceptions can come from within, from clinging to being self-righteously right rather than risking an understanding that would require a lot of thinking and transformation. Or they can come from the expectations of others. So often people have a fixed idea of who we are and it's deeply discomfiting to them if we begin to show signs of change. People can invest in us staying the same and, at this time of the year, this can include how we are expected to play certain roles within family or community events that have always been done in a particular way.

So taking some time to contemplate how you want to evolve as a person is integral to this season. The winter is the perfect time to go deeply within. It is a time to curl up in the warmth with books and music, with films and images of art that feed this inner life. Winter is a time for imagination, for 'hibernating' with whatever nourishes this inner journey so that we have the resources to go out into the world again when the sun returns. Winter is a time for taking time out, making some spaces that are not about meeting demands or merely making it from one day to the next. Winter is time to recharge, to let the mind wander and let feelings surface.

Journal exercise

How do you nurture your inner life?

What part does your writing play in constructing who you are and who you want to be?

What needs to die back to give your inner life the space to flourish?

Ritual

If you have a hearth or wood burner, or a part of a garden where it's safe to burn a log, burn one today. Or simply light a candle. As you contemplate the light and warmth, make a commitment to rebirth, to giving your inner life space to grow and thrive.

As the log or candle burns down toast your inner, creative life — with wine, with juice, with kombucha…

December 22

What do we bring to the table?

On December 14 we thought about the food of this season. Particularly if we keep Chanukah or Solstice or Christmas, there are likely to be elements that are traditional, either to our wider group, culture or family. These elements shift over time, of course. Goose was a traditional Christmas fare before turkey. Venison was the dish of choice for the rich at one time, though they would 'magnanimously' leave some of the offal and innards for the poor (the parts known as the 'umbles' and hence the origin of 'eating humble pie').

Cultures and eating habits change. We've already considered the food on our tables and we know this is a complex issue. What we eat will change with income levels, with wildly disparate beliefs about what it is ethical to eat and where it is ethical to buy from; with whether we see cooking as a joy and pleasure and something to always do from scratch or go for pre-made options. It's good to pause and think about our assumptions around food, but whatever food will be on our festive table, or whatever food we eat at this time of the year in any company but our own, food is only part of the alchemy. It's certainly a large part. We build stories around food, from family anecdotes to religious rituals and everything in between.

Cooking, like making art or writing a novel, involves innovation and risk and constant honing. The way ingredients change with heat or combination demands that we think ahead, imagine and go with the magic that sometimes goes wrong. Food and eating together is not only nourishing, but also transformative. We have winter foods and summer foods. We have foods that comfort us, that leave us feeling heavy or light, that bring back memories or create particular moods.

And, along with food, we bring other things to our tables. Alcohol or not? A bare table or one set with candles and decorations or particular crockery or glassware? And, crucially, ourselves. The people around the table will determine the flow of conversation, the expectations, the subtexts of belonging or resentments… But what is crucial is that the table is a place of unconditional welcome, a table where each person gives attention to those present, to the food, to the moment.

Journal exercise

What role does food play in your writing, whether in sustaining it or providing material for it?

Writing and cooking both require 'innovation and risk and constant honing'. Where do you find these elements in the food you eat and the writing you do?

In your writing, cooking and life, how do you make room for a 'the magic that sometimes goes wrong'?

Write about a table that has been or is important to you, or which is part of a significant memory. Or invent your perfect table.

Where and with whom are you most welcome?

Where, when and for whom do you offer welcome?

Ritual

Not everyone finds a table. Put aside some tinned or packet food or a donation for a local food bank and drop it off as soon as possible.

December 23

Whether you will be alone, with one other, or in a large family/friendship/community group this Solstice/Christmas/winter season, who will you bring to the table? Bringing ourselves can feel difficult. All families and cultures have certain expectations and sometimes these feel bent on making us be anyone but ourselves. The holiday season is often one in which we feel the world is doing its best, night and day, to make us conform — to how our family want or expect us to be, to how society wants us to spend money and time, to how particular religious ideologies want us to think and believe. Whether you write prose or poetry, memoir or blogs, you need, in this season to hang onto the feeling and quality of your inner life and experiences and keep feeding them into your writing.

Journal exercise

In the midst of this season, which may be frenetic and full of demands, or may be lonely and full of memories, or something else entirely, who are you going to bring to the table?

How will you show up as yourself this winter?

How would you describe this person?

Ritual

Listen to your feelings today and ask yourself which you need to act on and which you need to work with.

December 24

Awe and wonder are extraordinary emotions, so powerful that they have sometimes been harnessed to break those identified as 'the enemy' with 'shock and awe' tactics that overwhelm the other with such spectacular displays of power that they are paralysed. But at the other end of the spectrum, these same emotions can be sparked by a sudden realisation of cosmic grandeur, walking on a starry night, or by being in the presence of a newborn child.

We don't have to subscribe to a particular dogma to feel the power of birth, the heart-breaking combination of fragility, strength and possibility. It is breathtaking. We don't have to believe in a particular doctrine to have 'faith' in the sense of allowing there are mysteries we might never understand. Awe is not about answering questions, but being able to live with questions. Awe comes at unlooked for moments and enters us deeply.

Profound moments are not always 'big' experiences. Sometimes they come as a sudden welling of epiphany, sitting on a train watching a landscape flash by or as a quiet, shimmering sense of depth as you stand in a kitchen putting a kettle of water on the stove. Today, when you might be dashing to make last minute preparations or travelling to visit family or

• INTERLUDE 8: FINDING THE STILL POINT OF YOUR STORY •

cooking enough to feed a tribe, put yourself in the way of awe — take half an hour to walk, go outside and look at the stars...

Birth, which is the presiding theme of Christmas Eve, reminds us of the preciousness and precariousness of life; its power and vulnerability. In the words of Wordsworth:

> With an eye made quiet by the power of harmony, and the
> deep power of joy, we see into the life of things.

Journal exercise

What are your memories of profound moments?

Where are you most likely to encounter such moments? (In your writing, reading, in nature, going about simple daily tasks?)

Earlier in the month we thought about Kathleen Raine's poem, 'Northumbrian Sequence IV', with its injunction to let in the child. This isn't a call to immaturity or regression, but to the power of seeing things fresh and new; to have the courage to be fragile and open.

Where are you most fragile and open?

What power is there in this fragility?

In what ways can you let in your child? (Not to regress, but to be present in the moment, to look with awe and wonder?)

Ritual

Stand under the night sky alone for at least a few minutes before the end of today.

December 27

In the beautiful children's book, *Moominland Midwinter*, by Tove Jansson, Moomintroll finds a lovely snowy stroll turning into a frightening storm. Of course, in the howling gale with visibility diminishing, he becomes tense and afraid. And then he gets angry. He fills with fury in a way reminiscent of the story of Kierkegaard's father, desperate at his family's poverty, climbing a local hill and shaking his fists at the sky and cursing God. But this defiant resistance is useless until Moomintroll stops fighting it and becomes part of the elements, carried along by the blizzard and full of playful joy again.

The whole book is a superb metaphor for not trying to force a particular outcome. So often, in our writing and in our life, we become completely caught up in reaching a particular outcome or product. Then, when it doesn't go well, we feel despair and rage, with the universe, with anything we can project our disappointment onto and/or with ourselves. Sometimes in our efforts to control every variable, we feel more futile than ever. But it's when Moomintroll lets go, surrenders to the elements and goes with the flow that he experiences something completely different. He transcends his struggling, trying-to-control-it-all self and discovers something he hadn't looked for or expected, that is beautiful and thrilling.

It's a paradox that sometimes we have to let go of all the effort and forcing the work before creativity happens. And winter is, once again, a great metaphor for this with things germinating underground. The flowering will come, there is always change, always transformation, always a different story.

When the words are not coming and the creativity doesn't appear to be flowing, be confident that something will be going on deep within. Stop fighting yourself. In *The Conquest of Happiness*, the philosopher, Bertrand Russell, advises that when we are mulling over any problem we should stop thinking about it, give it to the unconscious, and later we will find the answer simply emerges. Winter can be a wonderful time to write. For a writer, every season is a time to write, but sometimes we have a 'winter spell' in our writing when we need to give it space and let the creativity take its own course while, in the meantime, we can do other creative and life-affirming things.

Journal exercise

What are the signs for you that you need to let a particular piece of writing alone for a while?

What are the emotions you feel when the writing isn't flowing?

What activities help you to stop fighting yourself, stand back and allow the subconscious to take over?

· INTERLUDE 8: FINDING THE STILL POINT OF YOUR STORY ·

Ritual

Do something you find creative or restorative today that isn't writing. It can be something really imaginative or utterly simple that gives you a sense of well-being.

December 28

We become reflective at this time of the year; the winter turning us inwards and the calendar signalling end and beginning combine to make us both look back and forward. Tomorrow we are going to look at tools for reflecting but, today, whether you have just had a big noisy Christmas and Boxing Day, or if you have survived a season that is all about groups on your own, or if you have opted out of the whole Christmas 'thing' but still felt it's everywhere you look, we are going to have some self-compassion.

The author of the fantastic book on the writing life, *Bird by Bird*, Anne Lamott, writes about mercy in her most recent book, *Hallelujah Anyway*. I don't share Lamott's religious faith (though I have a great respect for the broadness of her faith) but, regardless, I admire the way she foregrounds an unfashionable virtue, particularly one that relies on our choice between causing suffering or showing tenderness and grace. We often live in a harsh and judgemental world, but mercy is a gentler way of living; a quality we can extend not only to others but to ourselves, especially as we are often our own harshest critic.

We are all flawed. Did you have a perfect Christmas? Is winter going perfectly? Are you everything you want to be? I hope you answered 'No!' to most or all of that. Not because I want things to be going badly for you, quite the opposite, but because I hope we can all recognise that perfectionism is a toxic myth that stops us celebrating real, wonderful, messy lives; because I think it's essential to recognise that if we don't extend mercy to ourselves, we are lost. Go and look at the lyrics of Leonard Cohen's song, 'Hallelujah'. The jubilance is not for all that went right but despite things going wrong. Feeling grateful and extending mercy do not rely on everything being fine, or on perfect shiny lives. They are qualities for real people, real writers, living real, messy stories that nevertheless can change and change again, the more so with a bit of compassion and gentleness coming their way. So today, let's celebrate trying rather than succeeding; taking a risk over productivity; intention over triumph.

Journal exercise

How judgmental are you towards yourself? Why?

How can you shift this to show yourself more mercy?

How does self-respect impact on your sense of yourself as a writer?

Ritual

Forgive yourself for something. If it helps, write it down and burn the paper (safely) or write it in your journal and cross it out. But mean it. Let this bit of self-judgment go. Light a candle in honour of this mercy.

December 29

Every year, at some point between Christmas and New Year, I set aside some time for reflecting on the year in a way that will help me consider the direction of the next year. I have some issues with the language of 'measurement' for people. There are things that are certainly measurable, but overall I'm much more interested in the qualitative aspects of living and writing.

With that proviso, there are a couple of tools for thinking about the year gone and the year to come that are helpful. We can look at life from the perspective of what's missing — all the ways in which life is not the mythical ideal we might want, or we can see it from the viewpoint of the progress we've made — how far we have already come and all we've already achieved. If we focus on what is missing we cultivate a scarcity mentality and feel that nothing we have done is worth much, that we have hardly accomplished anything at all. We're fixated on some mythical outcome that only seems to get more distant in this mindset. But if we concentrate instead on progress, how much journeying we've done, then we shift to a mentality in which we can rejoice that we've moved forward; whether it's an increment or a million miles, we've achieved something and can feel grateful and more confident as we continue the quest.

This isn't a call to complacency or not examining those aspects of ourselves we know need more work, but if we berate ourselves it won't be motivating. Feeling that our lives are in deficit and that we are always chasing a gap that continually grows bigger will only overwhelm and demoralise us. We discover more optimism when we live with a sense of gain. Focussing on progress is energising, joyful and deepens our sense of well-being. So today, reflect on the last year from the perspective of progress. (It can also be enlightening to use these questions in relation to the last five years or the last decade. Sometimes I feel very little has shifted but when I take a longer view, I'm surprised.)

Journal exercise

Think about an average day this time last year. What is different now?

What are the things you're most grateful to have achieved this year?

What new insights, new ways of thinking and personal growth have you experienced this year?

What ideals did you set out with in January this year? How much closer are you to those ideals?

Given all of this growth, where will you be focusing next year?

Another tool I find useful is to ask these two simple questions of the various areas of my life: What needs more? What needs less? I use these questions in regard to my sense of spiritual and emotional health; physical health and well-being; relationships (from the closest family to friendships to those at work…); learning; rest and recuperation; work and financial survival. (Your categories might look different — sometimes I've used the system of chakras, each with a colour and aspect of life and there are lots of other models that might work for you.)

So, for each area of your life:

What needs more?

What needs less?

Ritual

Celebrate yourself today. This may be building on, or an extension of, what you did yesterday. But in addition, write a list of things you are grateful for and leave it somewhere you will see it for at least a few days.

December 30

How can you be a writer who changes the story of who you are and who changes the story of the world, if you are rushing around at a million miles an hour, have no time to think and breathe and are consumed with distractions, inessentials and just about making it from one day to the next?

Of course, you can't. We can only become the stories that make ourselves and the world different if we live each day differently. And this requires a particular perspective, convictions and ideals that constantly challenge the norms and constantly shake us awake. So, as the year ends, I'd like to offer some qualities for consideration, to open the conversation of how we might live as writers to make a difference, however small that difference might seem.

These qualities are a call to:

- find a humane pace
- be present

They are a call to have:

- compassion
- humility
- courage
- vulnerability
- generosity

There are many other important ideals and your list might be very different. We need that — different writers making their difference differently but each working with hope and love to refuse cynicism or doom. Over the next few days we'll take a closer look at the list and you can borrow what fits, and make your own. We'll return to the full list on New Year's Eve as we consider our quests for the next year but, today, I want to consider the first two qualities because I think they provide the context in which we can explore ideals to live by and quests we want to challenge ourselves with.

A humane pace

When we are rushing, we stay in the shallows. If I rush a yoga practice, I don't get into the positions correctly or feel the deep calming effects. If I rush a meal with family, I don't get into a deep conversation. If I rush a book I'm reading, I come away with an impoverished view of the story or metaphors or what I was hoping to learn. If I rush work, I make mistakes and the quality is skimped on. In *Either/Or*, Søren Kierkegaard puts it bluntly:

> Of all ridiculous things, the most ridiculous seems to me, to be busy — to be a [wo]man who is brisk about his[her] food and his[her] work.

He goes on to say that rushing stems from having what we might now call a 'productivity mindset' — it comes from caring less about the journey and more about arrival; less about the deep internal learning that takes place when we attend to and savour each moment and more about how we are seen, what our status is, how we 'appear'.

> The unhappy person is one who has his ideal, the content of his life, the fullness of his consciousness, the essence of his being, in some manner outside of himself. The unhappy man is always absent from himself, never present to himself.

Adopting a more humane pace gives us the opportunity to stop paddling in the shallows and launch into the depths. Once there, we may find that the rhythm shifts and sometimes we feel like we're moving at vast speeds, but, ironically, we have to first stop rushing headlong. Whatever else you do for your writing and your life in the next year, allow yourself a more humane rhythm and pace.

Be present

This is the only moment you have. Being present is intimately connected with giving your life rhythm and a humane pace. We don't orient ourselves to our moments if we are moving too fast to notice the days or even hours, let alone moments. We do it by learning, inch by inch, to pay attention. Psychologist William James says it with profound simplicity:

> My experience is what I agree to attend to.

If we live with or regularly spend time with young children, they are the best teachers of this type of deep attentiveness. They not only focus completely on the present, but are absolutely open to small joys. In a world in which the consumption of more and more and more shallow entertainment proliferates, taking time to savour the little joys can ensure we are really present in our own lives, not just showing up and looking the part, but moving at a humane pace, genuinely present and engaged.

Journal exercise

In what areas does your life need to change pace?

What are three realistic ways in which you can slow down in the coming year?

When are you most present and attentive?

When are you least present and attentive?

What does this tell you and are there ways you want this to change?

How will you do this?

How would your writing benefit if you stopped ever trying to rush or force it and were more present to the moment?

Ritual

Give yourself time today for at least one thing that you consider a 'small joy'.

December 31

Do you normally write resolutions at this time of the year? If you wrote them last year, did any survive?

Last year, I decided to ditch resolutions in favour of quests. I was more interested in how I thought and acted than in 'to do' lists. Looking back, I stayed on the path, though often as a very meandering one. That's the first big difference — not the end product but that you put yourself on a journey and delight in it. My path was about living by particular core qualities, prioritising my writing and my family and travelling to new places. It turned out to be a good path, but we're always works-in-progress and I realise that in the coming year I want to find a gentler rhythm, dig deeper and live more in the moment.

If I'm to prioritise my writing without making it product-oriented; if I'm to prioritise writing in a way that changes who I am and which allows what I write to make its way into the world and have its own impact, without me trying to control all of what that might mean, then the writing needs to be part of a wider context in which I'm living some fundamental qualities. We looked at these yesterday — a call to:

1. find a humane pace
2. be present

When work is all that you are, your work will dry up or stagnate. We have to live in order to produce art. We have to be able to appreciate the wind in the trees or the red kite flying high over the mountains. We have to turn off phones and apps and notifications and be still. Attend. Be present. We have to give time to people we love. One of the joys of being a writer is that you can also write yourself. Who we are is fluid. We don't come written in stone. Humans are adaptable. The environment we live in makes a huge difference, as do the choices we make. There are things we have little or no influence over in life, but we do have the capacity to change, to become the person we want to be.

Today is New Year's Eve and my suggestion is that we build on these fundamental attitudes of attending to the rhythm of life and being present not with resolutions or a to-do list, but with a to-be list. And that we build it slowly, with attention. This is my list at time of writing. I'll give some reasons for why each of these is important to my writing life over the next few days, as we move towards Twelfth Night and Epiphany. By then you might have an entirely different list for your quests for the next year.

- compassion
- humility
- courage
- vulnerability
- generosity

So, for today:

Compassion

We need kindness in our lives. We need to show it to others but we also need to show it to ourselves. We are often our own harshest critic and it's not motivating. It's just another drain on us. Moreover, when we are start picking ourselves apart, we become smaller in our thinking, less generous and more grudging with others. Our hearts and souls shrivel. Kindness, to ourselves as well as others, is expansive, it gives us a chance to be big-hearted and warm-souled.

We are all flawed. Faced with this, it's all too easy to resort to complaint, criticism and even cynicism. But tearing things apart doesn't motivate change, it just leaves destruction, hurt and anger in its wake. Both destruction and construction are powerful, but one diminishes and the other builds. Construction is harder, it's slower but also so much more rewarding.

Of course we should be aware of how we need to develop and become a different story, but as a joyful project of self-love, not a fight to the death between willpower and self-loathing. Of course we should not tolerate abuse or relationships that diminish us, but it's so much more life-affirming to wish them well and move on than to pour our energies into negative cycles of reaction, blaming and trying to change someone who has no interest in changing. And of course there are atrocities so unspeakable that we will always struggle to make sense of them or to know where lines of moral responsibility, evil and the unforgivable might be drawn (something illustrated in the conversation between Mary McCarthy and Hannah Arendt in *Between Friends*, after Arendt's publication of *The Banality of Evil*).

Notwithstanding that we don't want to self-delude nor stay in relationships that only harm us, nor trivialise atrocities, it remains the case that, in an everyday sense, real transformation and progress only happen when we are not on the defensive, when we feel loved, seen, heard and valuable and when we extend the same graciousness to others. In the normal course of life we do well to take the extraordinary philosopher, Simone Weil, seriously when she tells us in *First and Last Notebooks* to be wary of reacting to evil in such a way as to add to it. The world doesn't need more drama. Fyodor Dostoevsky says it with power in *A Writer's Diary*:

> A true friend of [hu]mankind whose heart has but once quivered in compassion over the sufferings of the people, will understand and forgive all the impassable alluvial filth in which they are submerged, and will be able to discover the diamonds in the filth.

Interlude 8: Finding the Still Point of Your Story

[...]

> Judge [others] not by what they are, but by what they strive to become.

Why is it particularly essential that writers should cultivate kind and generous souls? Because we write about the human condition in all its incarnations. We write flawed characters not only because perfect ones are boring but because, by writing them with empathy and kindness, we change human relations and the future.

Journal exercise

Who are you most and least kind to?

What do you want to change about how you show kindness and to whom?

What strains at the limits of your compassion?

Can you challenge this?

How does compassion show in your writing?

Ritual

What act of kindness/compassion can you perform today?

January 1

Continuing with the theme of the to-be list, today's quality is:

Humility

Humility gets a bad rap, all too often conflated with unctuousness, a false self-deprecation that is actually a way of demanding attention. But a more profound definition of humility comes from having a realistic sense of our place in the universe. We are at once a tiny speck and yet a part of

• Interlude 8: Finding the Still Point of Your Story •

everything... Nothing we do is as important as hubris wants to us to imagine, yet nothing we do is lost; it's a mark on the clay of reality. We are not the supreme centre of the universe and yet we can take responsibility for the world while we are here.

Accepting such responsibility is not the stuff of putting yourself down. True humility requires a measure of inner confidence that has no time for comparing yourself to others or for thinking yourself perfect. It is the confidence to not know everything, not be perfect, not protect our images with hubris. It's a good quality to start the New Year with. No matter how much money we make or how much status we accrue, we will never be immortal, infallible or all-knowing. No matter how much knowledge we possess, it will always be outstripped by what we don't know. Ignorance is simply part of the human condition so we have to come to terms with it by being humble, which in turn involves being cautious and kind, aware of our limits.

We can push these limits as humans and as writers, but we also need always to be tentative, to avoid pomposity and conceit. We do it when we have an inner confidence that allows us to look with kindness on others, so humility is intimately tied up with yesterday's quality, compassion. As writers, we illuminate the human condition, we tell stories and write poetry to make the world a more humane place. It takes great humility to take on this responsibility.

Journal exercise

What does humility mean to you?

How do you see humility in terms of your writing life?

'... nothing we do is lost.' How does this impact on your thoughts about being a writer?

Ritual

Do something that is both kind and anonymous today, that improves something for someone in however small a way without drawing attention to yourself.

Interlude 8: Finding the Still Point of Your Story

January 2

Continuing with the theme of the to-be list, today's quality is:

Courage

Courage for writers includes using language in fresh and inventive ways, not only for honest self-expression and genuine emotion but for telling the myths of their time and culture in ways that others don't always want to hear. In a world that screams at us to conform, the courage necessary to express our art with humanity and passion is enormous. Courage is crucial to our humanity. Maya Angelou talks about the need for and the power of courage in the face of racism, slavery and Holocaust.

True courage involves being true to your values and voice and to the larger truths of inclusivity and connection. It isn't about individualism but about the largeness of thought and action that propels us to move beyond what is culturally expected and acceptable when the need is urgent. Rachel Carson did this in her extraordinary book, *Silent Spring*, in 1962, catalysing the environmental movement. We become courageous not because we are necessarily extraordinary but because the situation demands it. Writers, like Fools, speak truth to power. This takes a great deal of courage and it arises when we care, passionately. We are courageous when we connect deeply and with fervour — with life, with each other, with our community or a cause or to the future. Courage is a facet of love, put to the test by what life throws at us.

Courage, in short, requires enormous integrity. It is the integrity not to sell out on what you truly believe, on what you know to be vital, on what and who you love. And writers have a special role to play in this because they are in the position to raise voices for what is lost, for how things might be different, for how we can hope and how we can be free. Writers are visionaries — not fantasists, but those who see what reality can be transformed into. This takes enormous courage.

Journal exercise

Do you think of yourself as courageous? Why/why not?

In what ways does your writing connect with 'real grounds for hope'?

Is your writing deeply seated in the body and in the world? In what ways?

• Interlude 8: Finding the Still Point of Your Story •

How could this be developed?

What truths does your writing communicate?

Ritual

Make a commitment to an act of courage in your writing. Write it out somewhere visible and revisit it often during the coming year.

January 3

Our next quality is:

Vulnerability

Courage, which we considered yesterday, and vulnerability are intimately linked and both require and nourish integrity. No matter how wealthy or privileged we are, we all know hard or dark times at points in life. No one is immune from suffering. Whether it's the loss of a loved one or an act of violence; a financial crisis or a period of depression, life can become raw and challenging and we find ourselves vulnerable. The dark night of the soul can overtake anyone and it's at its darkest when a chasm appears in our emotions or psyche at the same time as the circumstances of our lives seem overwhelming. Holding life together when this happens is beyond hard and we do it only when we are prepared to own the vulnerability, face both the inner and outer turmoil and ask for help.

Vulnerability is not parading our lives on Facebook as 'spectacle'; a 'selfie' doesn't reveal anything about us, except the image we're trying to create. Vulnerability is not drama, or forgetting the boundaries of privacy, but an openness, a susceptibility that renders us capable of being wounded and just as capable of being wholly in the moment, emotion and depth of all that life can be. Vulnerability is the courage to face both the inner voices of doubt, and the outer random events that come hurtling our way, with grace and equanimity.

Vulnerability is foundational to all creativity and particularly to the courage to share what we've created. Sharing our art is an extraordinary act of giving away power. Vulnerability resonates with compassion, humility and courage. The writing life requires all of these qualities as we persist one

• Interlude 8: Finding the Still Point of Your Story •

step at a time, dealing with rejection, being prepared to face whatever we find within ourselves, learning to nurture ourselves as well as others. We need all these qualities as we wrestle with the truth and with our craft.

Journal exercise

How does writing make a difference to the crises of your life, whether internal or external?

Where, in your writing and writing life, do you encounter vulnerability?

What is your experience of letting your work make its way in the world and how vulnerable does this make you feel?

Ritual

Give a piece of your writing to someone today as a gift.

January 4

Generosity

When we stop living from a sense of scarcity, life is transformed. This is not a matter of economics or somehow conning the universe to make you rich by visualising luxury cars each day. This is about a quality of living that connects us with the Numinous. To find this we need to be generous. The world, even on dark days, is full of wonder. Life is an extraordinary, ordinary miracle and too precious to be taken for granted. Generosity not only brings us full circle back to compassion, but also back to those underlying attitudes of finding a more humane pace and being present. Remember what Simone Weil wrote in *First and Last Notebooks*:

> Attention is the rarest and purest form of generosity.

I want that engraved on my soul. This is not an article of creed but the most humane way in which we connect — to the cosmos, to others, to ourselves — by paying attention; by being generous.

• Interlude 8: Finding the Still Point of Your Story •

- You cannot lack compassion if you live from a wellspring of generosity.
- You cannot be full of pride and hubris if you relax into the grace of generosity. It is a letting go that is filled with humility.
- You cannot be full of fear when you are generous: it is the courage to give no matter what the world says.
- You cannot be hard and impervious when you are generous; giving renders you vulnerable.
- Be generous, for all that is life-giving's sake, be generous.

Journal exercise

> Attention is [...] the purest form of generosity [and...] unmixed attention is prayer.
> (Simone Weil)

Write this in your journal and then keep writing — let it take you where it wills.

What is your personal 'to-be' list for the next year?

Ritual

Tell someone today how much they mean to you. It might be a letter, an email, a phone call, or in person, but give this person real attention.

January 5

There is plenty of winter left. The first green shoots of spring might be spearing through the earth by early February, the Celtic festival of Imbolc, but if you live anywhere like Wales it can be well into March or even April before spring feels established. Although the colder, darker months are good times for going inwards, we also need to look outwards. However incrementally, the days are lengthening now, the sun will return. So, on this Twelfth Night, the eve of Epiphany, we're going to look ahead.

Over the last few days we've thought about fundamental ways of being that can assist us to have a writing life of depth even in a frenetic world: pacing ourselves and being present. We've thought about qualities that a writer needs and you've constructed your own 'to-be' list, not as an impossible and overwhelming set of goals threatening to find you wanting when you don't become a saint by February, but as acts of inner commitment and hope to warm you along the path.

And now we're going to apply all this to the writing quests of this fresh New Year. Whatever we face in the next year and in our lives, creativity will make a difference. Creativity is a way of embodying what we know so it becomes a physical memory. Knowledge that stays in the mind is cold and remote, but when we move it to our fingertips as writers and creators, it inhabits every part of us. The Asaro tribe of Indonesia and Papua New Guinea has the perfect aphorism for this: 'Knowledge is only a rumour until it lives in the muscle.' Our writing moves all the journalling and deep thinking from heart to hands to world (wherever we share our writing).

Journal exercise

So the question is, what will you be writing this year and how will this fit in with the quests of your life for the next year?

Don't make this a list of resolutions. You might want the structure of word counts or numbers of articles. You might want a list of the places you want to visit, people you want to spend time with and experiences you would like to participate in. But once you have some notes, make it visual by using the ritual below.

Ritual

Take a double page in your journal, or a big sheet of paper you can pin up somewhere, and draw a horizon line across it near the bottom (perhaps with your city or villages' skyline). Now fill the sky (most of the paper) with big stars. Inside each star, write a quest that embodies the person and writer you want to become, a quest that embodies the qualities on your to-be list. Be imaginative. Be courageous. Be generous.

Now follow your stars.

And an extra:

If you have Christmas decorations, they traditionally disappear today but, this year, as we head towards the light, keep some greenery alive in your home at least until Imbolc.

Interlude 8: Finding the Still Point of Your Story

January 6

Life is precious and fragile. We get one chance to make it count. And significance is not about money or fame or Twitter followers, it's about the small and profound differences we make. Today is Epiphany. Epiphany rarely comes when we are consciously trying to force it and, when it does come, it is rarely what we expect, as Eliot expresses so brilliantly in his poem, 'The Journey of the Magi'. Sages searching for a child to save the world instead find a hard journey, strange people and a birth that makes them think of death, and yet they would do it again — this is 'death' as transformation, as epiphany...

Finding the still point of our stories is a dance with inspiration and flow; it's the courage to construct a life that says 'no' often, and always to those things that distract us from our quest and fritter our time into a frazzled sense of meaninglessness; it's the unexpected surprise that comes upon us when we make ourselves vulnerable by being present, attentive, humble, compassionate and generous. It happens when we allow for the possibility of the unknown to break into our lives. It happens when we loosen our hold on controlling every variable in life (or trying to), when we lose ourselves in creativity and in walks, making ourselves vulnerable to what life offers. We have to choose to become a different story, to cultivate a kind and generous soul, if we are to answer honestly and bravely how we intend to use this one fragile, beautiful and priceless life.

Chapter 24
Who Are You Becoming?

The idea that we can re-invent ourselves, that we live in stories and can shift those stories, is a vital concept for me. Being, I believe, is primary. Our values and how we live them matter so much more than how much money we earn or who has heard of us. The person at the core is everything, which is why I'm excited by the notion of quests. It fits the way I think of life in narrative terms, but as someone who journals a great deal, I've always spent a lot of time, especially as a year is drawing to its close or beginning, reflecting back on what I've learned, checking on how I am connecting to the people who matter most in my life, remembering events and what they mean — not just lists, but the texture and emotions of the year — and looking forward to what comes next. The primary question is not what do I want to have, but who do I want to be and how would such a person act in the world?

Who we are is fluid; we have the capacity to change, to become the person we want to be, but change can be difficult or completely thwarted if we are unable to match our external environments and relationships with the internal shift. A sober alcoholic has much less chance of thriving and staying sober if her environment is full of alcohol, if all her friends drink heavily and mock her abstention. We need a level of supportive congruence, whether in persuading others to view us as the self we want to be or in aligning our inner self-image and outer behaviour. As Mahatma Gandhi reputedly said,

> If your words, your thoughts, and your actions are all in harmony, then you can be happy.

If the world you live in is incongruous with the world you inhabit internally then the only way to become different is by dint of willpower. And eventually that will fail anyone. So that question, 'Who are you becoming?' has many layers to it. If you are a writer, you have to write. If you want to be a generous person, you have to give. You can't fool yourself. If you want to see yourself as a fit person, you have to do the exercise and eat healthily. If you don't, you are breaking promises to yourself, and you will know it and see yourself accordingly. On the other hand, when we live our values, our self-confidence rises.

It can be difficult to get people who've known you for a long time to believe you can make changes or set out on big quests. But no one is really 'self-made'. We all rely on a network of influences, environment and relationships and people who love you will support the journey if you let them in. Of course there will be some people who do not want you to change. A group of drinking friends with little else in common might not be the best supporters for someone giving up alcohol (though they could surprise you and start to make their own changes). Change can make you vulnerable to losing certain people. If the relationships have been purely transactional (about what one party is 'getting' from the other) then they may not survive. But the important relationships in your life will always be the transformational ones — the ones where sharing and mutual support become more than the sum of the parts. In these relationships, asking for support to make changes is likely to result in not only receiving support, but creative thinking and a ripple effect of changes in others' lives too.

As we come towards the end of this book, I hope you will be as excited as I am by the ideas of

- living a congruent life in which your inner and outer worlds match
- seeing yourself as the writer and person you want to become
- signalling to the important people in your life that you need their support

Becoming a different story is about making huge shifts by taking one step and then the next towards the writing life that delights you. You need to let your inner world emerge into the world. You need an environment and relationships that nurture your quest, rather than mocking or squashing it. This may demand a lot of courage and a great deal of change, but it doesn't have to happen all at once. The trick is to start heading in the right direction. Start with simple conversations. Let the dreams find voice and the voice start to affect what you do. Build small habits that signal the person you want to become until you realise it's now who you are. Life is too short for incongruity and internal conflict. Let's make the quest to live a different story, whatever than might mean for each of us.

Chapter 24: Who Are You Becoming?

What story do you want to write?

What story do you want to inhabit?

What story do you want to become?

One Final Exercise: A Mandala for Your Story

What story do you want to write?

What story do you want to inhabit?

What story do you want to become?

Becoming your story is never static. It has rhythm and quests and it changes, so this is an exercise you can repeat at intervals. This is a large exercise to end on so feel free to do the parts over several days.

You need two big sheets of paper and lots of coloured pens as well as your journal.

Part 1

Drawn a circle that fills the sheet with another circle inside it about 2 inches/5 cm from the circumference and a small circle at the centre.

In your middle circle write the title of your current writing project — it might be a full manuscript you are working on, so in my case, at the time of writing this, I put '*Saoirse's Crossing*', the novel I was beginning. It doesn't have to be the name of a manuscript: it might be to journal daily; write a haiku a day; a poem a week; a blog a fortnight… It's where your particular writing quest is now.

For the next circle divide it into seven wedges, labelling each in turn:

1. Vision
2. Rhythms
3. Environment

· One Final Exercise: a Mandala for Your Story ·

    4. Congruence
    5. Connections
    6. Re-creation
    7. Flexibility

Before filling in these wedges, we'll explore these areas in the following journalling exercises. (If you want to do lots of journalling for each feel free to spread it over as many sessions as is helpful.)

Vision

This is your manifesto, your values and your quests.

You wrote about this at the end of 'Writing the Soul' in the last of the six exercises in Soul-writing, 'Rhythm down deep'.

Look back at that exercise and note your manifesto again — you might want to revise or hone it.

What are the values you want to communicate in your life and your writing?

What quest/s are you on?

Rhythms

How do your rhythms support the story you want to write and want to become?

We have daily rhythms including habits that help us, like journalling, movement (whether walking or yoga or…), reading, nutrition, ablutions and, for some, meditation or prayer. There are seasonal rhythms of how we respond to summer or winter, spring or autumn. And there are rhythms that come and go in various proportions depending on our individual lives, for example my list includes:

    work — rest
    travel — home
    together — alone
    activity — stillness
    quests — ideas
    feast — fast

· One Final Exercise: a Mandala for Your Story ·

wake — sleep
write — think
play — imagine
create — meditate…

Trying to balance all the elements of your personal to your situation can feel overwhelming, but finding a rhythm is much more humane; sometimes one thing is in the ascendant, sometimes another; they don't all have to balance on a pinhead at once, but the rhythm needs to feel nurturing for you.

What are your rhythms? Write about them.

Environment

We need to design environments that support our vision and quest. Everything from the food in our cupboards to the sense of calm in our home, from the way we use our resources (emotional and intellectual as well as physical and financial) to how much time we give to distractions that might eat our energy, are all up for grabs. And of course how we use our time and space.

This has to work for you. There isn't a magic prescription. I find not having social media or TV and are big important, positive parts of my environment, and assist my writing. It might be something totally different for you.

How does your environment support or hamper your vision and quests? (For most of us, there's probably some of each.)

What small step can you take to improve this? (I'm not a minimalist but sometimes huge clear outs in particular areas can be liberating, especially if we find ourselves drowning in stuff that is neither useful not beautiful.)

Congruence

When your vision, your promises to yourself and others, your environment, and rhythms are in alignment, you become increasingly congruent. Congruence is an internal harmony between hopes and actions; values and behaviour.

How congruent do you feel in your life and in your approach to writing?

• ONE FINAL EXERCISE: A MANDALA FOR YOUR STORY •

Connections

How healthy and nurturing are your connections? These might be intimate relationships, those with family, friends, peers, colleagues or mentors or might be wider connections within your community or to nature.

What needs less?

What needs more?

Which connections are merely transactional and which are transformative?

How can you shift this?

Re-creation

The creativity to play, imagine and meditate. The fearlessness to pause, stop, rest, sometimes to do nothing, to allow ideas to germinate while you dive deeply into internal spaces or beautiful places or dream, walk, think or connect…

How do you find re-creation in your writing and life?

Flexibility

The courage to trust the process, to respond to the flow, re-consider and re-invent the path. The suppleness to learn and to constantly integrate new experiences and knowledge. The resilience to change and become a different story…

How flexible is your approach to your writing quests and your life journey?

Part 2

Now take key words from each of the areas you've journalled about above and write them onto your own version of the mandala. See my version opposite:

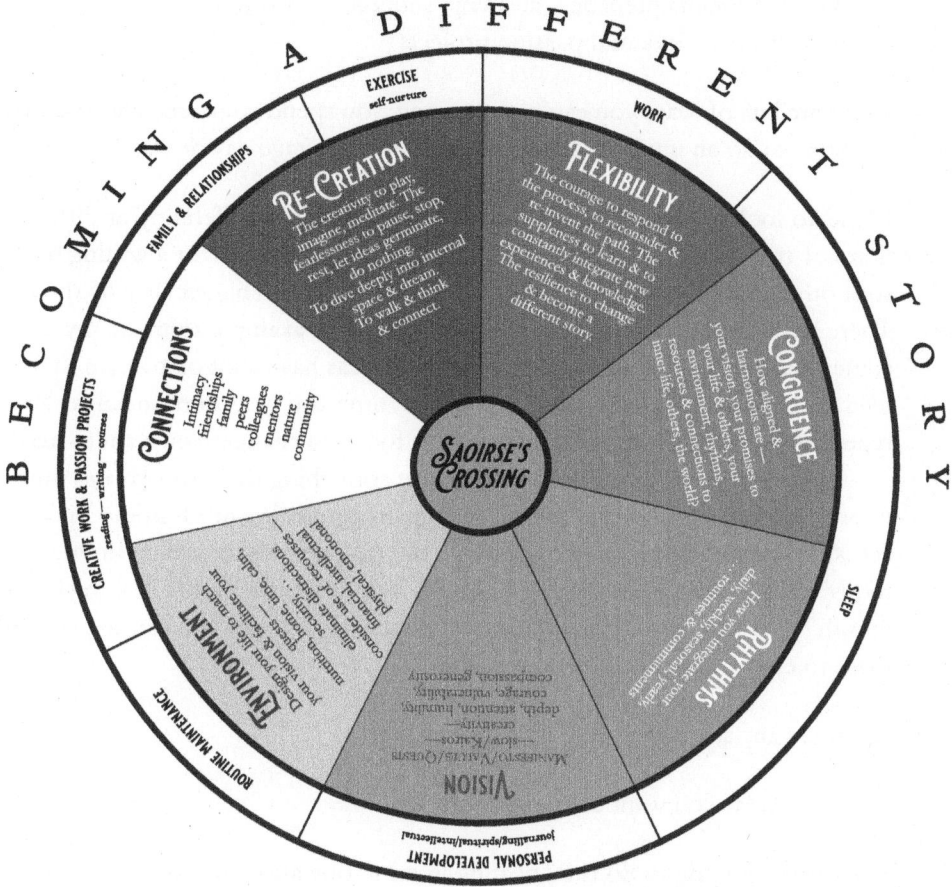

Figure 1: A plan of my mandala with all the categories filled in

Part 3

Next fill in the outer circle, which is how you use your time.

You can see on my version that I divided it into:

- sleep
- work
- exercise (and self nurture)
- family and relationships
- personal development (journalling/spiritual — however defined — and intellectual pursuits)

·One Final Exercise: a Mandala for Your Story·

- routine maintenance (cleaning, shopping, cooking…)
- creative work and passion projects

There are lots of ways you can visualise how you spend your time and you may just want to do an intuitive division based on an average day or week.

I tend to look at this every 90 days as I use time very differently at different times of the year. This mandala was drawn when I was away for a writing break so at other points in the year work would take up a much bigger slice of the pie. There are also compromises in what fits where, for example some of my work comes into my passion projects so these two areas have a lot of overlap. If you tend to have a more consistent pattern of time use, you don't need to keep repeating the exercise unless it helps you to focus on changes you want to make.

It doesn't have to be fixed in stone, just something that gives you an image of where time is going for you. I add up the guesstimate of hours on each activity over ninety days and divide by 2160 (the number of hours in 90 days) to get the percentage for each. You might want to do the hours in a week or a month. There are lots of free pie chart makers online and you can use one of these to create an image of your time use.

Are there any surprises?

Are there areas you want to spend more/less on?

How are you going to do that, bearing in mind one area will have to shrink for another to grow?

Part 4

Now you've got your basic mandala with its information in place, you can get more playful and creative.

Draw the large circle outline again on another large sheet. Then add a slightly smaller circle a couple of inches inside the first and the central circle as before.

Instead of writing a project title at the centre, this time draw a symbol that represents your writing project. It can be as simple or complex as you like. Choose a colour or colours that reflect its energy for you. (Mine was a maze as there is an extraordinarily complex maze at the place I've chosen as the home of my character, Saoirse.)

Next draw the seven pie graph lines quite lightly this time but where each of the titles fell on your first mandala draw a small circle instead, similar to your central one but slightly smaller; one for each element. And choose a dominant colour for each category:

- Vision
- Rhythms
- Congruence
- Environment
- Connections
- Re-creation
- Flexibility

(For example I chose green for connections and violet for vision)

In your journal draw an image for each area. These can be simple or complex, oblique or obvious. Make them positive images of how you want to be in that area, rather than necessarily how it feels at the moment, and make sure it's in a colour that resonates with that area for you. For example, my vision symbol is a violet star inside a sickle moon.

Part 5 (optional)

If images don't come easily you can design a symbol instead. Do this by writing a short phrase that sums up a clear goal for that area in your journal. For example for Vision I wrote: rhythm to allow *kairos* to break in. And for Congruence I wrote: values and behaviour in harmony.

Keep each one short and specific.

When you've written out each phrase, go through and take out all the vowels and any repeated constants. For example for congruence my phrase became:

```
v l s n d b h r m y
```

Use these letters to draw a symbol by winding the letters together in different sizes and rotations (you can see examples on my finished version below).

• One Final Exercise: a Mandala for Your Story •

Part 6

When you have your seven images or symbols, or both, use colours to design a mandala, starting at the edge of your centre circle and working the first perimeter. There are lots of websites on how to draw a mandala including one on WikiHow and videos on YouTube. Be as creative as possible. Don't get hung up on making it perfect, just go with the flow. Use the colours to reflect how much of that area you feel you want to develop or explore or how vital that area is for you. For example, if connections and flexibility are dominant for you, or you want to use the colours you've assigned these areas more than other colours. Most importantly, play and have fun!

Finally, you are going to do the border circle to represent time use. Again, assign a colour to each of your categories. Mine were:

- sleep
- daily maintenance
- family time
- self nurture
- work
- creative projects
- personal development

(For example, I put family time in dark red and creative projects in dark purple)

You could just draw bands in different thicknesses to represent the differing amounts of time or you could weave the colours together or find a repeating pattern that gives different weights to the elements. Experiment and play with it.

Finally, you have your mandala as both a written reminder and an image. Pin them up somewhere or scan them (especially the image mandala) to use as a screensaver. This is your visual image of the story you want to write and inhabit.

Mine came out like this:

• One Final Exercise: a Mandala for Your Story •

Figure 2: My finished mandala

Part 7

Look back at your phrases and use them to write yourself a blessing that sums up where your quest and your story are headed. This is the one I wrote and I added it as an outer spiral of words around the mandala:

· One Final Exercise: a Mandala for Your Story ·

May you find the rhythm to allow *kairos* to break in
and the courage to ebb and flow.
May your values and behaviour be in harmony
and your environment be designed for energy.
May you have connections that nurture
and the fearlessness to pause.
And may you always trust the flow.

Afterword

We all need companions along the quest, at least for some of the time. This book is one of those companions, written for the wild idealists and alchemists of the imagination who believe that writing is so powerful that it should change us as we write. I hope you have found inspiration here. For those who see writing as an act of radical transformation, I blog at 'Becoming a Different Story' (*https://janfortune.com/*). You'll find lots of free resources there as well as journalling courses and information about different ways of working with me. In particular, I have two routes for writers who want a supportive environment of others on similar quests either through a highly accessible online community with regular support and online workshops or through inclusion in a small group that also involves a residential and one to one mentoring. Join me on a quest to build daily rhythms that nurtures and support living and writing deliberately. I'd love to help you become a different story. And I also love hearing from readers so feel free to email.

References and Further Reading

I think writers should read widely, deeply and constantly. Ideas are in the ether and exposing ourselves to as many as possible helps us to hone the stories we want to become and the stories we want to write.

In crafting *Writing Down Deep* I've read some extraordinary books. I have only quoted from books that are in the public domain (where authors or translators died 70 years ago or more) but many more books have sparked ideas or are referred to without the use of quotations and all of these bear further reading. You will also find some films referred to and listed here.

Biblical quotations are taken from the NIV under the following copyright provision: Scripture quotations taken from The Holy Bible, New International Version® NIV® Copyright © 1973 1978 1984 2011 by Biblica, Inc.™ Used by permission. All rights reserved worldwide:

Genesis 32:22-32; 1 Kings 19:3-13; Ecclesiastes 1:9; John 10:10.

Alighieri, Dante, *Inferno*, accessed at:
https://www.gutenberg.org/ebooks/1001?msg=welcome_stranger
Allen, Woody (dir.), *Hannah and Her Sisters*, MGM Video (DVD), 2002
Allen, Woody (dir.), *Annie Hall*, MGM Video (DVD), 2000.
Angelou, Maya, 'Still I Rise' in *And Still I Rise*, Virago, 1986.
Angelou, Maya, *I know why the caged bird sings*, Virago, 1984
Arendt, Hannah & McCarthy, Mary *Between Friends*, Thomson Learning, 1995; Arendt, Hannah *The Banality of Evil*, Rowman & Littlefield, 1998.
Blake, William 'Auguries of Innocence' in *Poets of the English Language*, Viking, 1950
Chekhov, Anton see: Yarmolinsky, Avrahm (trans.), *The Unknown Chekhov: Stories and Other Writings Hitherto Untranslated by Anton Chekhov*, Noonday Press, New York, 1954.
Atwood, Margaret, *Negotiating with the Dead*, Anchor Books, 2003
Auden, W H, 'Atlantis', Collected Poems, Faber & Faber, 1994.
Augustine, St Aurelius, *Sermon on 1 John 4:4-12*
Austen, Jane, *Pride and Prejudice*.
Barbour, Julian, *The End of Time: the next revolution in our understanding of the universe*, W&N, 2000.

References and Further Reading

Barrie, J M, *Peter Pan*, Frederick Orville Press, 1916.

Barrie, J M, *The Little Minister*

Beauvoir, Simone de., *All Said and Done*, Penguin, 1977.

Beckett, Samuel, *Not I*, Faber & Faber, 1973.

Bede, the Venerable, *The Reckoning of Time*, Liverpool University Press, 1999.

Benjamin, Walter, *The Storyteller: tales out of loneliness*, Verso, 2016.

Bly, Robert and Booth, William (ed.), *A Little Book on the Human Shadow*, HarperCollins, 1998

Bonhoeffer, Dietrich, *Dietrich Bonhoeffer's Christmas Sermons*, quoted at: https://www.firstthings.com/web-exclusives/2014/12/bonhoeffer-in-advent

Brontë, Charlotte, *Jane Eyre*.

Brooks, Phillips, 'O little town of Bethlehem', 1868.

Byatt, A S, *Ragnarok, the End of the Gods*, Cannongate, 2016.

Cameron, Julia, *The Artist's Way*, Pan McMillan, 1995

Camus, Albert, *The Myth of Sisyphus*, accessed at: https://archive.org/stream/AlbertCamusTheMythOfSisyphus/Albert%20Camus%20-%20The%20Myth%20Of%20Sisyphus_djvu.txt

Camus, *The Rebel*, Penguin Classics, 2000

Carey, Nessa, *The Epigenetics Revolution*, Icon Books, 2012.

Carson, Rachel, *Silent Spring*, Penguin, 2000.

Carter, Angela, 'The Company of Wolves' in *The Bloody Chamber*, Vintage Classics, 1995

Carter, Elizabeth, *All the Works of Epictetus, which are now extant*, Dublin, 1759.

Cervantes De, Miguel, *Don Quixote*, Wordsworth Classics, 1992, or available at: https://www.gutenberg.org/ebooks/996

Clarke, A C, *In the Margin*, Cinnamon Press, 2015

Crum, John Macleod Campbell, *The Oxford Book of Carols*, OUP, 1928

Csikszentmihalyi, Mihaly, *Flow, the psychology of happiness*, Rider, 2002

Cuaron, Alfonso, *Children of Men*, Universal, 2007.

Delacroix, Eugène, *Journal*.

Dickens, Charles, *A Tale of Two Cities*, Penguin Classics, 2003.

Dickens, Charles, *Bleak House*, Wordsworth Classics, 1993.

Dostoevsky, Fyodor, *A Writer's Diary*, Northwestern University Press, 2009

Eliot, George, *Letters and Journals*.

Eliot, George, *Middlemarch*

Eliot, T S, 'The Journey of the Magi' – listen a recording of Eliot reading the poem at: https://www.poetryarchive.org/poem/journey-magi

Eliot, T S, *The Cultivation of Christmas Trees*, Farrar Straus Giroux, 1956

Elson, Rebecca, *A Responsibility to Awe*, Carcanet Press, 2018

Emerson, Ralph Waldo, *The Essential Writings*, Modern Library, 2000

Eno, Brian & Schmidt, Peter, *Oblique Strategies* (cards), 1979.
Epicurus, *The Essential Epicurus,* Prometheus Books, 1993.
Farman, Jason, *Delayed Response,* Yale University Press, 2019
Fitzgerald, F Scott, *The Great Gatsby,* Bantam Books, 1945, or access at: *http://gutenberg.net.au/ebooks02/0200041h.html*
Flaubert, Gustave, collected in *Reports,* Boston Athanaeum, 1961.
Fletcher, Joseph F, *Situation Ethics,* Westminster John Knox, 1997.
Fortune, Jan, 'How to rise again', *Particles of Life, Bluechrome,* 2005.
Fortune, Jan, *Stale Bread & Miracles,* Cinnamon Press, 2012.
Fortune, Jan, The Casilda Trilogy: *This is the End of the Story; A Remedy for All Things; For Hope is Always Born,* Liquorice Fish Books. 2017, 2018, 2019.
Frost, Robert, 'Stopping by Woods on a Snowy Evening', *The Collected Poems*, Vintage, 2013.
Gale, Catharine, & Martyn Christopher 'Larks and owls and health, wealth, and wisdom' @ *https://www.bmj.com/content/bmj/317/7174/1675.full.pdf*
Gaston Bachelard, *The Poetics of Reverie,* Beacon Press, 1992
Gaston Bachelard, *Water and Dreams an Essay on the Imagination of Matter,* Dallas Institute of Humanities & Culture, 1994
Goethe, Johann Wolfgang von, *The Sorrows of Young Werther* (*Die Leiden des jungen Werther*), accessed at: *https://www.gutenberg.org/ebooks/2527*
Hall Young, Samuel, *Alaska Days with John Muir.*
Hammarskjöld, Dag, *Markings,* Faber & Faber, 1964.
Harris, Joanne, *Chocolat,* Black Swan, 1999.
Hawthorne, Nathaniel, 'The Haunted Mind' in *Twice Told Tales,* public domain.
Hawthorne, Nathaniel, *The Marble Fawn.* (aka: *The Romance of Monte Beni* or *Transformation*)
Hesse, Herman, *If the War Goes On, reflections on war and politics,* Farrar Straus & Giroux, 1971.
Hesse, Herman, *Wandering: Notes and Sketches,* Farrar Straus & Giroux, 1972
Hume, David, *My Own Life,* Fugazi Press, 2012.
Husserl, Edmund, *Ideas for a Pure Phenomenology and Phenomenological Philosophy,* Hackett Publishing, 2014.
Iyer, Pico, *The Art of Stillness, Adventures in Going Nowhere,* Simon & Schuster, 2013.
James, William, *The Principles of Psychology, Vol. 1*, accessed at: https://www.gutenberg.org/ebooks/57628
James, William, *The Heart of William James,* Harvard University Press, 2010.
Jansson, Tove, *Moominland Midwinter,* Puffin Books, 1973.
Jeremias, Joachim, *The Parables of Jesus,* 2d ed., trans. S. H. Hooke (1972; German ed.: 1958)
Jodorowsky, Alejandro (dir.), *The Holy Mountain,* Tartan Video (DVD), 2007.

References and Further Reading

Johnson, Robert A, *Inner Work: Using dreams and active imagination for personal growth*, HarperOne, 1991.

Jung, Carl, *Psychology and Alchemy*, Routledge, 1980.

Kafka, Franz, *Diaries*

Keats, John, 'Lines to Fanny'.

Keats, John, *Letters of John Keats, No. 44* (Frederick Page, ed.), quoted at:
https://www.poemhunter.com/john-keats/quotations/

Kierkegaard, Søren, *Either/Or: A Fragment of a Life*, accessed at:
http://sqapo.com/CompleteText-Kierkegaard-EitherOr.htm

Kierkegaard, Søren, *The Concept of Anxiety*, 1844, Eng. trans. Lowrie, Walter as *The Concept of Dread*, 1944.

Kolk, van der, Bessel, *The Body Keeps the Score*, Penguin, 2015

Kyllonen, Robert C, & Roberts, Richard D, Morningness-eveningness and intelligence, in *Personality and Individual Differences* 27, Permagon

L'Engle, Madeleine, *Glimpses of Grace*, Harper, 1997.

Lamott, Anne, *Hallelujah Anyway, Rediscovering Mercy*, Riverhead Books, 2017.

Lamott, Anne, *Hallelujah Anyway: Rediscovering Mercy*, Riverhead Books, 2017

Lamott, Anne, op.cit.

Le Guin, Ursula K, *A Wizard of Earthsea*, Gollancz 1971.

Le Guin, Ursula K, *The Dispossessed*,

Le Guin, Ursula K, *The Wave in the Mind: Talks and Essays on the Writer, the Reader, and the Imagination*, Shambhala Publications, 2004

Le Guin, Ursula, *Lao Tzu: Tao Te Ching*, Shambala Publications, 1998.

Lightman, Alan, *A Sense of the Mysterious*, Vintage, 2006

Lightman, Alan, *Searching for Stars on an Island in Maine*, Corsair, 2018.

Marcus Aurelius, Meditations, Penguin, 2006.

Marvell, Andrew, 'To His Coy Mistress', accessed at:
https://www.poetryfoundation.org/poems/44688/to-his-coy-mistress

Mashni, John, 'Now Is The Time To Be Unreasonable',
https://medium.com/@JohnMashni/now-is-the-time-to-be-unreasonable-8ca84900709e

Maslow, A H, *Motivation and Personality*, Harper & Row, 1987.

May, Rollo, *Freedom and Destiny*, W W Norton & Co, 1982.

May, Rollo, *The Courage to Create*, W. W. Norton & Company, 1994

Merleau Ponty, Maurice, *Phenomenology of Perception*, Routledge, 2013.

Merwin, W S, 'Berryman', accessed at:
https://www.poetryfoundation.org/poems/58530/berryman

Michaels, Anne, *All We Saw*, Bloomsbury, 2017

Muir, John, *My First Summer in the Sierra*, Canongate Books, 2014

Muir, John, *Nature Writings*, Library of America, 1998.

Newport, Cal, *Deep Work, rules for focussed success in a distracted world*, Piatkus, 2016.

References and Further Reading

Newport, Cal, *So good they can't ignore you*, Piatkus, 2016.
Nietzsche, Friedrich and Kaufman, Walter (trans.), *The Will to Power*, Random House, 1968.
Nietzsche, Friedrich and Kaufman, Walter (trans.), *The Gay Science*, Random House, 1974.
Nietzsche, Friedrich, *Daybreak: Thoughts on the Prejudices of Morality*, accessed at: http://users.compaqnet.be/cn127103/Nietzsche_the_dawn_or_daybreak/the_dawn.htm
Nietzsche, Friedrich, *Twilight of the Idols*, 1888.
Oakes, Lauren E., *In Search of the Canary Tree, the story of a scientist, a cypress and a changing world*, Basic Books, 2019.
Oatley, Keith, *Such Stuff as Dreams*, Wiley, 2011.
Oliver, Mary, 'Of Power and Time' in *Upstream*, Penguin, Random House, 2016.
Oliver, Mary, *Dream Work*, Atlantic Monthly Press, 1994, see also *Staying Alive*, Bloodaxe, 2002.
Orwell, George, *Animal Farm*, Penguin Classics, 2000.
Otto, Rudolph, *The Idea of the Holy (Das Heilige)*, OUP, 1924.
Pearce, Patricia, 'Finding the Still Point', accessed at:
  https://www.patriciapearce.com/finding-the-still-point/
Pollan, Michael, *How to Change Your Mind*, Penguin, 2019
Proust, Marcel, 'Swann's Way' from *In Search of Lost Time*.
Raine, Kathleen, 'Northumbrian Sequence 1V', *Collected Poems*, Hamish Hamilton, 1972.
Rich, Adrienne, *'Natural Resources'* in *The Dream of a Common Language*, Norton, 1978.
Ricoeur, Paul, *Time and Narrative*, vol. 1, University of Chicago, 1990.
Rilke, Rainer Maria and Linton, John (trans.), *The Notebook of Malte Laurids Brigge*, London, 1930
Rilke, Rainer Maria *Letters on Life*, Modern Library 2006.
Rilke, Rainer Maria, 'Already the ripening berries are red', from *Poems From The Book Of Hours*, accessed at: https://archive.org/stream/in.ernet.dli.2015.136247/2015.136247.Poems-From-The-Book-Of-Hours_djvu.txt
Rilke, Rainer Maria, *Letters to a Young Poet*, accessed at:
  https://archive.org/stream/lettersofrainerm030932mbp/lettersofrainerm030932mbp_djvu.txt
Rilke, Rainer Maria, *Letters to a Young Woman (Briefe an eine junge Frau)*, accessed at: http://gutenberg.net.au/ebooks09/0900041h.html
Robinson, J A T, *Jesus and His Coming*, SCM Press, 1959.
Rousseau, Jean Jacques, *Emile, or On Education*, 1763.
Rumi, *Masnavi*, Kegan Paul, trans. 1898,
Russell, Bertrand, *The Conquest of Happiness*, Liveright Publishing Corporation, 2013.
Russell, Bertrand, *The Scientific Outlook*, Routledge, 2009.

References and Further Reading

Sacks, Oliver, *The Island of the Colourblind*, Picador, 2012
Saint Exupéry, Antoine de, *The Little Prince*, Egmont, 2004.
Sartre, Jean-Paul, *Being and Nothingness*, Routledge, 2003.
Shakespeare, William, *Macbeth*, accessed at: http://shakespeare.mit.edu/macbeth/full.html
Shakespeare, William, *Romeo and Juliet*, accessed at:
  https://www.gutenberg.org/ebooks/1112
Shaw, George Bernard, *Maxims for Revolutionists*, 1903.
Solnit, Rebecca, *Hope in the Dark, Untold Histories, Wild Possibilities*, Canongate, 2016.
Sontag, Susan, *Against interpretation & other essays*, Penguin, 2009
Sontag, Susan, *Reborn: early diaries & As Consciousness is Harnessed to Flesh*, Penguin, 2009 & 2013.
Spender, Dale, *Man Made Language*, Thorsons, 1985
Stephenson Bond, D, *Living Myth: Personal Meaning as a Way of Life*, Shambala, 2001.
Swift, Jonathan, *The Works of Jonathan Swift*, Vol. 13, 1751.
The Twelve Labours of Hercules, Leopold Classic Library, 2015.
Thomas, Lewis, *The Medusa and the Snail*, Penguin, 1995.
Thoreau, David Henry, *Walden or Life in the Woods*, Henry Frowde Oxford University Press, 1906
Thoreau, Henry David, 'A Winter Walk', *Excursions*, accessed at:
  https://www.gutenberg.org/ebooks/9846
Thoreau, Henry David, diary entry, January, 1857, quoted at:
  https://www.brainpickings.org/2018/03/08/thoreau-and-the-language-of-trees/
Tillich, Paul, *Dynamics of Faith*, Harper & Row, 1957.
Tolkien, J R R, *The Lord of the Rings*, Ballantine Books, 1975.
Tolstoy, Leo, *War and Peace*.
Twain, Mark, *Autobiography of Mark Twain*, University of California Press, 2012.
Weil, Simone, *First and Last Notebooks*, Wipf and Stock, 2015.
Weil, Simone, *Gravity and Grace*, Routledge, 2002
Whitman, Walt, notes, 1855/6, from Yale Collection of American Literature, accessed via The Walt Whitman Archive, at:
  https://whitmanarchive.org/manuscripts/transcriptions/yal.00138.html
Woolf, Virginia, writing to Vita Sackville-West, 1926,see: *The Letters of Virginia Woolf, Volume II: 1923–1928*, Harcourt Brace Jovanovich, 1978.
Woolf, Virginia, *A Room of One's Own*, accessed at:
  http://gutenberg.net.au/ebooks02/0200791.txt
Woolf, Virginia, diary entries, see *The Complete Works*, Musaicum Books, 2017.
Wordsworth, William, 'Lines Composed a Few Miles Above Tintern Abbey', accessed at: https://www.poetryfoundation.org/poems/45527/lines-composed-a-few-miles-above-tintern-abbey-on-revisiting-the-banks-of-the-wye-during-a-tour-july-13-1798

· REFERENCES AND FURTHER READING ·

Wright, C D, 'More Blues and the Abstract Truth', from *Steal Away, Selected and New Poems,* Copper Canyon Press, 2003, and at PennSound's page: *https://media.sas.upenn.edu/pennsound/authors/Wright-CD/Port-Townsend_1999/Wright-CD_15_More-Blues-Abstract-Truth_Copper-Canyon-Session_Port-Townsend-WA_7-16-99.mp3*

About the Author

Jan Fortune runs the website 'Becoming a Different Story' to share a passion for the writing life and to help others develop their writing practice, at all stages. She believes that writing is powerful, that the world is shaped by the stories we tell and that imagination makes things happen.

She has authored several novels and poetry collections as well as numerous articles and has taught writing courses across Europe. Jan also co-runs the independent publishing house, Cinnamon Press, where she has edited over 400 books and mentored many writers. She loves books that are engaged, raise questions, take risks with form, voice or subject, or that push the boundaries of mainstream writing.

She is married to Adam, a writer, editor and designer. They live in a tiny village in North Wales, in a quirky house with no central heating and no TV, but magnificent views of mountains and lots of rain. She has four wonderful (adult) children, who were all educated at home, plus a fantastic son-in-law and daughter-in-law and an adorable grandson.

Jan has a PhD in feminist theology and is passionate about issues of equality. She enjoys cooking and slow travel. She writes in a trance and does yoga most days.

https://janfortune.com/